The People's Faith

The People's Faith

The Liturgy of the Faithful in Orthodoxy

Nicholas E. Denysenko

LEXINGTON BOOKS/FORTRESS ACADEMIC
Lanham • Boulder • New York • London

Published by Lexington Books/Fortress Academic

Lexington Books is an imprint of The Rowman & Littlefield Publishing Group, Inc.
4501 Forbes Boulevard, Suite 200, Lanham, Maryland 20706
www.rowman.com

6 Tinworth Street, London SE11 5AL, United Kingdom

British Library Cataloguing in Publication Information Available

Library of Congress Cataloging-in-Publication Data Available

ISBN 978-1-9787-0459-6 (cloth : alk. paper)
ISBN 978-1-9787-0460-2 (electronic)

♾™ The paper used in this publication meets the minimum requirements of American National Standard for Information Sciences Permanence of Paper for Printed Library Materials, ANSI/NISO Z39.48-1992.

Printed in the United States of America

To Fr. Michael Courey—mentor, friend, and brother in Christ

Contents

List of Textbox and Tables

Acknowledgments

It is often the case that several people contribute to the publication of a book, even if it is attributed to the work of a single author. Such is the case with this book, a work inspired by countless conversations with colleagues, and especially by the experience of standing in the midst of the assembly and worshiping God, side-by-side with the rest of the people.

I begin by thanking the pastors and people who agreed to contribute to this project by participating in the focus groups. Fr. Rick Andrews and the people of St. George Greek Orthodox Church in St. Paul, Minnesota, Fr. Robert Arida and the faithful of Holy Trinity OCA Cathedral in Boston, Fr. Gabriel Rochelle and the flock at St. Anthony of the Desert Mission (UOC-USA) in Las Cruces, New Mexico, and Fr. Michael Courey and the people at St. Katherine Greek Orthodox Church at Redondo Beach in southern California—you are the true authors of this book, and you shared your reflections on the Liturgy with an authentic love for God and reverence for the Orthodox tradition. May your testimony inspire others to share their love for the Liturgy in written and spoken word, and in act.

Many colleagues assisted with preparing for the focus groups and the clergy survey. Sincere thanks to Julie Paterson, Senior Institutional Review Board (IRB) coordinator at Loyola Marymount University (LMU) for guiding me through the approval process. Thanks also to Dr. Laura Massa, Director of Assessment at LMU, who both assisted and provided helpful feedback on creating, disseminating, and interpreting the clergy survey.

Friends in the academy encouraged me to pursue this project and complete it, especially during a time of self-doubt. Special thanks to the members of the Christian Initiation seminar of the North American Academy of Liturgy, who responded to my initial report in January 2017 with ideas and encouragement. I am also deeply grateful to the Collegeville Institute at St.

John's University in central Minnesota for engaging me in dialogue about this project at my resident scholar seminar in October 2017. Carla Durand, Vivian Krueger, Jim Hoffman, Toppo Takamura, David Smoker, Jaisy Joseph, Don Ottenhoff, Bill Cahoy, and Fr. Columba Stewart offered helpful feedback on the project. I am also grateful to Fr. Michael Plekon for reading chapter drafts and referring me to the seminal literature on the topic from the perspective of the scientific study of religion, and to Fr. Alkiviadis Calivas for encouragement. Thanks to my editor, Michael Gibson, who supported the project and granted me an extension after 2017 posed unanticipated challenges that paused the writing process temporarily, and to production editor Jehanne Schweitzer. The project was conceived and commenced during my tenure as associate professor of Theological Studies at LMU, and completed as a resident fellow at St. John's University, and Jochum Professor and Chair at Valparaiso University. Thanks to my colleagues of these three fine institutions who supported this work. The most important of the contributors to this work are the family members who provide the space to work, and who offer the best feedback in daily, domestic conversation. Thanks to Tresja and Sophia, as always, for your patience with me.

Chapter One

Introducing the People's Faith

The People's Faith explores the liturgical theology of Orthodox Churches of America, as understood and interpreted by the laypeople of those churches. Liturgical theology is the confession of God that occurs in the Church's liturgical event. Liturgiology and the diverse scholarly works of liturgical theology tend to be works produced by experts: scholars with access to liturgical manuscripts, clergy with vast experience of liturgical presidency, and brilliant amateurs bearing the talent to decipher liturgical patterns and relationships. Liturgical experts draw from the sources and explain the meaning of the liturgy to the laity. When such explanations are firmly grounded in the sources, the academy accepts and celebrates them as genuine works of liturgical theology, and they have the capacity to become authoritative for pastoral liturgy.

Liturgical theology requires an examination from a different perspective: the laity's. How do lay men and women explain their understanding of the liturgy, in their own words? Does the laypeople's explanation of the liturgy correspond to the liturgical theology defined by the experts? How do the laypeople understand Baptism, Holy Communion, and their participation in the liturgy? How do laypeople describe the significance of the special offices of the liturgical year, such as Christmas and Pascha? How do the people describe divine activity in liturgy and sacraments?

To date, there is no inventory of the people's perspective on liturgy in the Orthodox Churches of America. Liturgical theology is incomplete without making a more concerted effort to draw from the theology expressed by the very laypeople who offer the liturgy to God. The absence of information on what the laypeople believe impoverishes the pastoral liturgical enterprise. The primary contribution of this proposed study is that it significantly elucidates Orthodox liturgical theology, especially its development and pastoral

1

application in America. Without this body of information, the method of liturgical theology is robbed of its most important component: the very lay-people who comprise the assembly, the Church.

ORTHODOX LITURGICAL THEOLOGY AND THE CONTRIBUTION OF THE LAITY

Eastern Orthodox liturgy has been a source of inspiration for Western liturgical reform from the early twentieth century to the present, so new information on how Eastern Christians understand liturgy can benefit pastors and theologians of the Western tradition as well as the East. This proposed study on the liturgy of the people fills a significant gap in scholarship on the participation of the laity in the Orthodox Churches of America. In this vein, the project enriches the extant scholarship by Alexei Krindatch and Amy Slagle, two sociologists of religion who have produced informative studies of Orthodoxy in America. In addition to presenting new information on the laity's engagement of the liturgy, the study establishes a third foundation of liturgical theology that complements the contributions of liturgical historians and sacramental theologians. An analysis of the laity's engagement of the liturgy serves as an informative resource for Western liturgical scholars who refer to studies on Orthodox liturgy as crucial sources for comparative analysis.

The prevailing pastoral model of Orthodox liturgical theology is to explain the history of the liturgy and catechize people on the meaning of the extant liturgical components. While this method has yielded useful contributions, it has not sufficiently taken into account the evolution of liturgy within the local American environment. The continued use of the received Byzantine liturgical tradition in America amounts to the celebration of liturgies developed in late antiquity and the medieval era and communicated through the theological and cultural idioms of those historical periods. Orthodoxy in America has witnessed two attempts at liturgical reform, one pioneered by Alexander Schmemann (former professor and Dean of St. Vladimir's Seminary) and the other implemented by New Skete Monastery in Cambridge, New York.[1] Schmemann's reform integrated the achievements of the liturgical *ressourcement* movement, but only began to consider the cultural implications of celebrating a liturgy formed primarily in Byzantium and Rus' in the medieval era. New Skete's reform has taken the local culture into serious consideration in its liturgical revision.

Schmemann's and New Skete's liturgical renewal programs elucidated the need for contemporary liturgy the laypeople can comprehend. Detailed reports on how the laity engage and understand the liturgy can strengthen contemporary Orthodox liturgical renewal. Liturgical theologians contributing to renewal programs need quality sources on how laypeople engage the liturgy to produce transformative work: this is the primary objective of my proposal. This research project has the capacity to elucidate the realities of parish liturgical life by establishing the sources and methods clergy and parish leaders use to teach liturgy.

Methodology

The primary feature of this project is an articulation of the people's theology of the liturgy. The study employs the method presented by Margaret Mary Kelleher in her description of the theologian's task in carrying out a project of ritual studies in "Liturgical Theology: A Task and a Method."[2] The project also draws from the methodologies of Mark Searle, Nathan Mitchell, and Kevin Irwin in the field of liturgical ritual studies.[3] Information will be collected from people of four Orthodox parishes and includes an examination of the rituals in which they participate. The investigator will work with the pastors of the communities to select men and women who represent parish demographics. The communities selected for this study represent the regional and ethnic diversity of Orthodox jurisdictions in America. Parishes from California (Greek Archdiocese), New Mexico (Ukrainian Orthodox Church in the USA), Minnesota (Greek Archdiocese), and Massachusetts (Orthodox Church in America) are participating in the study.

The study occurs in three substantive parts. Part 1 explains the background of liturgical practices in the Orthodox communities of America by defining the primary schools of liturgical theology that influence parish practice and presenting information on parish liturgy taken from a survey of pastors. The second component presents and categorizes the people's perspectives on the liturgy by presenting summaries and a description of the data collected from interviews about the liturgy with a selection of laypeople representing four Orthodox parishes. The focus group questions collected narrative information on the people's understanding of the liturgy. The third component is substantive: it brings the people's theology into dialogue with the teachings of authoritative theology. This part of the study presents the most prominent liturgical figures and teachings that have influenced liturgical practice in the Orthodox Churches of America. A comparison between the authoritative liturgical theology and the laity's liturgical theology follows.

LIVED RELIGION AND LITURGICAL THEOLOGY

There is a vast body of scholarly literature on lived religion, collected in influential studies on religion in America, spiritual practices, and the daily prayers and rituals performed by ordinary laity. Collecting and elaborating information on "ordinary" people is not designed to demean or belittle the ordinary person (as if God did not hear their prayers!), nor to diminish the profundity of liturgical theology. The study of lived religion provides precious insights into the rituals people perform, and the place of priority of community ritual celebration in the context of daily life. Employing sociological methods of ethnography, many scholars have produced studies presenting the religious and spiritual narratives of ordinary people to provide the reader with a sense of religious life interpreted and practices in non-official capacities, by nonexperts. For the purposes of this study on the liturgical theology of Orthodox laity, the recent work of Nancy Ammerman and Ricky Manalo are the most compatible studies.

Ammerman presents her methodology in detail in the introduction of her study.[4] Ammerman suggests that the yield from studying everyday spiritual life is much more robust than limiting one's examination to official texts, rituals, and statements, as "contemporary spiritual realities encompass a much broader range of practices, experiences, beliefs, and affiliations."[5] Ammerman asserts that people's spiritual practices are nourished over a period of time and are much more important than philosophical systems.[6] But individual spiritual practices are not mutually exclusive from official religious communities. Ammerman suggests that individual narratives contribute to and are derived from congregational identity, as the narrative of everyday life represents the meaning gleaned from community associations and other influences.[7] Ammerman observed that the actual narratives presented by individuals encompassed much more than spiritual practices or religious devotions. The narratives were complicated and multilayered.[8] Ammerman's reflection on the complexity of the narrative and its capacity to encompass themes outside of religion and spirituality is intriguing: she picks up on the way one's description of spirituality naturally includes all of the other contexts and factors contributing to the way we live in daily life.

Ammerman's commitment to presenting spiritual and religious perspectives through the careful collection of narratives from nonexperts also inspired Ricky Manalo's study on the relationship between official Catholic liturgy and liturgical theology and lived religion among Catholic people.[9] Manalo sought to broaden the scope of "what constitute worshipful practices in the everyday lives of Christians" by putting daily prayer, devotion, and spirituality into dialogue with official liturgical rites.[10] Manalo draws upon a plethora of Christian thinkers and practitioners in his attempt to deepen our understanding of liturgical theology by presenting the narratives of a variety of Catholic people. Manalo depends mostly upon the work of Peter Phan, who argues that Vatican II's teaching on liturgy as the source and summit of Christian life means that the object of liturgy is not an aesthetically pleasing liturgical celebration, but an encounter with the living God.[11] Phan's insistence that one must consult practices in addition to the official liturgy to see how Christians seek and find God is a substantial contributor to Manalo's work.

Manalo's study gives credence to the place of popular religion in understanding liturgy, which is a bit dissonant with the reforms implemented in the wake of the liturgical movement and by the authority of Vatican II, which liberated liturgy from the dominance of popular devotions, at least in part. Manalo writes that Catholic concern about popular religion "seems to arise from the side of official and elite groups."[12] Manalo attempts to reconcile liturgical theology with popular religion by considering "more intentionally" the people's perspectives on faith and spirituality, essentially granting nonexperts a place at a table of discourse normally dominated by experts.[13]

Ammerman and Manalo establish solid models for the method of recording spiritual and religious narratives. Ammerman's scope was broad and ambitious, as she sought to "recruit a group of participants that would, as closely as possible, mirror the religious demography of the United States."[14] Her study entailed interviewing ninety-five total participants over the course of several months.[15] She also sought to portray religious diversity by selecting participants from two contrasting cities, Boston and Atlanta. Both cities are religiously diverse, but the urban cultures differ, especially given Atlanta's historical context of "southern evangelical heritage."[16] Ammerman's own description of the process for selecting congregations and participants illuminates the attention for proper representation in order to yield solid results in the study:[17]

> We started by selecting specific congregations proportionate to the various traditions we wanted to include and then selected participants from within them to fill the demographic and participation target numbers. We attempted to tap diversity in social class by selecting parishes from neighborhoods that varied from typically working class to typically more affluent. Because we wanted to have some sense of the interaction between individual stories and the collective public narratives of religious communities, we selected a cluster of five respondents from each of the congregations that agreed to participate. Seventeen parishes, congregations, temples, a ward, and a sacred circle signed on.

Most of the participants from Ammerman's study came from mainstream organized religious communities. She and her team sought participants who tended to participate in cyberspace religious discussions, and she also noted that many of the participants were "disproportionately well-educated and well off," though this was not intentional.[18] Ammerman states the purpose of the study in plain words: "this is a book not about spiritual adventurers but about the broad mainstream of ordinary, more and less spiritually engaged Americans."[19] In other words, Ammerman's net was defined, yet broad, seeking to account for the religious and spiritual experiences of people who were mostly nominal members of a particular religious organization, but did not necessarily define themselves as very active in parish life.

Ammerman's method entailed multiple visits with the cohorts of participants. Her team prioritized an interview approach that resulted in the telling of stories, not in providing short, terse responses to a range of possibilities on a checklist.[20] Ammerman stated the necessity for developing intimacy in congregational visits, requiring a level of trust in which participants would be willing to share photos and to lead the way by telling their stories in their own words.[21]

Ammerman's study endeavored to present the narratives of people representing a broad spectrum of mainstream American religion. Manalo's study has a narrow focus. He performed ethnographic research with eight members of St. Agnes Church in San Francisco, a Roman Catholic parish.[22] Manalo also observed Mass at the parish from February 2010 to June 2012, a reasonably deep immersion into the life of one particular parish community.[23] Mary McGann's study of liturgical music at Our Lady of Lourdes parish in San Francisco, an African-American community, is an even deeper immersion into the particular liturgical practices of a parish.[24] Sally Gallagher's recent study of gender in the decision to join or belong to a community is also notable, as she closely examined the lives of three parish communities of the Pacific Northwest from 2002 to 2009 (Orthodox, conservative Protestant, and mainline Protestant).[25] Gallagher's study is groundbreaking in the method used to consider the multiple dimensions that shape a sense of belonging. She looks at a broad spectrum of communications within a parish setting to obtain a sense of people's core beliefs and depth of affiliation within the denomination.[26] Liturgy is a significant factor in Gallagher's study, but she is aiming at a focused study of identity in parishes clustered in a region, a noble undertaking that goes beyond an inventory of lay views on the liturgy.

Amy Slagle's ethnographic profiles of recent converts to the Orthodox Church shares similarities with both Ammerman's and Manalo's projects. Slagle professes to follow the patterns and practices established by Ammerman, David Hall, and Robert Orsi by embracing lived religion as breaking the division between ordinary nonexperts and official figures and teachings on conversion in Orthodoxy.[27] Slagle's objective is to present the narratives of conversion in the context of the American spiritual marketplace, while also accounting for the "ongoing post-conversion identities" of the informants as they settle into parish life.[28]

Slagle differentiates her study from comparable works by including intermarriage converts among her informants. She selected three primary field sites for her research: St. Michael's parish in Pittsburgh, a community over one-hundred years old belonging to the Orthodox Church in America, and Ascension Greek Orthodox parish, also in Pittsburgh. Slagle's choice of two Orthodox parishes in Pittsburgh coincided with her attempt to bring contemporary conversions to Orthodox Christianity into dialogue with "the supposed mainstreams of American religious life."[29] Pittsburgh is affectionately known as the "Holy Land" of Orthodoxy in North America, and has over 35 parishes with multiple ethnic jurisdictions.[30] St. Michael's was an intriguing choice as a parish established by Carpatho-Rusyn people who observed the Russian tradition. The demographic changes in St. Michael's neighborhood affected the life of the parish, especially when steel mills closed in the area. Slagle states that the local neighborhood "had a reputation for being a dangerous, high-crime area," and that most of the parishioners commuted to St. Michael's and lived as far as 45 minutes to an hour away.[31] St. Michael's was experiencing a kind of rejuvenation during the time of her study, both through pastoral outreach, and through welcoming new immigrants from Russia and Ukraine. Slagle observed worship at St. Michael's, but pointed to "informal encounters with priests and parishioners" as the ultimate key to understanding the social dynamics at play in the parish.[32]

Slagle's selection of Ascension in Pittsburgh afforded her the opportunity for diversity within her pool of informants. Ascension was not as old as St. Michael's, and most of the parishioners were affluent, open to the neighborhood, active, had high membership numbers, and also a high rate of intermarriage, one of the keystones of Slagle's study.[33] Slagle supplemented her Pittsburgh fieldwork with interviews at five additional parishes in the general region, three near Pittsburgh and two near Cleveland.[34]

Slagle further strengthened her selected field of informants by conducting an additional round of research at St. Seraphim's, an OCA parish in Jackson, Mississippi.[35] Her research in Jackson provided a regional contrast to the holy land of Pittsburgh, given the dominance of Protestantism in the south.[36] The Jackson parish also granted her access to a convert-oriented Orthodox community, diversifying her field of research. Slagle's research was a deep immersion into the lives of the parishes and her informants. She engaged the ethnographic methods of participant observation (over a period of seven months) and semi-structural interviewing.[37] Slagle conducted a total of 48 interviews, and supplemented the data provided by her informants with documentary evidence and published conversion narratives.[38] Slagle humbly asserted that her book "does not present a comprehensive or even representative portrait" of the so-called conversion experience, but her contribution provides a reasonable baseline for understanding conversion and its impact on parishes by taking a solid sample from diverse communities within one of the most vibrant Orthodox metropolises in North America (Pittsburgh) and supplementing that sample through her Mississippi fieldwork.

The studies of Ammerman, Manalo, McGann, and Slagle do not exhaust the scholarship on lived religion, but I have reflected on them here as they are the primary methodological inspirations for this study. Ammerman's study represents an attempt to unveil the lived religion belonging to the most prominent American religious organizations. The scope of her project permitted her to execute the work with a high number of participants over a long period of time. Manalo's project is similar to mine in his endeavor to bring the lived religion of his informants into dialogue with his Church's official liturgical theology. Like Ammerman, he observed and interviewed his informants over a sustained period of time. Slagle's project is particularly pertinent because of her understanding of the history and demographics of contemporary Orthodoxy in North America. She executed her research with informants from select communities who corresponded to significant identity markers in contemporary Orthodoxy: Pittsburgh represents Orthodox tradition in North America, whereas Jackson, Mississippi reflects its contemporary mission. My proposed project is similar to all three projects in the method of collecting data from selected informants via interviews.[39] My method differs, as I have collected reflections on the meaning of liturgy in the words of informants in small group settings. The scope of my project is designed to be exploratory and an initial survey. In this vein, it is not compatible with the depth and sustained period of study characterizing the three model studies presented here.

CONTEMPORARY ORTHODOXY IN NORTH AMERICA

While the Orthodox Church is among the smaller Christian communities of the United States, comprising about 0.5% of the overall US population, Orthodoxy's roots in America began with Russian missionaries to Alaska in 1794.[40] The Alaskan mission is the exception to the rule of Orthodoxy coming to America, especially the "lower-48," through immigration, a process that began when European migrants arrived in America in search of work in the nineteenth century, and continued with succeeding waves of immigrants up until today. Unlike the Roman Catholic Church, the Orthodox Church is generally distributed among semi-independent Churches that have roots in a "mother" Church overseas. Ethnicity is the face identifying Orthodox jurisdictions in America today. The Orthodox jurisdictions in America are generally separated by ethnic affiliation, with each jurisdiction enjoying an autonomous status of self-governance, even if they still adhere to a larger mother Church abroad. Most of these jurisdictions cooperate by having their bishops assemble together—the quasi-official Orthodox episcopal assembly is called the Assembly of Canonical Orthodox Bishops in America (ACOBA), the "canonical" status distinguishing these churches from Orthodox bodies that have ethnic affiliations, but are separated from their canonical counterparts on account of disputes over the calendar governing the liturgical year, the position on ecumenism, or political issues. The canonical ethnic jurisdictions in America are Greek, Antiochian, Serbian, Bulgarian, Romanian, Russian (patriarchal), Russian Orthodox Church Outside of Russia (ROCOR), Ukrainian Orthodox Church of the USA (UOC-USA), Albanian, Georgian, and Carpatho-Russian. The Orthodox Church in America (OCA) is a canonical Church with a seat on ACOBA, but they differ from all of the ethnic jurisdictions in their claim to autocephaly, canonical Church self-governance independent of a mother Church. The Greek, Ukrainian, Albanian, and Carpatho-Russian churches are all part of the Ecumenical Patriarchate of Constantinople, the Russian patriarchal churches and ROCOR belong to the Moscow Patriarchate, and the Antiochian, Serbian, Bulgarian, and Romanian churches belong to their respective mother Churches in Antioch, Serbia, Bulgaria, and Romania.

Relations among these churches have endured their ups and downs in the twentieth century, often in reaction to the persecution of mother Churches in the Soviet Union and during the Cold War. When the Moscow Patriarchate created the OCA by granting the Metropolia autocephaly in 1970, the previously uneasy relations between Moscow and the Ecumenical Patriarchate worsened. These ups and downs continue in the twenty-first century. On the one hand, relations have improved. ROCOR and the UOC-USA were alienated from most of the canonical Orthodox Churches in America until the Ecumenical Patriarchate received the UOC-USA in 1995, and ROCOR reconciled with the Moscow Patriarchate in 2007. There is a living sense of cooperation among Orthodox of varying jurisdictions, and in general, laity and clergy can worship in one another's churches without prohibitions. On the other hand, clergy and laity can experience the down side, too. There is no single English translation of the Liturgy used by the jurisdictions, which can make worshipping in another parish challenging. In some cases, it can be very difficult for clergy of one jurisdiction to concelebrate in a parish of another jurisdiction. Sometimes, laity will find that they are not allowed to receive Holy Communion in a parish of another jurisdiction unless they have been to Confession first. Most of the jurisdictions also have their own seminaries for clerical formation, despite the national trend of small theological schools struggling to survive. A detailed analysis of the problems emanating from Orthodox divisions is outside the scope of this study.[41] The weight of the separation causes enough problems that the Holy and Great Council of Crete in 2016 addressed the question of the diaspora, although assessments of the council's statement on the diaspora vary.

Despite the jurisdictional differences, ACOBA has committed to publishing sociological research on the Orthodox Churches in America. Alexei Krindatch's ongoing research on the profile of Orthodoxy in America establishes a baseline for my selection of parishes and approach to the topic. According to Krindatch's brief presentation titled "Ten Facts About Geographic Patterns," there are currently approximately 800,000 people who identify themselves as participating in parish life in the canonical Orthodox parishes of America, belonging to approximately 1,900 parish and mission communities.[42] Orthodoxy is distributed into regional clusters: the majority of parishes are in the states of New York, California, Illinois, Pennsylvania, and Massachusetts. In terms of jurisdictional distribution, readers should note that the Greek Orthodox Archdiocese of America is dominant; it is larger than all of the other Orthodox jurisdictions combined and consists of approximately 60% of all Orthodox people in America.

My selection of parish communities from which I have recruited adult informants follows the pattern of taking samples from important clusters while also seeking contrast established by Ammerman, Manalo, and Slagle. I expect the total number of informants to be between 35 and 40 for this study, and two of the four parish communities belong to the Greek Orthodox Archdiocese. Given the preponderance of the GOA in American Orthodox life, it made sense to take a larger sample size from the GOA.

Likewise, two of the four communities studied belong to the small cluster of states dominating Orthodox demographics, namely St. Katherine Greek Orthodox parish in Redondo Beach, California, and Holy Trinity Cathedral (OCA) in Boston. Holy Trinity Cathedral is particularly important because of the geographical density of Orthodox parishes in the Boston area. In this vein, the selection of St. Anthony of the Desert Orthodox mission in Las Cruces, New Mexico, provides the necessary contrast for this study. New Mexico ranks low in terms of geographic density for Orthodox parishes, although it has potential for growth. St. Anthony is also a mission community of converts in the Ukrainian Orthodox Church of the USA. The selection of St. George Greek Orthodox Church in St. Paul, Minnesota, presents some regional diversity to the study, as the four parishes come from north, south, east, and west. Krindatch's research emphasizes the relatively low numbers of active participants in parish life. The United States has fewer than one million active participants in Orthodox Church life, and the numbers vary according to jurisdiction. For the purposes of this study, the notable characteristic of Orthodoxy as a very small Church in the American religious context is somewhat helpful, as the cohorts of informants I have selected will represent patterns of Orthodox belief in America. The informants of this study are essentially actively participating members of Orthodoxy, though they are diverse in age, background, and gender.

Sources: Clergy Survey and Parish Focus Groups: Introducing the Communities

A variety of primary and secondary sources have been consulted to provide the information of this study. It begins with a description of the liturgical environment of Orthodoxy in America, including descriptions of a typical worship experience that honors the pluralism characterizing the Church in

America. The environment description moves from the general to the specific, with a survey of parish clergy providing a sample of how liturgy is celebrated in a parish. The next part of the analysis focuses on the specific by presenting the people's reflections on their experiences and understanding of liturgy in their own words.

Methodologically, the study attempts to honor regional and jurisdictional diversity.[43] The scope of the project permitted me to hold a focus group session of 2.5 hours with small groups of laity from the four parishes. The four parishes are St. George Greek Orthodox Church (SG) in urban St. Paul, Minnesota, consisting of approximately 225 members, slightly larger than the median parish size (200) and lower than the mean (321) of the Greek Orthodox Archdiocese of America as a whole. Six adults participated in the focus group on July 13, 2016.[44] The next site is Holy Trinity Orthodox Cathedral (HTC) in Boston, an OCA urban parish of approximately 125 people, larger than both the median (70) and mean (104) of the OCA. The focus group session at HTC took place on November 12, 2016, with eleven adults participating. St. Anthony of the Desert Mission (SA) is the next parish—it is a mission of the Ukrainian Orthodox Church of the USA in Las Cruces, New Mexico, a community of approximately 60 people.[45] This session took place on January 28, 2017, and seven adults contributed to the discussion. The final session was at St. Katherine Greek Orthodox parish (SK) in Redondo Beach, California, in the South Bay region of the greater Los Angeles area. St. Katherine's is a large parish of approximately 600 members. The focus group had 15 adult participants, and occurred on February 8, 2017.

In summary, the two Greek Orthodox parishes represent the dominance of the Greek Orthodox Archdiocese in the Orthodox communities of America. The selection of HTC and SA honor jurisdictional plurality, and SA offers a non-urban, mission setting representing many Orthodox communities in America. A total of 39 adults contributed to the focus group sessions. I selected the adults with the cooperation of the pastor of each parish. The adult respondents are a balanced mix of men (19) and women (20): they tend to be older, as 23 of the respondents are older than 55, with the other 16 respondents younger than 55. The convert constituency of Orthodoxy had 13 respondents, and 6 of those belong to SA, a mission parish. The other 26 respondents were born and raised Orthodox, along with a nice sampling of immigrants for whom English is their second language.

FOCUS GROUP SESSIONS:
THE INVESTIGATOR'S OBSERVATIONS

With decades of Church ministry in my portfolio, I adopted an ascetical approach to the focus group sessions. It was not merely a matter of expecting the unexpected, but to present the purpose of the project and establish an environment of careful listening. Given the small size of the Orthodox community in America, many people knew of me prior to my arrival for the focus group sessions. SG was the proverbial "guinea pig," being the first focus group, so I followed my script of simple questions on the liturgy and deviated from that list only when a respondent remark would benefit from elaboration. None of the respondents were experts, and some of them responded to my questions by asking me for an authoritative explanation of the issue. In those instances, my responses were always the same: I am here to listen to what you have to say, and there are no wrong answers. I urged respondents to say as much or little as they wished.

The dynamics of group discussion picked up momentum once respondents took the initiative to speak before the other people in the group. All of the 39 participants contributed comments, some more so than others. The decision to interview focus groups instead of individuals requires a different heuristic lens since people were sharing their views in front of others. Individual interviews permit the investigator to probe into issues with depth. In the context of the focus group, the cohorts of respondents were not only responding to the session's questions, but were also taking cues from one another. It is entirely possible that some elaboration on any given question was withheld as a consequence of group dynamics, especially for respondents who did not venture beyond their comfort zones with their comments. In two cases at SK, respondents shared additional information with me privately. In one respondent's case, he was uncomfortable sharing a view he thought others might disapprove of. Another respondent was aware that she might not have an opportunity to say everything she hoped to cover, so she handed me a printed document with additional thoughts on the Liturgy she thought of beforehand. Furthermore, in the group setting, respondents may have limited their comments to allocate more time for others to respond. This study's information is based on comments taken from one session: one might have received a more complete respondent view from follow-up visits.

My own observation of the dynamics of the sessions is that group dynamics also had positive results, mostly from the pattern of respondents picking up the threads of earlier comments or returning to the subject after they had thought about it. In many cases, obtaining information from respondents was more a matter of observing them engaging one another in a lively conversation on Liturgy. One pattern stood out among them all: the focus group discussions gained momentum and the sessions went longer than I had expected. The dynamics of group discussion demonstrated that respondents had no experience of reflecting on the meaning of Liturgy in a group context; these sessions were an invitation for respondents to speak about issues they had never been asked about, as attested to by several respondents. In each session, the discussions took on an energy and rhythm of their own. The group format seemed to encourage some respondents to offer a perspective on the Liturgy: it was more of a group discussion than an interview. Readers should therefore interpret the testimony of the respondents with the understanding that their comments on the Liturgy are an initial response to questions they have not spoken about in public, and are therefore not exhaustive of what they might have said in an elongated study of the matter. Two additional dynamics are also featured: some respondents might have withheld information, whereas the group discussion persuaded some respondents to speak about their perspectives.

Findings: A Preview

The focus group sessions contained a series of questions inviting participants to reflect on their experience of the Liturgy, exhibited in textbox 1.1. Two questions concerned how participants experienced the Divine Liturgy and Holy Communion, and asked them to identify features, experiences, and memories particularly meaningful to them. One question asked respondents to reflect on their understanding of the most holy occasions of the liturgical year, and the meaning of those rituals in their daily lives. Two questions revolved around strong experiences in the Liturgy, asking respondents to recall and reflect upon occasions they cherish, the setting for those occasions, and the contribution of those ritual moments to their lives. One question asked respondents to reflect on the role of women in liturgical ministry and their opinion on whether or not the order of deaconess should be restored. The final question asked respondents to explain how they learn about Liturgy and its meaning, and liturgical questions they'd like pastors and theologians to address. Each focus group session followed this script loosely; I deviated from the script to ask respondents to elaborate or clarify issues. I also asked respondents to explain their parish's ritual environment to gain a sense of particular parish traditions that contribute to their viewpoints.

The responses show that the four parishes of this study are imbued with the spirit of liturgical renewal, especially since respondents receive Communion frequently. Respondents lingered on their awareness of celebrating Liturgy with others, and tended to admire the ritual participation of children. They also worried that they might be unworthy of receiving Communion frequently, especially those who were raised in an era when people received Communion a few times each year at most. Many respondents noted the centrality of the homily and the narratives of saints' lives, testimony showing that the Liturgy of the Word is a priority in their parishes. While most respondents expressed relief for God's mercy tolerating their lack of attention and focus, several respondents stated their desire to be more involved in liturgical ministry. The debate on the legitimacy of women serving at the altar as assistants or deacons was vibrant, though not heated, during the focus groups: these discussions echo the dispute on restoring the deaconess raging today, especially among Orthodox Christians in America. Respondents were grateful to understand the Divine Liturgy, they tended to depict the people's participation in the contemporary Church as comparatively weaker than the rigorous preparation required in their countries of origin, and they were deeply sensitive to the fundamental moral teachings communicated through solemn occasions like Palm Sunday and the reading of the vita of St. Mary of Egypt.

Textbox 1.1. Focus Group Session Discussion Questions

The Divine Liturgy

What parts of the Divine Liturgy appeal to you the most, and why?
In your own words, briefly: what is happening in the Divine Liturgy? What does it mean?
What does it mean to receive Holy Communion?
How often do you receive Holy Communion?
How do you prepare for Holy Communion?
What is the relationship between the Sunday Divine Liturgy and your daily life?
How has the Liturgy developed since you began going to church? Is it exactly the same as it was? Has it changed? How?

The Liturgical Year

What features of the liturgical year engage you the most?
Holy Week and Pascha: how do you understand this week? When you go to church, what are you remembering? How does the theme of that week speak to you and your life?

Liturgical Intensity

Tell me about one moment in church that was particularly memorable and important in your life: when did it happen, and why was it memorable?
Tell me about one moment outside of church that was particularly memorable in a Christian way: when did it happen and why?
How do you learn about the liturgy?
What aspects of the Church's Liturgy would you like to learn more?

What would you like to see changed in the liturgy, and why?

Liturgy and Gender

Is gender equality or differentiation important to you in terms of liturgical ministry and participation? If so, why?

In terms of significant findings, we learn that respondents are acutely attuned to the personal dimensions of Liturgy in both positive and negative ways. The sense of joy that occurs when people receive Communion with the rest of the parish is both personal and a confirmation of the effect of liturgical renewal. The lament coming from the knowledge that some are ineligible for Communion, or fear that others in the community might disapprove of them shows the negative side of the personal dimension. The rituals suggesting that Christ, Mary, or the saints are present with the people easily resonated the most with the people: they consistently suggested a desire for evidence of divine compassion in the Liturgy.

We use the people's yearning for divine compassion and their attention to those excluded from the Liturgy to suggest areas theologians might engage in updating liturgical theology. In terms of updating the agenda of liturgical theology, it is not sufficient to identify a few lacunae of liturgical catechesis and schedule research and publication of materials that would fill the gap. The outcome of this study leads to bolder aspirations: the people's experience of Liturgy can result in profound reflections on God as the lover of humankind and how receiving the gift of divine grace from God can build up community in this world. There is no reason to limit the enterprise of exploring ways to enrich the liturgical event to experts when the voices of the nonexperts are so valuable. In the existing paradigm of authoritative liturgical theology, the mechanism for instruction is predominantly vertical, a system in which the experts administer liturgy and sacraments to the people. The outcome of this study demands an adjustment on the part of pastors and theologians to include more intentionally the people's perspective in the liturgical enterprise. Their attention to the people is not a matter of mere acknowledgment that the "Mrs. Murphys" and "Mr. Pappas's" of Orthodox parishes understand the Liturgy. The experts are called to locate themselves as part of that assembly, to relate their own experiences to those of the people, so that their theological reflection originates from the same context of divine-human encounter experienced by the people. In other words, the pastors and theologians are called to offer a permanent seat at the table of authoritative theology to the people, whose responses to liturgical events might lack the sophistication of experts, but are just as potent. Our thesis is that the enterprise of liturgical theology will be deeply enriched if the theologians accept this invitation, and we are confident that the testimony of the people in this book will persuade them to agreement.

The analysis of Orthodox liturgical theology and practice in America and the observations taken from the four focus groups yield substantial insights on the ways people experience the Liturgy. A review of major schools of liturgical theology in America shows that the Church in America has proven to be a laboratory for liturgical renewal and a bastion of conservatism, or fidelity to maintaining the status quo. Alexander Schmemann and Alkiviadis Calivas exercised substantial influence in implementing liturgical renewal through their respective tenures as professors of liturgical theology at St. Vladimir's Seminary and Holy Cross Greek Orthodox School of Theology. Their initiatives encouraged parish clergy to engage the people in liturgical celebration, enhance the Liturgy of the Word, improve preaching, and cele- brate in a style that illuminates the Liturgy as a foretaste of life in the kingdom of God. Through their efforts along with those whose teaching supported them, multiple generations of Orthodox clergy in America set the stage for a Eucharistic revival that substantially increased the people's en- gagement of the Liturgy, primarily through using English for worship and in receiving Communion frequently.

These schools of liturgical renewal are joined by conservative schools of liturgical theology in America. Liturgical maximalism is one variant of these schools, and this mindset shares the notion that the people are to be trans- formed through the Liturgy, but differs by promoting more frequent liturgies in individual parishes and celebrating Liturgy without any abbreviations. Liturgical maximalism is also hesitant to impose change or abbreviations, as it views the Liturgy as akin to a plant or tree that develops according to a divine growth cycle—liturgical revision or change is viewed as disrupting that growth. One should also note that high-profile seminary teachers like Schmemann and Calivas are not the only shapers of the liturgical mindset: clergy are influenced by parish mentors, friends, and their own independent reading as they develop their own styles of liturgical leadership. The coexis- tence of multiple liturgical schools and styles of celebration in Orthodox America foregrounds the analysis of the people's reflections on the liturgy, especially since one cannot conveniently depict Orthodox liturgy in America as Westernized. Liturgical pluralism describes liturgy in America more accu- rately, and the people testify both to the pluralism they experience, and the conflicts that occasionally emerge when the liturgical schools collide with one another.

The people's reflections on their liturgical experience testify to liturgical pluralism and offer insight on the fissures between authoritative liturgical theology and the people's understanding of what liturgy is. Authoritative liturgical theology refers to multiple layers of teaching on the Liturgy that carry authority in some way. The highest level of authoritative liturgical theology is teaching deemed official, especially teachings emanating from the legacy of the seven ecumenical councils recognized by the Orthodox Church. Without an apparatus of documents codifying this official theology, examples of the highest level of authoritative theology would be located in liturgical components bearing the conciliar legacy, such as the Nicene-Constantinopolitan Creed recited at each Liturgy, the *Monogenes* hymn on the second antiphon, the teaching on icons, and the Eucharistic theology of the three anaphoras used for Orthodox liturgy, especially the distinctive pneumatology of the epicleses.[46]

The next level of liturgical theology is the one most prevalent in the Orthodox world: the broad notion of a neo-patristic synthesis, a heritage of patristic liturgical theology in which the fathers speak univocally on the liturgy. This quasi-official approach to liturgical theology uses the fathers as a source to test the legitimacy of liturgical practices and interpretations. I mention it here because it is a living method of teaching Liturgy at the parish level. A simple example: one can learn Orthodox Eucharistic theology by reading the mystagogical catecheses of St. Cyril of Jerusalem. The next and final level of authoritative liturgical theology comes from the liturgical academy. In some instances, the works of Schmemann are held with an authority equal to the fathers in Orthodox America; other works are considered authoritative because they are produced by experts.

This study argues that the people have received some of the teachings of authoritative liturgical theology in America, but their responses to these teachings raise new questions on crucial liturgical practices and Church positions. The people occasionally struggle to articulate their understanding of the liturgy, but their reflections demonstrate a sense of participating in the life of God and striving to remain faithful disciples that goes beyond concrete and neat phrases. Understanding the Liturgy is a lifelong process that has no end-date, and it cannot be evaluated through cognitive mechanisms. Parish liturgy has evolved in America, with the most significant change being the introduction of English. English is not the only language used, as some respondents remarked about the continued use of Greek, but the gradual transition to English has dramatically changed the experience of participants, who now have some sense of what is happening in Liturgy. The switch to the vernacular elucidates a crucial shift in the people's engagement of the Liturgy: they became active hearers of the Word of God, and experienced the process of witnessing to epic narratives proclaimed in the Liturgy that raised questions for them on the human condition. The shift to English functioned as a portal for the people to see themselves included in the narrative stories of salvation history.

This study also shows the limits of the changes effected by liturgical renewal. Most of the people hailed the Eucharistic revival and expressed joy and relief at the privilege of experiencing unity in worship, with everyone receiving together. Their comments testified to the strengthening of their bonds with God and with one another. But the people's remarks on their experience in church also show how the Eucharistic revival collides with the piety associated with the fear of damnation from receiving Communion unworthily, as many people wondered if they had prepared for Communion with enough rigor. Sorrow over the knowledge that other Christians are not permitted to partake of Communion suggested that the desire that all participate in the Liturgy still has its limits. The analysis wrestles with the irony that the participants are overjoyed to belong to a community, yet yearn for more instances of experiencing divine compassion in the Liturgy. Participants express confidence that the Liturgy is a bearer of the Church's teaching on theological anthropology, but they disagree on how that theological precept is manifest. For some, the current form of a male-only clergy continues the structural tradition passed on from Christ, through the apostles, to today's Church, while others view the continued absence of deaconesses from ministry as a distortion of the new humanity inaugurated by Christ. Both sides agree on one thing: the Liturgy should manifest the Church's theological anthropology.

Besides the primary findings gleaned from the people's responses to the focus group questions, this analysis yields four significant conclusions. The first concerns the complexity of the American Orthodox context. While this study confirms that American Orthodoxy has been generally hospitable to both conciliarity and liturgical renewal, it also dispels the notion that Orthodoxy has become quite Westernized. Despite its small size among other churches and religions, Orthodoxy in America is quite diverse, and has multiple models of liturgical renewal. The focus group sessions elucidate the complex and uneven process of implementing liturgical renewal, and how some opponents to change sought Byzantinization as an alternative to the notion that the Church was being Americanized. In this sense, one can define the status of American Orthodoxy as a Church shaped by immigrants that evolves independently of the mother Churches, largely because of the pluralism among Orthodox in America. The second major finding concerns tradition, as the evidence suggests that people understand tradition as that which has been received from the previous generation, even if these traditions are actually innovative and have limited roots in Church history. One also learns that liturgical traditions are deeply personal: faithful honor them and feel a strong sense of responsibility for passing them on to the next generation because of the love they have for the elders who introduced them to tradition. The recent and personal qualities of dimension supersede the academic contributions that locate rites and practices at particular points in Church history. In terms of the people's experience of tradition, the personal dimensions are more influential than evidence of historical precedence, and illuminate how people interpret their local liturgical traditions.

This observation on tradition shapes the third major conclusion, that the experts of the academy have the most capacity to enrich liturgical life by living side-by-side with the people, witnessing to their experiences, and treating them as partners in the enterprise of liturgical theology as opposed to subjects. In this sense, the role of the people as the Church's theologians takes on a new quality beyond those ascribed to Kavanagh's "Mrs. Murphy": expert theologians are to seek them out and view their verbal reflections on Liturgy as authentic first-order theology, even if these narratives lack the precision of expert theological jargon. In other words, the Church should ever seek to hear the testimony of its faithful on the Liturgy, not as an academic attempt to honor the legitimacy of popular religion, but to respect their testimony as evidence of real, personal and communal encounters with God and the world. Concluding with these recommendations does not assume that the people will conform to the hegemony of authoritative theology, but that authoritative theology will embrace the people's testimony as an authentic witness to tradition and truth.

NOTES

1. See surveys of these two reforms in Nicholas Denysenko, *Liturgical Reform After Vatican II: The Impact on Eastern Orthodoxy* (Minneapolis: Fortress Press, 2015).

2. Margaret Mary Kelleher, "Liturgical Theology: A Task and a Method," *Worship* 62, no. 1 (1988): 2–25.

3. Mark Searle, *Called to Participate: Theological, Ritual, and Social Perspectives,* ed. Barbara Searle and Anne Y. Koester (Collegeville, MN: Liturgical Press, 2006); Kevin W. Irwin, *Context and Text: Method in Liturgical Theology* (Collegeville, MN: Liturgical Press, 1994); Nathan Mitchell, *Liturgy and the Social Sciences* (Collegeville, MN: Liturgical Press, 1999).

4. Nancy Ammerman, *Sacred Stories, Spiritual Tribes: Finding Religion in Everyday Life* (Oxford, New York: Oxford University Press, 2014). See also idem, ed., *Everyday Religion: Observing Modern Religious Lives* (Oxford, New York: Oxford University Press, 2007).

5. Ammerman, *Sacred Stories,* 6.

6. Ibid., 7.

7. Ibid., 8.

8. Ibid., 9.

9. Ricky Manalo, *The Liturgy of Life: The Interrelationship of Sunday Eucharist and Everyday Worship Practices* (Collegeville, MN: Liturgical Press, 2014).

10. Ibid., 11–12.

11. Peter C. Phan, *Being Religious Interreligiously: Asian Perspectives on Interfaith Dialogue in Postmodernity* (Maryknoll, NY: Orbis Books, 2004); idem, "Liturgy of Life as the 'Summit and Source' of the Eucharistic Liturgy: Church Worship as Symbolization of the Liturgy of Life?" In *Incongruities: Who We Are and How We Pray,* ed. Timothy Fitzgerald and David A. Lysik (Chicago: Liturgy Training Publications, 2000), 5–33.

12. Manalo, *The Liturgy of Life,* 97.

13. Ibid., 98.

14. Ammerman, *Sacred Stories, Spiritual Tribes,* 10.

15. Ibid.

16. Ibid., 11.

17. Ibid.

18. Ibid., 12.

19. Ibid., 13.

20. Ibid., 14.

21. Ibid., 15–17.

22. Manalo, *The Liturgy of Life*, 15.

23. Ibid.

24. Mary E. McGann, *A Precious Fountain: Music in the Worship of an African American Catholic Community*, Virgil Michel Series, ed. Don Saliers (Collegeville, MN: Liturgical Press, 2004).

25. Sally Gallagher, *Getting to Church: Narratives of Gender and Joining* (Oxford: Oxford University Press, 2017).

26. Ibid., 10–11.

27. Amy Slagle, *The Eastern Church in the Spiritual Marketplace: American Conversions to Orthodox Christianity* (DeKalb: Northern Illinois University Press, 2011), 12.

28. Ibid., 13.

29. Ibid., 25. Note that Slagle used pseudonyms for the names of her field sites, applied to parishes in this case (see p. 173, n. 1).

30. Ibid., 25–26.

31. Ibid., 27.

32. Ibid., 29.

33. Ibid., 31–32.

34. Ibid., 33.

35. Ibid.

36. Ibid.

37. Ibid., 36.

38. Ibid.

39. See also Clare Johnson, "Researching Ritual Practice," *Studia Liturgica* 35, no. 2 (2005): 204–20.

40. See "Orthodox Christianity in the 21st Century," Pew Research Center Study, November 8, 2017, http://www.pewforum.org/2017/11/08/orthodox-christianity-in-the-21st-century/ (accessed March 7, 2018). For the history of Orthodoxy in America, see Thomas E. FitzGerald, *The Orthodox Church*, Denominations in America 7, ed. Henry Warner Bowden (Westport, CT: Greenwood Press, 1959); Mark Stokoe and Leonid Kishkovsky, *Orthodox Christians in North America: 1794–1994* (Syosset, NY: Orthodox Christian Publications Center, 1995).

41. Some Orthodox Churches withheld participation in the council. For a sharp critique of the 2016 council in Crete, see Peter Heers, "The 'Council' in Crete and the New Emerging Ecclesiology: An Orthodox Examination," Orthodox Ethos, March 21, 2017, https://orthodoxethos.com/post/the-council-of-crete-and-the-new-emerging-ecclesiology-an-orthodox-examination (accessed March 7, 2018). See the council's statement on the "diaspora," titled "The Orthodox Diaspora," Holy and Great Council, https://www.holycouncil.org/-/diaspora (accessed March 7, 2018).

42. Alexei Krindatch, "Ten Facts About Geographic Patterns of Orthodox Church Life in North America," http://hirr.hartsem.edu/research/TenFactsAboutGeographicPatterns.pdf (accessed December 6, 2016). See also the informative demographic report and analysis of Michael Plekon, "Belonging to the Church in the Twenty-First Century, When 'The Church Has Left the Building'," in *The Church Has Left the Building: Faith, Parish, and Ministry in the Twenty-First Century*, ed. Michael Plekon, Maria Gwyn McDowell, and Elizabeth Schroeder (Eugene, OR: Cascade Books, 2016), 1–16.

43. For current information on parish size per jurisdiction in America, see Alexei Krindatch, "Orthodox Christian Churches in the 21st Century: A Parish Life Study," ACOBA, http://www.assemblyofbishops.org/assets/files/studies/2018-01-OrthodoxChurchesIn21Century AmericaFinal.pdf (accessed March 7, 2018).

44. Ibid.

45. Krindatch's study of parishes did not include UOC-USA communities. The 60 members of St. Anthony of the Desert makes it smaller than the mean (171) and median (100) of all parishes participating in the study (ibid.).

46. See Robert F. Taft, "Monogenes," in *The Oxford Dictionary of Byzantium*, vol. 2, ed. Alexander Kazhdan (New York: Oxford University Press, 1991), 1397; Cyril of Jerusalem, *Lectures on the Christian Sacraments: The Procatechesis and the Five Mystagogical Catecheses Ascribed to Cyril of Jerusalem*, trans. Maxwell Johnson (Crestwood, NY: St. Vladimir's Seminary Press, 2017). For the seminal study on pneumatology and the epiclesis, see Anne McGowan, *Eucharistic Epicleses, Ancient and Modern: Speaking of the Spirit in Eucharistic Prayers*, Alcuin Club Collections, no. 89 (London: SPCK, 2014).

Chapter Two

Mainstream Orthodox Liturgical Theology in America

Orthodox Liturgy in America: how is it celebrated and taught? Do clergy have programs of liturgical formation in the parish? When they teach people about liturgy, what sources do they use? This chapter presents a profile of Orthodox liturgical practices in America, in as much as this is possible. Describing Orthodoxy in America as diverse is an understatement: in addition to jurisdictional multiplicity, liturgical diversity exists within the Orthodox Churches in America, even in individual jurisdictions. One cannot account for all differences in liturgical practice from one parish to another.

On the surface, liturgical language is the most diverse component in parish liturgical practice. While all jurisdictions use English to some degree, parishes also worship in Greek, Church Slavonic, Arabic, Ukrainian, Romanian, Georgian, and Spanish, not to mention the different languages used for worship in Alaskan parishes.[1] Furthermore, any given parish might employ multiple liturgical languages for services. Parishes of the GOA employ varying mixes of Greek and English. Several English translations of the Liturgy are used in the jurisdictions, with multiple translations often used within a single jurisdiction.[2] There is no guarantee that the liturgical text prayed by the people matches the official text printed in the book: I have stumbled while reciting the Creed with the assembly on more than one occasion, when the text memorized by the assembly differs from the version printed in the book. These differences apply to ritual patterns as well. Numerous patterns are used for the censing appointed to the Alleluiarion: practices vary from censing during the Prokeimenon and Epistle, the Trisagion, and the Alleluia. One parish censes the altar, iconostasis, and all the people, and in another, the priest or deacon simply waves the censer over the open Gospel book.

Clearly, these examples illustrate diversity, and differences not only between jurisdictions, but among parishes within jurisdictions.

If this brief description paints a picture of absolute chaos, that is not the intent. My description of Orthodox Liturgy in America demonstrates two points well-known to students of liturgical history. The reality of liturgical celebration in America demythologizes the notion of liturgical uniformity in any given Church, even if the leaders of the Church promote and encourage uniformity. As Robert Taft has said many times, the liturgy is a local event.[3] Second, a structural unity exists in the midst of all this diversity. The fundamental order of the Liturgy is the same in all places. Each parish's Liturgy has litanies, the proclamation of the Word, and the preparation, offering, and partaking of the gifts consecrated by God. The divergent practices characterizing contemporary Orthodox Liturgy in America were caused by the circumstances of jurisdictional plurality and adjustments to the Church's development in the context of immigration, attrition, and the reception of converts into the Church. The Liturgy is in a constant state of development and adjustment, especially in the use of English translations.

This chapter analyzes the current state of Orthodox liturgical theology and celebration in America by introducing the primary schools of liturgical theology and describing parish liturgical practices. Diversity characterizes the present state of liturgical theology and practice because of jurisdictional plurality and the transition of the Church from an immigrant community to a multi-generation American Church that has received many converts. While I will not account for all liturgical variants in Orthodox America—especially since I am not aware of them all—I will present the primary schools of liturgical theology in America. The primary schools are liturgical renewal, exemplified by the teaching of Alexander Schmemann and Alkiviadis Calivas; liturgical maximalism, promoted by the Russian Orthodox Church Outside of Russia; and maintaining the liturgical status quo, a collection of practices that threads through all jurisdictions. Robert Taft's influence on the interpretation and teaching of the Liturgy is also included, given Taft's stature as the preeminent historian of the Byzantine liturgy who taught many of today's liturgical theologians who contribute to the formation of Orthodox clergy in America. A description of Orthodox liturgical practices follows, based on a survey administered to Orthodox clergy and information on liturgical practices in the four parishes constituting the focus groups of this study. The presentation on parish liturgy descends from the general to the particular, to provide the reader with a general sense of Orthodox liturgy, along with specific information on the parish liturgical environments shaping the respondents from the four focus groups.

LITURGICAL RENEWAL: ALEXANDER SCHMEMANN

Alexander Schmemann's reputation as the pioneer of the Eucharistic revival in the Orthodox Church is well-known and documented in several scholarly books and essays.[4] Schmemann's popularity as a teacher is often attributed to his dynamism as a teacher and public speaker, but it is likely that Schmemann resonated with Orthodox in the West because he was formed by the best theologians of the East and West. Schmemann's theological vision was shaped by Sergius Bulgakov, Kyprian Kern, and Nicholas Afanasiev, but he also engaged his Western interlocutors with the same vigor.[5] Schmemann's course syllabi included readings on liturgical history and theology from renowned thinkers like Odo Casel and Oscar Cullmann, so students were exposed to the larger picture of Christian liturgical development.[6]

We tend to compartmentalize Schmemann as a liturgical theologian whose primary legacy was in restoring the right relationship between liturgy and theology, and while I do not contest this assertion, he also made a significant practical contribution. In many ways, Schmemann revived the liturgical proposals that the Moscow Council of 1917–18 was unable to consider, and applied them to Orthodox Church life in the West.[7] Schmemann's applications of liturgical renewal were designed to reveal the liturgy as the authentic source of theology: liturgical celebration was to be a real epiphany of the kingdom of God, an encounter of the assembly with the living God. Schmemann privileged select changes in liturgical practice over the performance of cosmetic surgery on the entire liturgy. These changes were manifest in the style of liturgical celebration by the priest and the participation of the people in the Liturgy. The priest, along with all the clergy, would celebrate clearly and comprehensibly with the prayers said aloud for the people to hear. Hearing was one aspect of the people's participation that granted them access to the Liturgy: they were to engage all appointed ritual gestures of the Liturgy as well.

Schmemann's Eucharistic Revival

The most visible change enacted in Schmemann's reform was the shift of the people from passive spectators during Holy Communion to an active assembly of participants.[8] The regular reception of Holy Communion was the most visible change, but even this revision belonged to a larger enterprise: the people were to participate not only as the recipients, but also those who offered the Liturgy, to become not those who witnessed the miracle of bread and cup becoming the Lord's body and blood, but participants in and witnesses to the promise of Christ's resurrection given freely to all, and the transfiguration of humankind and creation. In other words, the effect of regularly participating in the entire Liturgy was for the people to become a body

that witnesses, confesses, and testifies to the joy of God's promise in everyone and everything. The gift of receiving Communion was to see the world in
a new way, to see things as they really are, creatures and creations God
described as "good."[9] On the surface, the actual liturgical change seems
limited: the structure and content of the Orthodox liturgy changed subtly in
its performance. The priest led the people in prayer, and they were able to
hear him and thus join him in offering and praying. Instead of abstaining
from Communion, they engaged the rite and received it. The objective of this
change in the style of liturgical celebration was for the people to truly see the
theophanies of God present throughout the world: in creation, matter, and
especially in one's fellow human beings. The capacity to see and express
thanks for God's goodness in all things is the realization of the objective of
liturgical theology, that the Liturgy is the epiphany of the kingdom of God.

Schmemann's imprint on liturgical renewal is best-known for the introduction of frequent Communion and increased lay participation in the Liturgy, but his contribution was not limited to the Eucharist. Schmemann's restoration of the primacy of Liturgy in its relationship with theology generated a
new interest in Liturgy, one that was also vibrant in the Western Christian
Churches. Schmemann generated excitement among the clergy who learned
from him at St. Vladimir's, and he also had a public profile as a lecturer who
traveled across North America, sharing his vision on liturgy's capacity to
reveal the kingdom of God and bring the Church into communion with God.
Schmemann's essays on liturgical theology and his short books on Sacraments and Orthodoxy and Great Lent became instant classics in the North
American context and beyond, as his books were also translated in Greek and
circulated among clergy and laity in Greece.[10] Although he was trained as a
historian, Schmemann's published works were not studies in liturgical history. He demonstrated his knowledge of the history published by his contem-
poraries in the field of Byzantine liturgy, as demonstrated by his public letter
to Metropolitan Ireney (Bekish) on the rationale for liturgical reform in the
American context in 1972.[11] This letter contains several references to the
studies of Juan Mateos, whose work on the Liturgy of the Hours and the
proclamation of the Word in the Divine Liturgy established the DNA of early
liturgical development.[12] But history was secondary for Schmemann: his
critique of Vatican II confirmed that he was not interested in substantial
revisions of the Orthodox liturgy, so radical reform does not belong to his
legacy.

Schmemann's Influence on the Parish

Schmemann's success resides in his ability to make the Orthodox Liturgy
accessible to the people in the North American context. Thomas Pott's taxonomy of Byzantine liturgical reform is helpful in this regard.[13] Schmemann's

reform certainly does not conform to the model of revising the Liturgy to fit the people, but it doesn't perfectly fit the related model of converting the people to the Liturgy. In Schmemann's case, a slightly revised model based on Pott's useful taxonomy works best: the clergy were converted to teach and celebrate the existing liturgy in such a way that the people could engage it. Schmemann's legacy was passed on to multiple generations of clergy who served the OCA, Antiochian Archdiocese, Serbian Church, and the clergy of jurisdictions who learned at St. Vladimir's or learned from Schmemann via his publications or public lectures. Parish clergy introduced the practices of liturgical celebration involving the people's participation, worshiping in a way that joined the people to the Church's prayer, and encouraging the people to receive Communion regularly. These changes would have been impossible without parish priests introducing them to the people.

Schmemann's influence entailed the involvement of experts who shared his commitment to liturgical renewal. A crucial component of the laity's liturgical participation was liturgical music. St. Vladimir's hired Boris Ledkovsky to teach liturgical music, and he formed musical leaders according to the spirit of the Moscow Synodal choir's legacy. This legacy sought to revive canonical singing, with an emphasis on chant-based singing, resetting the proper relationship between liturgical texts and music, and encouraging assembly singing. The Moscow synodal musical heritage permeated much of the life of the OCA as Ledkovsky passed on the tradition to his protégé, David Drillock, whose tenure lasted as music professor lasted into the early twenty-first century.[14] Musicians who learned at St. Vladimir's applied this philosophy of liturgical singing to parish life in the same parishes the clergy led.

Schmemann's contribution to the experience of parish worship involved the entirety of the liturgical experience. People were not only encouraged to partake of Communion regularly, but they prayed in English increasingly, heard more of the services in a language they understood, were encouraged to sing their portions of the liturgy, and were exposed to liturgical dimensions and components that were previously less known to them. The hymns appointed to Vespers and Matins provide a good example for us. The hymns sung on Psalm 140 (Lord, I Call) at Vespers were often abbreviated (with only one or two sung by the choir) or chanted very quickly by an appointed reader. This practice originated from choir directors with limited musical training; many directors were able to read music and time signatures, but lacked the training needed to lead recitative chants. Musicians trained at St. Vladimir's learned how to lead chant-based singing, teach diction to singers, and mastered the tones appointed to the hymns. Training choir directors to conduct chant-based hymns changed the people's experience of the services: they heard more of the hymnography, and it became more comprehensible to them, when a choir director or chanter did not rush through the setting.

It is crucial to note that this was not a matter of restructuring the services, composing new poetic hymns, or abbreviating the services. The principle was to revive the services themselves so that they would be celebrated in a style appropriate to their form and function. Schmemann was responsible for cultivating a liturgical environment that promoted good liturgy: the primary reform was in the style of liturgical celebration. He did not invent these principles on his own, but inherited them from the teachings of theologians like Nicholas Afanasiev and musicians like Ledkovsky and Johann von Gardner.

It is also noteworthy that these reforms mirrored those that occurred in the West: the principles of Schmemann's liturgical renewal also underpinned the aspirations of the ecumenical liturgical movement. Celebrating clearly in the language of the people in a style conducive to comprehension was a value transcending denominational boundaries. The difference between the Western reforms and Schmemann's is the scope of reform: the reforms of the Western Churches were much more expansive in the rearrangement of services, creation and introduction of new material, and authorization of new styles of aesthetics and celebration. Schmemann's introduction of liturgical renewal to the Orthodox Church in the West carries a hint of irony. On the one hand, he introduced a program of renewal originally intended for the mother Church in Russia, so the liturgical renewal occurred in a new habitat, outside of the original context for which it was intended. The introduction of these changes to an Eastern body of Christians in the West also coheres with the general trend of liturgical reform, as the changes unleashed by Vatican II were designed for the Latin rite Churches of the West, with the same holding true for the mainline Protestant Churches that implemented similar programs of liturgical renewal. On the other hand, Schmemann's program of liturgical renewal also coincided with the establishment of an autocephalous Orthodox Church when the Moscow Patriarchate granted autocephaly to Schmemann's Orthodox Church in America in 1970. The contemporaneous co-existence of a local Orthodox Church in America that sought to bring all Orthodox clergy and people into one body along with a Liturgy promoting the corporate worship of this people—clergy and laity offering and receiving the Liturgy together—seems to fit hand-in-glove, with local Church independence and an authentically local liturgy compatible partners. In other words, the creation of an autocephalous Church would conceivably provide fertile soil for the cultivation of an ecclesiology that brought clergy and laity together, instead of promoting the clergy administering the sacraments to the laity. The success of the establishment of an autocephalous local Church depended on the participation of all the Orthodox jurisdictions in America, and this has yet to come to realization, largely because of the active opposition of the mother Churches abroad to such an arrangement. Despite the lack of success by the OCA in establishing a single, united autocephalous Church in America, the program of liturgical renewal has endured, and continues to have life outside of the narrow context of Schmemann's OCA. This means that the OCA itself was not the only Church providing fertile soil for the proliferation of a liturgy that promoted the concelebration of clergy and laity together.

ST. VLADIMIR'S AFTER SCHMEMANN

Schmemann's position as dean and professor of Liturgy at St. Vladimir's Seminary made the school the center for liturgical renewal in America. In addition to Schmemann's courses, St. Vladimir's also hosted a summer liturgical institute for parish clergy and musicians for several decades as a way of extending the ministry into the life of the Church. Following Schmemann's death in 1983, St. Vladimir's maintained its heritage as a center of liturgical renewal and enjoyed continuity through Paul Meyendorff's teaching of liturgical theology and the active presence of Schmemann's disciples in seminary education.

St. Vladimir's shifted its focus from liturgical renewal to patristics when John Behr was appointed as dean of the seminary. This change in focus conformed St. Vladimir's approach to clerical formation with the majority of the Orthodox world. The dominant model of Orthodox education emphasizes mastering the fundamentals of the patristic tradition and adopting the mindset of the fathers. Active and frequent participation in the Church's liturgical life is a staple feature of restoring the mind of the fathers to the Church. Schmemann himself was a frequent critic of the idealization of the fathers in American Orthodox culture, even though he contributed to this phenomenon. Schmemann distinguished between a negative and misled idolizing of the fathers—a type of harmful antiquarianism—and a positive adoption of the mind and spirit of the fathers, whose theology was capacitated by their constant engagement in corporate worship.[15] Schmemann's appeal for adopting the mind of the fathers lacks historical precision, as he synthesizes the fathers into a convenient theological harmony that only enhances the temptation to idealize the patristic age. His conditional reception of the neo-patristic way offers a secondary insight on the place of liturgical theology in the larger field of theological studies.

The Patristic Synthesis

For the Eastern Christian academic tradition, the study of patristics was the primary method employed to learn liturgical history. One learned about Baptism in late antiquity by reading the works of Cyril of Jerusalem, Ambrose of Milan, John Chrysostom, and Augustine of Hippo, among others. The same method applied to learning Eucharistic tradition and theology: Chrysostom's homilies offer plenty of pastoral insight on the assemblies in late-antique

Antioch and Constantinople, and for the Eastern tradition, medieval fathers such as Maximus Confessor, Andrew of Crete, Germanos of Constantinople, Nicholas Cabasilas, and Symeon of Thessalonika proved to be precious primary sources of Eucharistic celebration and interpretation.[16] St. Vladimir's encourages the scientific method of studying the patristic tradition, and this approach is compatible with studying Scripture and Liturgy. The same methods are applied to studying Byzantine liturgical texts.

A dilemma emerges from this paradigm, however: it is difficult to establish objective criteria for determining if contemporary liturgical theology conforms to the patristic synthesis. Orthodox theologians claim that the patristic age never ended, with today's holy fathers continuing the apostolic tradition. In parish practice, it is convenient to teach liturgical theology through patristic texts, as it is common for clergy to apply the teachings of Cyril of Jerusalem or John Chrysostom to the present liturgical life of the Church. The opposite approach of ascertaining whether or not a new offering is legitimately patristic or Orthodox is more difficult if we are committed to refraining from imposing the present on the past. The easier approach is to continue to turn to the fathers, and this is how clergy are taught to interpret the liturgy.

The restrained quality of Schmemann's reform does not mean that ordinary parishioners did not experience changes. Those who lived through the transition inspired by Schmemann heard prayers in their native language, learned new styles of music, experienced components and entire liturgies with which they were previously unfamiliar, and began to receive Communion regularly, whereas they had previously partaken about once a year. Not everyone welcomed the change introduced to the Orthodox Liturgy: for some, the changes were unwelcome and attributed to non-Orthodox influences. But despite some hesitance on the part of some Orthodox faithful to adopt the changes introduced to the liturgy, Schmemann's legacy has survived for multiple generations following its initial planting, and one can conclude that it is now a fixed feature of Orthodox liturgical life in America.

LITURGICAL RENEWAL: ALKIVIADIS CALIVAS

Alkiviadis Calivas taught liturgics at Holy Cross Greek Orthodox School of Theology from 1978 until his retirement in 2003. I present a profile of his contribution to liturgical theology here as he was a leading figure in shaping liturgical theology and praxis for a generation of Greek Orthodox clergy in America. Calivas's scholarly apparatus is prodigious: he has authored books on Holy Week and Pascha, and theology as conscience, along with numerous articles on liturgical history and the application of the Byzantine liturgical heritage to today's Church.[17]

Calivas was and remains an active proponent of liturgical renewal for the Church in America. His contribution belongs to the cohort of teachers who sought to renew the existing liturgical tradition instead of performing major surgery on it. His background as a pastor of two large parishes in New York city for twenty years (1956–76) deeply informed his scholarship. Calivas's essays on liturgical practice speak directly to the realities of parish life, and his work exemplifies a bridge of the pastoral and academic.

Adjusting to the American Context

In his scholarship, Calivas exhorts clergy and Church leaders to view Church life in America as an opportunity that is much greater than mere survival and retaining the traditions inherited from immigrants. In this sense, Calivas was keenly attuned to changes in the American cultural and ecclesial landscape and sought to develop strategies for pastors to lead effectively in the new American context. Calivas witnessed the socioeconomic changes affecting all Americans, which inevitably resulted in changes in parish membership. He observed that Greek Orthodox communities experienced numerous layers of change in America, initially through the processes of adaptation, acculturation, and assimilation, and more recently, on account of social mobility.[18] Recent shifts in education and employment have rendered "the neighborhood urban parish almost a thing of the past."[19]

Calivas views the emergence of the suburban parish as a positive development, but states that the necessity of commuting to the parish changes the rhythm and content of its activity, as the parish is no longer the locus of non-liturgical community gatherings, and the people will be unable to participate in its life with the same frequency.[20] The tendency for clergy and parishes to remain frozen in idealized historical periods with a preference for a monastic model of liturgy has resulted in depreciated worship that lacks the energy to stir the minds and hearts of the people.[21]

Excellence in Pastoral Liturgy

Effective pastoral leadership would be rooted in a vibrant liturgical life. Calivas did not outline a detailed plan for liturgical renewal, but emphasized specific areas of importance in the liturgy that had the capacity to engage the people. The first area of emphasis is a fervent commitment to cultivating quality liturgical music in parish life, since the primary means of celebrating and proclaiming the Orthodox liturgy is through chanting and singing.[22] Preaching is the second area of emphasis. Calivas depicts preaching as an act of evangelism and mission, an opportunity to tell the greatness of God's story, and the primary means of leading the people into truly becoming a "new creation."[23] Pastors are to devote themselves to mastering the Scriptures and other sources of Church Tradition, and to come to know their people so that preaching will address the realities of their lives.[24] Preaching is not synonymous with catechetics, and should not be the "dry recital of facts," but it must be persuasive and engaging, and most importantly, it cannot be omitted from Liturgy, but should rather be a part of it at every gathering of the faithful.[25]

Calivas differs from other Orthodox theologians in his view on pastoral leadership and the world: he does not simply dismiss secularism, but states that it has contributed good to the Church and the world, and the pastoral strategy is to consistently lead people into adopting a way of life that nourishes their recognition of the spiritual dimension.[26] The Church's task is to avoid the strain of secularism that relies solely on materialism, to the point of concealing the life of God that is the source of human life. Calivas frames the pastoral task as cultivating a liturgical life, rooted primarily in frequent and quality preaching, that narrates the story of God who shares life with humankind and proclaims the eternal victory of life over death.[27] The Liturgy illustrates a model of living that shapes one's identity: in this process, the Liturgy exposes human failure while training the Christian on the process of becoming an "authentic human being," a person whose experience of communion with God, the saints, and living humanity translates into a thankful way of life.[28]

Calivas does not outline a detailed program of liturgical change, but focuses on liturgical elements that bear particular power to touch people. Underpinning his philosophy of liturgical renewal is a Eucharistic ecclesiology that views the clergy and laity as engaging, offering, and receiving the Liturgy together, at all times, with the clergy always a part of the assembly with the laity.[29] Christ's high priesthood establishes the unified worship of clergy and laity and their ecclesial identity through Baptism, Chrismation, and Eucharist. The ecclesiological underpinning of liturgical renewal had a crucial practical dimension, as Calivas encourages clergy to be "open, engaged, versatile, flexible, and resourceful."[30] He illuminates a method of openness in contrast to the prevailing tendency of clergy to live in "an idealized past . . . aloof from the demands, the problems, the challenges of the times."[31] The decision to live in the past is motivated by fear of change and skepticism of new ideas. Calivas asserts that liturgical renewal is absolutely required to stir the hearts and minds of people and captivate them, especially younger people who tend to drift away from the Church. This renewal will be a local phenomenon growing from the parish as the "Eucharistic cell" of the Church.[32]

Calivas assures clergy that the liturgical renewal is a worthwhile labor of love, as the local quality of liturgical renewal has universal implications, since "the evangelization of the world begins locally."[33] His vision for liturgical renewal has two primary objectives: to vivify Greek Orthodox parish life in the American context, and to continue the apostolic work of preaching the Gospel to the ends of the earth. The first objective acknowledges the new reality confronting Greek Orthodox communities in America: community life here is not temporary, and there will be no return of immigrants and their descendants to Greece. Adaptation and acculturation are inevitable: clergy and parish leaders must learn how to adjust to the challenges of the times to ensure sustainability. Calivas is careful to acknowledge that parishes and clergy must remain faithful to the legacy they have inherited from the past, but the mission is to structure and cultivate parish life, especially liturgy, in such a way that it fits squarely in the present—attempts to recreate the past are doomed to fail.[34]

Calivas's formation of clergy serving the Greek Orthodox Archdiocese emphasized veneration for the liturgical tradition inherited form the past, with the hope that it would develop into a healthy organism that bears fruit in the American environment. He focused on correcting liturgical practices that had fallen into decay, with preaching first and foremost on this list, along with music. Calivas presents a vision of Byzantine Liturgy as appropriate for the religious context of America, despite its Eastern roots. Pursuing excellence in liturgical celebration is the objective, as a clear and comprehensible Liturgy that truly engages the people is one that will lead them to Communion with the living God. This kind of Liturgy is therefore appropriate for any place and space of the world.

Calivas's emphasis on mission in the American context assists in illuminating the differences between two approaches to liturgical renewal in the contemporary Orthodox academy. Calivas's teaching emphasizes liturgical renewal for evangelization and mission, an approach that differs from enhancing the Byzantine features of Liturgy to restore it to its authentic Byzantine form. The differences between the approaches are somewhat implicit; the second approach (Byzantinizing Liturgy in America) seeks to excise external influences from the Liturgy and projects a solely Eastern ecclesiology. Calivas's view is an admission that the Liturgy's celebration in the American context will result in some adaptation. It is entirely possible for that Liturgy to become a Western rite of worship while remaining completely Orthodox.

Sources for Orthodox Mission in America

Learning how to minister in the American religious context requires thinking dependent on a broader spectrum of sources. Calivas's presentations on Liturgy consult traditional Orthodox sources, and also draw from a variety of Western thinkers such as Taft, Susan Wood, Mark Searle, Gregory Dix, Steven Platten, David Batchelder, and Don Saliers, among others.[35] Calivas also exposed his seminary students to an ecumenical lineup of theologians as they studied liturgy. His course syllabi feature diverse Orthodox thinkers such as Schmemann, Florovsky, Bobrinskoy, Clement, and Yannaras, among many others.[36] Calivas also assigned readings from Western historians and theologians such as Baumstark, Fagerberg, Searle, Baldovin, Bouyer, Grisbrooke, Susan White, and Paul Bradshaw. On the one hand, Calivas's ecumenical lineup resembles Schmemann's, which also included non-Orthodox readings. On the other hand, Calivas's syllabi reflect his vision for Orthodox mission in the American religious landscape. Clergy would need to engage the leading thinkers of other Christian traditions in America to succeed in constructing parish liturgies that effectively engage the people. Through his teaching and scholarship, Calivas formed prospective parish clergy to be masters of the fundamentals of Orthodox Liturgy capable of celebrating it in a period of transition from sustaining the inherited tradition to mission in America. Calivas's emphasis on preaching and openness to new ways of thinking and leading will be manifest in some of the examples of parish liturgy we encounter in this study.

LITURGICAL MAXIMALISM: ROCOR

An alternative to the style of liturgical renewal promoted by Schmemann and Calivas is the approach adopted by the Russian Orthodox Church Outside of Russia (ROCOR). This approach views the Liturgy as a living organism that is in a constant state of natural growth and development, and is thus on a course of development that does not need to be altered. All alterations of the Liturgy remove it from its natural course of development—examples of such changes include removing content from the liturgy (e.g., removing or shortening repetitive litanies appointed to the Liturgy), taking new approaches to liturgical aesthetics (e.g., using few icons for the iconostasis or changing the interior design to grant the laity greater visual access to the sanctuary), altering the style of celebration (reading prayers aloud instead of quietly, having the whole assembly recite prayers together), and changing the way that people participate (altering the process of preparation for Communion so people can receive more frequently without having to make a Confession before each Eucharist).

The view of Liturgy emerging from this approach is maximalistic: omissions, abbreviations, and changes seem to promote liturgical minimalism, to persuade the people to engage it with more interest and enthusiasm, since the longer version of Liturgy has the reputation of being long and boring. Proponents of liturgical maximalism believe that there are no deficiencies in the full version of the Liturgy: the problem resides with clergy who are not committed to teach the people about the riches and blessings that liturgical maximalism imparts. The maximalists seek to convert the people to the Liturgy, an approach conforming to one of Pott's descriptions of liturgical reform.[37] The problem is not the Liturgy, its length or content; the lack of commitment of the people and the clergy to devote themselves to the fullness of the Liturgy is the issue.

ROCOR has featured a full liturgical life as an ideal to be pursued in essays and public lectures. St. John Maximovich himself displayed liturgical maximalism as an ideal when he prohibited gathering for community dances and Halloween celebrations if they would require an abbreviation of the appointed services.[38] The instance of this prohibition illuminates the collision of contemporary culture with the core values of the Church: true, devoted disciples of Christ must set aside the cheap thrill of entertainment offered by the world and devote themselves to the rule of prayer established by the Churches and observed in her Liturgy. Disciples are as devoted as their teachers, meaning that laity will never be committed to a full engagement of the life of prayer if clergy fail to show them how and set an example in doing so themselves.

The Monastery and Seminarian Formation

In forming clergy who are enabled to lead parish liturgy with competence and piety, proponents of liturgical maximalism find convenient partners in Orthodox monasteries. It is no accident that ROCOR's seminary for clerical formation is Holy Trinity Monastery in Jordanville. All of ROCOR's liturgical books are edited and published by the monastery press, a tradition of monastics serving as liturgy's guardians and curators for over a millennium that has carried over into the present. The coexistence of the seminary with the monastery is the key to understanding the liturgical formation of the clergy, though. The primary liturgical formation for seminarians is experiential: they form one community with the monks and pray with them, as one body, through the cycle of services and Liturgies. The monastery functions as a type of liturgical center for the whole Church, then—through its publication of books and as the training ground for the clergy who lead the Church. Liturgy is the heart of monastic life, and the monks as guardians of the Church's liturgical tradition sustain the Liturgy they inherited.

The clergy, then, depart from the seminary having been formed by multiple years of worshiping at the Church's primary monastery. ROCOR's practice is not innovative, but continues a pattern well-known throughout the Church, and the key for clerical liturgical formation is the intensity of the liturgical experience at the monastery. Seminarians who begin their studies with some parish experience certainly have other practical experiences as source for leadership and catechesis (more on this below), but the experience of worshiping at the Church's designated center with special intensity, as part of a broader program of preparation for parish ministry, becomes primary.

Earlier, I mentioned that liturgical music is a particularly crucial component in the program of liturgical renewal: the same is true for liturgical maximalism. In the maximalism model of ROCOR, many musicians are also formed at the liturgical center of Jordanville, where they learn the skills for liturgical leadership. Mastering the requirements of the full observation of the services is a required component of the course: the director must know the appointed modes and tones, and be competent in teaching them to the choir, and performing them beautifully.[39]

I have referred to ROCOR as the primary example of liturgical maximalism, but it is not the only Church in North America that prefers this approach. The OCA has three seminaries: St. Herman's prepares clergy for ministry in Alaska, and St. Tikhon's has been the sister seminary to St. Vladimir's since 1938. Like Holy Trinity in Jordanville, St. Tikhon's Seminary prepares candidates for ministry in cooperation with the life of St. Tikhon's Monastery, as the liturgical life of the community functions as the primary curricular component for students.[40] St. Tikhon's has traditionally formed clergy for service in the OCA, and now accepts students from a variety of jurisdictions.

Liturgical Renewal among Progressives and Maximalists

The maximal approach is not bereft of the principles of liturgical renewal. Some of the renewalist principles underpin both liturgical renewal enthusiasts and maximalists: they tend to share the same view of Liturgy as the Church's heart and the event that nourishes her people. They also share a common concern for competent performance of the Liturgy and cultivation of the *ars celebrandi*. Boris Ledkovsky's legacy of passing on the tradition of canonical singing to Orthodoxy in America occurred both at St. Vladimir's and at ROCOR, and Holy Trinity and St. Vladimir's have sponsored programs outside of the academic year to train musicians and offer additional education for clergy. The primary difference between the approaches to Liturgy of the two schools is that renewalists identify several instances of revisions made to the Liturgy that were necessitated by challenges to the Church and cultural factors. Episodes of liturgical revision in Church history justify revising the Liturgy in the present, so that its language, form, and style of celebration occur in ways recognizable to the people. Renewalists view the inherited form of the Liturgy as beautiful, but like a plant needing to be trimmed and pruned lest it become completely inaccessible and unrecognizable. Therefore, trimming away repetitions of components or altering styles of celebration that belong to a past historical period are legitimate ways of removing accretions that became affixed to the Liturgy by accident. Maximalists view trimming as removing healthy branches from the Liturgy and causing it sickness, with the new additions from contemporary culture alien to a Liturgy that should not be of this world.

Two issues associated with the divergent schools of liturgical theology require careful analysis. One is the degree to which the Liturgy can embrace the world's modes of communication in language, art, image, and ritual performance. In short, the differences in the theologies supporting the liturgical schools is shaped by desires to flee the world coming into conflict with the reality of living firmly within it. The other issue is the ecclesiology promoted by the Liturgy: strong lay participation suggests a horizontal approach to clergy-lay relationships in Church life, and this creates tension within Orthodoxy's traditional hierarchical culture and mode of operation. A strong preference for maintaining one's position on the Church's relationship with the world and the hierarchical ecclesiology tend to fuel the enthusiasm for promoting the renewalist or maximalist approaches to liturgical theology.

The outcome of the coexistence of diverse schools of liturgical theology is that Orthodox people have a wide variety of liturgical experiences in the American Churches. Some liturgies are shorter, whereas others are longer. Some people have never heard the prayers appointed to the priest, whereas others can paraphrase the most often-repeated presidential prayers. The musical aesthetic differs from one parish to the next. Liturgical diversity proliferates within Orthodox America, and this trend will continue as long as the Church remains divided in its position on engaging the world and maintaining a hierarchical ecclesiology.

MAINTAINING THE LITURGICAL STATUS QUO

Not all parishes, clergy, and people fit in one of the above categories. Parish clergy might have been under the influence of one of the liturgical schools we are profiling here, and may have adhered strictly to a parish Typikon, or simply adopted a path independent of liturgical renewal. Simply put, many clergy simply maintain the status quo with parish liturgy. Maintaining the status quo is following the basic requirements of the liturgical ordo. The parish meets for Sunday Divine Liturgy and the most solemn feasts of the liturgical year, but there is no promotion of liturgical renewal or maximalism. Status quo parishes are not necessarily liturgically deficient, since the Word is proclaimed and God is praised, but there is usually no energy behind introducing new music or encouraging people to participate in the liturgy through more frequent Communion or education on liturgical offices. In many cases, clergy do not pursue liturgical renewal or maximalism because external factors prohibit it. In smaller parishes, clergy have to work full-time and can only devote a small percentage of hours each week to parish ministry. Many parishes do not have trained choir directors and rely on volunteers and amateurs to lead the singing or perform it on their own, which renders musical innovation beyond reach. Other parishes are aging or have such dwindling numbers that it is enough for a community to meet for the Liturgy. Some mission parishes lack the resources and time to find space for gathering: in some of these places, the time they have for Divine Liturgy might be constrained by the parameters established by their hosts. Finally, some clergy simply aren't interested in liturgical renewal or see no need to change anything. Our primary liturgical schools have not permeated all parishes in North America, for reasons of survival, lack of resources, and not recognizing a need for any kind of liturgical change.

Robert Taft and Scholarship on the Byzantine Liturgy

Scholars of Byzantine liturgy know that Robert Taft has established a high bar for historical scholarship on the Byzantine Liturgy. While Taft is not nominally Orthodox, he has influenced Orthodox liturgical practice through his scholarship and the number of scholars he mentored in the larger Byzantine liturgical academy. St. Vladimir's Seminary is a good example: Schmemann's legacy still persists in the OCA, but several generations of clergy were also trained by Paul Meyendorff, who recently retired, and Fr. Alexander Rentel, who teaches canon law and select courses on liturgical history, theology, and pastoral liturgy. Taft passed on his method of sound liturgical historical methodology to Meyendorff and Rentel, and Taft's school of liturgy has also shaped select theologians whose work contributes in some way to their Orthodox Church.

At the Society of Oriental Liturgy meeting in 2014 that gathered at St. Vladimir's, Rentel organized a photo of the scholars who can be traced to Taft's school through the tree of teachers that learned directly from him. So, for example, while Taft's own proteges were included in the photo—including the well-known liturgists Meyendorff, Rentel, Mark Morozowich, Daniel Galadza, Gabriel Radle, and Nina Glibetic—several scholars who learned from Taft's disciples also appeared in the photo, such as Vitaly Permiakov and me. I traced my training to Taft as I was Morozowich's student at The Catholic University of America, and this illustrates the degree to which Taft's liturgical method has influenced the field of liturgical studies.

The primary rationale underpinning Taft's method is sound historical scholarship. Taft connects the value of understanding the past to present practice: liturgical history helps us understand how we arrived at today's practices and shows us what is possible in liturgical celebration. The point of liturgical history is to inform richly, but not necessarily reform, because the historian is not called to revive the past, and the work of liturgical reform belongs to bishops, not professors of liturgy. Taft's great gift to Orthodox America is a robust understanding at how and why we celebrate our Liturgy. The scholarship of Taft's school equips clergy and local leaders with the tools they need for sound liturgical catechesis, and many clergy are familiar with Taft's histories of the Liturgy of St. John Chrysostom and the development of the liturgical offices of Holy Week. Taft's work complements Schmemann's macro-level liturgical theology, and neither approach calls for surgery, but for deepening understanding of the Liturgy today's Orthodox Christians received.

Taft's Tree of Liturgical Scholars

Taft's contribution to the formation of clergy and their liturgical ministry is indirect. His cultivation of multiple generations of scholars has expanded the information available to students of Byzantine liturgical history, of which clergy are a primary audience. He has also contributed to the practice of liturgical catechesis, as clergy have numerous reference works to consult in understanding how the Liturgy developed throughout history. While Taft himself has performed the yeoman's work on constructing a history of the Byzantine Liturgy, the scholars belonging to his school have essentially sketched a history of the main parts, with many details still in need of explanation. Following the lead of Juan Mateos, who wrote the initial histories on the typikon of the Great Church in Constantinople and the proclamation of the Word in the Liturgy, Taft has authored most of the volumes on the history of the Liturgy of St. John Chrysostom, with Vassa Larin expanding and completing the work initially undertaken by Mateos.[41] Stelyios Muksuris covers the liturgy of preparation, Vitaly Permiakov the rite of the dedication of the church, Mark Morozowich the liturgies of Holy Thursday, Gabriel Radle on the rites of marriage, Gabriel Bertonière on Pascha and the Sundays of Lent, and Daniel Galadza on liturgical Byzantinization in Jerusalem.[42]

This list merely scratches the surface of Byzantine liturgical history: a diverse collection of historians has thoroughly covered the development of the monastic Typikon, published translations of influential typica, analyzed the anaphoras of the Byzantine tradition (including a history of the anaphora of Basil), and covered the history and theology of several rites. An international array of liturgiologists writes the history of regional liturgical development, with special emphasis on the manuscript tradition of liturgical books in those regions. The study and presentation of these sources enables the analytical historical work that has benefitted the liturgical academy. With the publication of detailed studies of liturgical history, clergy are able to reference these works and promote an understanding of liturgical history in parish life. I am not proposing that the majority of clergy read these volumes, but the key points of historical information have a way of reaching clergy through essays and related pieces published online. The question of the origin of the Liturgy of St. John Chrysostom is a good example. Liturgical scholarship has dismissed the oft-repeated claim that the anaphora of St. John Chrysostom is an abbreviation of Basil's Byzantine anaphora. Taft's scholarship alone has demonstrated that the Chrysostom anaphora originated from the Antiochene anaphora of the Apostles, which Chrysostom edited; he introduced his redaction to Constantinople at the end of the fourth century, and over a period of centuries, it became the primary anaphora for Sunday liturgies, gradually displacing the one attributed to St. Basil.[43]

Sound history is the most important source for liturgical catechesis, and Taft's school of liturgical historians has done more to promote an understanding of what actually happened and how the Liturgy developed more than any other. One cannot claim that most Orthodox clergy read the historical studies by Taft and his disciples, especially since there are cohorts of clergy that reject Taft and his method of liturgiology because Taft is Jesuit, leading to the notion that comparative liturgy is alien to Orthodoxy.[44] On the other hand, one cannot deny the general hunger for knowledge of Byzantine liturgical history among rank and file clergy and laity in the Church. Larin's popular YouTube series "Coffee with Sister Vassa" offering short takes on Church and culture, along with her lecture series on the Byzantine liturgy, has substantial support among people desiring more information on liturgical history.[45] Larin's success in public theology is a brilliant distillation of the Taft school's publications on liturgy designed for other scholars in the field. Taft's development of Orthodox scholars who are experts in liturgical history and contribute in some way to informing the Church on liturgical history and how it can be useful in understanding and reforming liturgical celebration is substantial.

SOURCES FOR CLERICAL LITURGICAL FORMATION

To this point, I have presented the primary figures and schools of influence in clerical liturgical formation in Orthodox America. The liturgical schools and leaders I have described have contributed to the formation of clergy, but they are not the only sources clergy consult. Parish clergy have different journeys on the way to and through pastoral appointments, and other people and factors influence liturgical leadership. The most important source for the celebration of liturgy is personal mentoring. For generations, Orthodox clergy learned liturgical celebration through their own parish experience or from an ordained relative, a tradition that migrated from countries with a substantial Orthodox population to America. While the paradigm of sons learning the liturgical craft from their fathers has shifted somewhat, it is still common for men who are baptized and raised in the Church to learn the local liturgical practice of their parish and its clergy. Currently, many clergy in America have dedicated themselves to pastoral service either as second or midlife vocations, or entered into Orthodoxy as converts.[46] These clergy tend to learn liturgical celebration either at intense diocesan or Churchwide gatherings offering crash courses in Liturgy, or from their local clergy. When ordained, some clergy have temporary appointments to larger parishes that introduce them to the entire context of parish ministry, including liturgical leadership. Such appointments are designed to provide new clergy with the initial mentoring required to preside. Clergy also form friendships within their ranks and seek out their own mentors, who counsel them on all kinds of matters, including liturgical celebration. Like laity, clergy use technology and electronic content as liturgical sources. YouTube and other video sources provide access to an international forum of liturgies that were unknown to the previous generation, and clergy discuss and debate these practices while also occasionally learning from them.[47] Clergy also write pieces on liturgical celebration on their own blogs, or peruse material on the Liturgy published online. This development in clerical learning on the Liturgy is not surprising; it simply shows how digital communities and social media have expanded the options available to clergy, while also making the process of searching for sources much more selective and subjective.

Survey of Orthodox Clergy on the Liturgy

The examples of liturgical teachers and parish pastors grant us particular insights into the foundations of today's liturgical theology and praxis in the American Orthodox environment. I administered a detailed survey of Orthodox clergy on liturgical practices and catechesis in the parish to obtain information about the liturgical practices of Orthodox parishes in America. The survey was open to Orthodox clergy and lay leaders in May 2016. A total of 57 people fulfilled the survey. Thirty pastors participated (52.63%), along with nine associate pastors and 10 deacons. Three retired priests and 5 lay assistants were among the respondents.

Jurisdictional Profile of Respondents

The survey provides some information on practices in Orthodox parishes in America. Most of the respondents hailed from the Antiochian Archdiocese of America (27). Fifteen represent the OCA, 14 represent the Greek Orthodox Archdiocese, and one respondent is from the Moscow Patriarchate. Several churches were not represented: no clergy from ROCOR, the Ukrainian Orthodox Church, the Serbian Church, the Carpatho-Russian Church, and the Romanian and Bulgarian patriarchates participated. Therefore, the survey results provide helpful information on liturgical practices, but the reader should not interpret these as an exact representation of Orthodox liturgical practices in America.

Table 2.1. Survey Respondent Profile

Jurisdiction and Number of Participants	Percent
Antiochian Archdiocese of America: 27	47.4
Orthodox Church in America (OCA): 14	24.5
Greek Orthodox Archdiocese: 14	24.5
Moscow Patriarchate: 1	1.8
Unidentified: 1	1.8

Distribution of Parish Size in Study

Survey results primarily represent large and medium sized Orthodox parishes. Nineteen parishes have 300 or more people; 12 have 75–149. Only nine of the clergy participating come from small parishes (1–75).

Table 2.2. Clergy Survey Parish Size

Number of Parishes and Member Range (55 responses)	Percent
300+: 19	34.55
200–299: 9	16.36
150–199: 6	10.91
75–149: 12	21.82
25–75: 8	14.55
1–24: 1	1.82

Of the parishes, 62.5% have a fairly full Sunday liturgical schedule, with Saturday Vespers, Sunday Orthros, and Divine Liturgy all taking place. Only 2 of the 57 parishes have Sunday Divine Liturgy only; 11 have Sunday Orthros and Divine Liturgy, a practice typical of Greek and Antiochian liturgical traditions. Therefore, the parishes represented by the survey have a fairly full slate of weekend services.

Table 2.3. Weekly Services

Weekly Service Schedules	Percent
Sunday Divine Liturgy and Saturday Vigil: 1	1.79
Sunday Orthros and Divine Liturgy: 11	19.64
Sunday Orthros and Divine Liturgy and Saturday Vespers: 35	62.5
Sunday Divine Liturgy and Saturday Vespers: 7	12.5
Sunday Divine Liturgy only: 2	3.57

In terms of liturgical language, 55 of the 56 respondents to this question reported using English. Twenty-two use Greek, 18 Arabic, and 6 Church Slavonic. A few comments from respondents indicate that non-English languages are used to serve non-Anglophone worshippers. One respondent stated that the Lord's Prayer is recited in "whatever language is represented by native speakers on any particular Sunday," and cited Eritrean and French as examples of languages used for the Lord's Prayer. Another respondent stated that "a petition in Greek or Arabic form an ektenia" will occasionally be taken, with at least one response in Greek, Slavonic, Arabic, or Spanish taken on Saturday Vespers. Therefore, in specific situations, a sampling of the native language of attendees is used. In summary, English is the prevailing liturgical language of parish liturgical celebration, but liturgy is multi-lingual.

Table 2.4. Liturgical Language

Language Used for Liturgy	Percent
English: 55	98.21
Greek: 22	39.29
Arabic: 18	32.14
Church Slavonic: 6	10.71
Romanian: 2	3.57
Spanish: 2	3.57
Ukrainian: 1	1.79
Serbian: 1	1.79

My observation that English is the dominant language in a generally multi-lingual Orthodox liturgy in America finds support in Alexei Krindatch's data on the use of English and other languages in Orthodox jurisdictions.[48] Krindatch observes that "English is much more widely used" in the liturgical services of all Orthodox jurisdictions.[49] Other languages are important in the liturgies of a few jurisdictions (e.g., ROCOR and UOC-USA), but even in these groups, English is prominent as a language of worship and sermons.[50]

Recitation of Prayers and Communion Practices

Responses to the question on reciting prayers aloud varied, elucidating diversity in liturgical practice. A total of 25 respondents reported reciting all of the prayers of the Divine Liturgy aloud. Another 15 reported reading the anaphora aloud, with 13 reporting reading a portion of the anaphora aloud—only 5 respondents reported reading all prayers quietly. Respondent results on the frequency of participation in Holy Communion were closer to unanimity: 27 reported the laity always receiving Communion, with 26 reporting the laity receiving frequently. Only 3 respondents reported that the laity receive occasionally. No respondents reported the laity receiving rarely or once a year.

Table 2.5.   Parish Practices on Prayer

Parish Practice and Number	Percent
Read all prayers of Divine Liturgy aloud: 25	45.45
Read anaphora aloud: 15	27.27
Read a portion of anaphora aloud: 13	23.64
Do not read any prayers aloud: 5	9.09

Respondent information on the relationship between Confession and Communion represents liturgical renewal in parish liturgy. Twenty-seven respondents encourage Confession, but do not strictly require it before Communion, whereas 24 treated Communion and Confession separately. Only 5 respondents encourage Confession before Communion, and zero respondents require and strictly enforce Confession before Communion.

Table 2.6.   Relationship between Confession and Communion

Parish Practice and Number	Percent
Confession encouraged; not strictly required: 27	48.21
Confession and Communion treated separately: 24	42.86
Confession before Communion encouraged: 5	8.93

Women in Liturgical Leadership

Respondents were surveyed on the participation of women in liturgical leadership. In general, women exercise some liturgical leadership, primarily in liturgical music. Some 52 respondents reported women singing in the choir, and 34 (60.71%) reported that women lead the choir. Women also take an active role in reading the liturgy of the Word, as 42% of the respondents stated that women read and chant the hours and the epistle. Some parishes do not set aside specific roles for women: 19 (33%) reported that women pray with the rest of the laity but do not have designated roles.

Table 2.7.   Women's Roles in Liturgical Ministry

Ministries Engaged by Women and Girls	Percent
Women sing in the choir: 52	92.86
Women read and chant epistle and hours: 42	75.00

Ministries Engaged by Women and Girls	Percent
Women lead the choir: 34	60.71
Women pray with laity; no designated role: 19	33.93
Women carry epitaphios during Holy Week: 12	21.43
Women hold Communion cloth: 11	19.64
Women serve in the altar: 2	3.57
Women serve as acolytes but do not enter altar: 1	1.79

Parish Liturgical Catechesis

A question integral to this study was on liturgical catechesis. A total of 35 respondents stated that liturgy is taught informally, at the pastor's discretion. Seventeen reported a liturgical curriculum for catechumens, with 14 reporting a liturgical curriculum for children. Eleven respondents stated that there is no organized program for teaching, with 6 reporting that the parish has a liturgical curriculum for the entire parish. Two respondents commented that they used liturgical texts such as litanies as sources for their sermons. Multiple respondents noted that they use liturgical texts, patristic sources, and Scriptures as sources for teaching the liturgy.

Respondents also identified Thomas Hopko's well-known introductory series on the Orthodox Church (also known as the "rainbow" series since each book was printed with a distinct solid color) and Stanley Harakas's *Living the Liturgy* as sources for liturgical catechesis.[51] One respondent offered a detailed description of parish liturgical catechesis: "we have a three-year rotating children's ed program, year 1 is Old Testament, year 2 is New Testament, year 3 is Liturgy and Sacraments, so children in second and third grade study liturgy and they'll get it again in 6th grade and then in 9th grade." Several respondents described general sources used to teach liturgy, including books and liturgical music, and offered brief references to writers such as Hugh Wybrew, Meletios Webber, Robert Taft, Hilarion Alfeyev, Frederica Mathews-Green, and Nicholas Denysenko. The section on liturgical catechesis yields two primary observations: clergy teach liturgy in the parish setting, but there is no universal program or single source used for catechesis, as clergy customize liturgical catechesis to conform to pastoral need.

Liturgical Music in the Parish

Liturgical diversity also marks the performance of liturgical music among respondent parishes. Seventeen respondents reported that a choir leads the singing with the people singing along. Another 17 reported that the people are encouraged to sing along with the choir. Only six parishes reported that the choir sings with no assembly singing, while 5 respondents reported that the people sing most or all of the liturgy, with a cantor leading. Some 17 respondents reported that the choir stands in front, with 14 reporting the choir standing in a loft above the nave, and 10 reporting that the choir stands in the back of the church. The musical program of respondent parishes tended to be a mixture of traditions: 32 respondents stated that the choir sings chant-based music, and another 28 reported that the choir sings diverse musical selections (including polyphony and chant). Only ten respondents reported that the choir sings contemporary music set to part-singing.

Table 2.8. Music in the Parish

Music Practices	Percent
Choir sings all responses, people sing along as desired: 17	30.36
Choir sings all responses, people encouraged to sing: 17	30.36
Choir leads singing, people sing along for most of liturgy: 11	19.64
Choir sings all responses with no assembly singing: 6	10.71
People sing all of the liturgy with some assistance: 5	8.93

Parishes had diverse practices in providing textual and musical aids to the assembly for singing along during the liturgy. Some 37% reported providing some texts for singing along, but no music. Another 20% provide some of the music for singing along, and 22% do not distribute anything for the congregation to follow. Only 5 respondents indicated that the people have the music for singing the liturgy.

Education of Parish Musicians

The importance of music to liturgical celebration is evident in commitment to training choir directors. Some 47% of respondents reported that choir directors have both musical and liturgical training; another 26% reported musical training. A total of 22% stated that the parish choir director has neither musical nor liturgical training. The high number of people leading music with no training illustrates a number of challenges in contemporary Church life. The primary problem is a shortage of candidates capable of leading a music program that can fulfill the requirements of Byzantine liturgy. Many parishes simply lack the resources to compensate a director with musical training. This compensation problem is exacerbated by the demands of the liturgical year: the Church calendar is demanding, and even the regular weekly cycle can require choral leadership on both Saturday evening and Sunday morning. Parishes lacking the resources to support and sustain a music program must rely on lay volunteers to perform this function.

Liturgical Catechesis of Converts

Because of the number of converts to Orthodoxy in America, the survey included a question on the methods clergy use to introduce converts to the liturgical and sacramental life of the Church. The results favored a customized approach to teaching converts on the basis of their experience and background. A total of 42.6% of respondents offer a survey of the liturgy and sacraments as part of a larger program on Orthodoxy. Another 29.6% customize liturgical instruction to fit the convert's experience and background—instruction can change as needed. Some 11% focus exclusively (or primarily) on liturgy and sacraments, whereas 11% do not have a formal program of instruction for converts. A solid majority of respondents reported offering catechesis to people preparing for Baptism and Marriage (85.45%); the other 8 respondents responded "it depends," indicating an explanation of the sacraments in some circumstances.

Table 2.9. Parish Liturgical Catechesis

Description of Catechetical Method	Percent
Basic Survey on Liturgy as part of larger curriculum: 23	42.59
Liturgical catechesis depends on convert's experience: 16	29.63
Program primarily liturgy and sacraments: 6	11.11
No parish program for catechizing converts: 6	11.11
Converts learn liturgy by participation: 3	5.56

Parishes also provided information on the liturgy through social media or in the Church itself (40%)—only nine respondents reported that they do not provide any literature on the liturgy to the people. Furthermore, 60% of respondents stated that they provide links to sites on the liturgy on their web sites. Most of these parishes link to the primary web site of their mother church (66.6% to OCA.org or goarch.org) or Ancient Faith Radio (30.5%).

Analysis of Survey Results

Clergy responses to our survey depict the Orthodox parish liturgy in America to be in a state of transition. The most obvious pattern is the prevalence of diversity in all liturgical practices. There is no uniform pattern governing liturgical celebration in American parish life; one can refer only to the emergence of certain trends. The absence of uniformity is obvious, but also noteworthy, as it demythologizes the myth of liturgical uniformity in the Orthodox Church. No two worship experiences are alike, even if the general order for the Liturgy is essentially the same, as the music, placement of the choir, participation of women, and style of the recitation of prayers differ among parish practices. This liturgical diversity is attributable to numerous factors, including the coexistence of multiple Orthodox jurisdictions in one country, and divergent degrees of the application of liturgical renewal principles.

The survey elucidates a few emerging trends in Orthodox Liturgy in America. The frequent recitation of prayers aloud and practice of frequent communion demonstrate the reception of the core values of liturgical renewal. Parishes do not apply these principles to liturgical practice in the exact same ways, but the fact that most parishes of the survey read some prayers aloud and encourage frequent Communion demonstrates a transition from the inherited practices of reciting all prayers silently and reserving Communion for the most solemn occasions of the liturgical year (e.g., Lent or Pascha). The information on liturgical music also demonstrates liturgy in transition. While clergy valued both musical and liturgical education of musicians, many parishes rely on volunteers with no formal training. This form of liturgical leadership includes women who lead choirs. The survey's report that women's leadership is limited to choral leadership and chanting the epistle or psalms does not suggest a forthcoming transition for women to assume new roles of liturgical leadership. The absence of formal training of musicians also confirms Calivas's lament on the deficiency of quality liturgical music in parish life, especially since liturgical music has been a fixed feature of renewal.

The absence of formal programs of liturgical catechesis and the inconsistency in the selection of liturgical languages illustrate the emergence of the trend of adaptability. This trend corresponds to the demographic pattern of parish attrition, with people coming and going from parish life. The need to occasionally insert a variety of liturgical languages suggests that some Orthodox parishes minister to diverse peoples, including those with a limited command of English. Reciting the Lord's Prayer or a minor liturgical component in their native language is a small, but meaningful gesture of inclusion. This pattern speaks to the global and international composition of the Orthodox Church, especially since a variety of people might congregate in one parish in America.[52]

The use of multiple languages in one Liturgy also discloses the Orthodox preference for a local variant of ecclesiology. Orthodoxy does not permit priests to preside at multiple liturgies on a Sunday or solemnity, so there is no option for a given parish to offer Liturgies in multiple languages at the same site on a given day. Only a handful of parishes in America can offer two Divine Liturgies, which requires two presiders and a second altar. Therefore, an urban assembly will be multicultural or multinational by nature, so it is not unusual for clergy to perform a portion of the Liturgy in another language for non-English speakers. That said, the selection of the Lord's Prayer or a portion of a litany is not prescribed by any Church authority: it comes from the practice of customizing the liturgy in accordance with need.

The customizing approach is much more prominent in parish liturgical catechesis. Essentially, clergy create liturgical catechesis from scratch. The frequent citation of biblical, patristic, and liturgical texts as the sources used to teach the liturgy suggests that parish clergy view the Liturgy itself as catechetical. Clergy consult online sources such as Ancient Faith Radio to bolster their catechesis, and this trend fits the larger pattern of using the Internet to find sources for learning and teaching. We see the Liturgy in transition as clergy employ different sources and methods to respond to the need for some level of liturgical catechesis at the parish level. There is no evidence of an emerging demand for more formal liturgical catechesis in Orthodox parishes in America. It is clear that parishes are making minor adjustments within the inherited tradition of Byzantine Liturgy to meet the many needs presented by ever-changing parish constituencies.

PARISH PROFILES AND LITURGICAL PRACTICES

A brief examination of the liturgical environments of the four parishes featured in this study brings us from a general description to a particular one. St. George Greek Orthodox Church in St. Paul, Minnesota, was established by Greek immigrants in 1940. It is one of two Greek Orthodox parishes in the Twin Cities area, serving families in St. Paul, with St. Mary's parish serving faithful in Minneapolis. St. George parish currently has approximately 225 member units. Most of these units are married couples of Greek descent, either first or second generation. St. George also has converts, who compose about 20% of the parish. Fr. Andrews reports that the parish is holding steady in its membership.

Fr. Andrews states that the parish's liturgical practices have evolved since its inception in 1940. Only a small portion of the Liturgy is celebrated in Greek (about 10%), with the majority in English. The parish is slowly easing Greek out of the Liturgy. The Gospel was read in both English and Greek up until 2015 when the parish dropped the Greek reading. In 2017, the parish stopped reciting the Creed in Greek. Fr. Andrews observed that a few parishioners lamented the loss of the Greek Gospel, as it symbolized the Greek legacy of the parish. He noted that no one made any remarks about the dropping of the Greek version of the Creed.

The transition to a predominantly English liturgy is significant for St. George's, as it is for the entire Greek Orthodox Archdiocese of America. Fr. Andrews remarked that "language is a barrier for people even if there is only a little Greek" in the Liturgy. He suggested that celebrating 10% of the Liturgy in Greek feels like 60% to English-language faithful, and noted that the use of non-English languages in parish liturgy can stifle efforts of welcome and outreach. Fr. Andrews attributed his emphasis on the Liturgy of the

Word and the sermon in parish liturgy to the formation he received from clergy who mentored him during his time as a young priest, along with the instruction of Fr. Calivas at Holy Cross School of the Theology. Fr. Andrews' pastoral strategy is to make worship the focal point of the Sunday assembly, with liturgical participation the springboard for further learning. In other words, the Liturgy is a ritual rehearsal for formation as Christian disciples in everyday life.

The Liturgy at St. George's prominently features Scripture and the Liturgy of the Word. Fr. Andrews restored the position of the sermon to follow the Gospel, and he adds a special sermon for children before Communion. The active participation of children in the entire liturgy is another change for the parish community. For much of its history, the children attended Sunday school while the adults were in Liturgy, but instruction for children now occurs after the Liturgy. Fr. Andrews promotes liturgical participation by reading the priest's prayers aloud, including the anaphora, and he hopes to enhance worship at St. George's by adding more weekday liturgies to the schedule.

St. George parish in St. Paul, then, is an Orthodox community in transition. The parish has a distinctly Greek legacy, but its liturgical environment is experiencing a slow transition from Greek-language liturgy involving adult faithful primarily to an English Liturgy that includes all ages of the community, promotes Scripture, and provides the people with access to the priestly prayers that were once said quietly. The emphasis on Scripture and the preference for English are themes that cohere with the testimony of the focus group respondents from St. George.

Holy Trinity Cathedral (Boston)

Holy Trinity Cathedral was founded in 1910 by immigrants from Russia and the Austro-Hungarian empire. It was originally established as a parish of the Russian Orthodox Church under Tsar Nicholas II.[53] Holy Trinity has approximately 125 adults and children. As the case for many cathedrals, visitors are drawn to Holy Trinity because of its convenient urban location. The constituency of the cathedral community has changed over the course of its history: today, approximately 50% of the parish consists of converts to Orthodoxy, a statistic cohering with the pattern of Orthodox Christians belonging to the OCA. Another 20% of the parish consists of immigrants from the former Soviet Union, many of whom were baptized and chrismated as adults.

Worship is at the center of the cathedral's life: each week revolves around the celebration of the Resurrection, beginning with Vigil on Saturday evenings and culminating with the Divine Liturgy Sunday morning. The parish promotes learning with liturgy as the primary source for education: Church school for children meets on Saturdays before Vigil, and again on Sunday morning to review the Gospel lesson appointed for that day. Middle and high school students meet after Liturgy on Sundays, and the parish promotes adult learning through education during coffee hour and a seminar with the rector one day per week after Vespers. Fr. Robert Arida encourages the people to attend the entire cycle of the resurrection, beginning with Vigil—this is unique as most parishes of the OCA do not have Vigil on a regular basis. Vespers are celebrated each Tuesday and Thursday, and the cathedral observes the feasts of the liturgical year, so its liturgical life is quite full, with multiple worship opportunities made available to the people. Fr. Arida notes that attendance at weekday services is inconsistent, ranging from 5 for Vespers to 40 for Vigil.

Fr. Arida's style of liturgical celebration was shaped by a number of theologians and thinkers, including Saints Gregory of Nyssa, John Chrysostom, and Maximus Confessor, and modern theologians such as Georges Florovsky, Nicholas Afanasiev, John Meyendorff, Irenee Dalmais, Juan Mateos, Robert Taft, Dmitru Staniloae, Jean Danileou, Christos Yannaras, Vladimir Lossky, Thomas Mathews, and Roland Mainstone, along with Alexander Schmemann. I have listed these theologians to illustrate the breadth of ecumenical thinkers who have influenced Fr. Arida and his approach to liturgical presidency. Fr. Arida teaches Liturgy intentionally through his sermons, education classes, and small discussion groups. When they ask for recommended literature, he refers them to Schmemann's books in English, and selections from Florovsky, Afanasiev, Leaonid Ouspensky, Lossky, and Yannaras, and selections from Paul's letter to the Ephesians.

The cathedral uses English only for the Liturgy and most of the prayers are read aloud for the people to hear, including the prayer of the Trisagion, the prayer before the Gospel, the prayer for the catechumens (when there are catechumens in the parish community), the anaphora, and the prayers before and after "Our Father." Fr. Arida follows Schmemann's credo of corporate prayer, and the configuration of the interior space brings the people together into a common space for worship. Seating is available along the walls with some chairs interspersed, but there are no private or segregated areas of assembly. The choir leads the singing from the front of the Church, so all the people are encouraged to join in the singing: the choir leads the people, and does not perform for them. The corporate character of the cathedral's liturgy coheres with the pastor's encouragement of the people to partake of Communion frequently, without neglecting attention to their relationship with a confessor. [54] Fr. Arida observes that the entire parish receives Communion at most Sunday liturgies.

The liturgical experience at Holy Trinity represents Schmemann's legacy, especially the priorities of corporate prayer and the participation of all the people in the parish's liturgical life. The cathedral observes a full cycle of services, with the two weekly Vespers offices affording faithful an opportunity to gather for non-Eucharistic prayer. The weekly celebration of the Divine Liturgy is the focal point of parish life, and like St. George parish, the springboard for education of all cathedral members. Technology permits faithful to tune into services afterwards, as the parish posts Fr. Arida's homilies on the parish web site. In terms of liturgical catechesis, Fr. Arida's approach is outstanding among the examples we have collected, as his own liturgical formation is deeply ecumenical and he intentionally shares his knowledge of the sources with his community.

St. Anthony of the Desert Mission (Ukrainian Orthodox Church of the USA)

In the desert of the southwestern United States, a small group of Orthodox Christians established a community in Las Cruces, New Mexico, near El Paso, in 2007. The community began with its rector, Fr. Gabriel (Jay) Rochelle and his wife, Susan Steinhaus, who prayed in their home alongside a handful of Orthodox people for two months until a community gradually formed around them and they created a mission parish of approximately 60 people that worships in a chapel of St. Andrew's Episcopal Church in Las Cruces. St. Anthony Mission was established to provide an Orthodox Church in a region that did not have any other parishes, as Las Cruces is a city of 100,000 people with a university, a desert city with the beautiful topography of mountains on the landscape. El Paso has Orthodox parishes, but they are over 50 miles away. Fr. Gabriel is a retired professor of theology who taught at the Lutheran School of Theology in Chicago for many years while also serving as a Lutheran pastor. Fr. Rochelle and Susan were received by the Ukrainian Orthodox Church in the USA (Ecumenical Patriarchate).

St. Anthony of the Desert is a small, tight-knit community. The worship space of their current chapel is conducive to corporate worship, and the chapel has to be arranged and dismantled every Sunday since the parish does not own the space. St. Anthony is an example of a community that adjusts to its context in scheduling liturgy. The community meets for Vespers every Saturday and Divine Liturgy on Sunday, with a fairly full schedule of Lenten services and Vesperal liturgies for the feasts of the liturgical year. The Liturgy is celebrated almost exclusively in English, with occasional Ukrainian interpolations in honor of the parish's official affiliation. The UOC-USA observes the Old (Julian) Calendar, and St. Anthony mission is an exception, following the revised Julian (Gregorian). Fr. Rochelle's experience as a professional theologian and pastor adds a strong educational dimension to the community. He has a public profile as a lecturer and offers a podcast series, while also blogging on the early church and liturgy. Fr. Rochelle taught liturgy in the Western theological academy for 26 years, and he was influenced by early Church documents such as the Didache, Egeria's diaries,

Cyril of Jerusalem, and Basil's treatise on the Holy Spirit. Given his formation in the Lutheran Church, numerous Western theologians contributed to
Fr. Rochelle's approach to liturgy. He cites Luther Reed, George Seltzer,
Arthur Karl Piepkorn, and Berthold von Schenk as his primary Lutheran
interlocutors on the Liturgy, while he also immersed himself in the work of
Josef Jungmann, Dom Gregory Dix, Geoffrey Wainwright, Aidan Kavanagh,
and Schmemann.

The style of liturgical celebration follows the standard practices of the
Orthodox Church, while Fr. Rochelle recites the anaphora aloud for all to
hear. His academic background in the Early Church occasionally results in
public readings from the fathers and sermons on their writings.[55] The current
configuration of the rented chapel space promotes a cozy assembly: the choir
is nestled into a front corner near the people and clergy, so everyone shares
the same space. St. Anthony mission is unique in that it observes the traditional Byzantine ordo, but does not favor a particular ethnicity since the
parish consists of mostly converts, with a handful of people born and raised
Orthodox. The community uses English settings of simple music familiar to
the East Slavic Orthodox traditions. While there is no sense of liturgical
transition within the parish history, St. Anthony exemplifies an Orthodox
community still in the process of establishing roots at the very beginning of
its life, as it is only ten years old. The people of the community know the
liturgical life of Orthodox primarily through their experience at St. Anthony,
as many of them are converts and the parish is still new.

St. Katherine Greek Orthodox Parish (Redondo Beach, CA)

Nestled in America's second-largest city of Los Angeles is St. Katherine
Greek Orthodox parish, four blocks from the Pacific Ocean in the co-called
"South Bay" community. St. Katherine's was established initially in 1956 by
a group of fifty Greek Orthodox families belonging to the cathedral community of St. Sophia near downtown Los Angeles.[56] These families started a
Bible study that eventually grew into the establishment of St. Katherine
parish in Redondo Beach, in 1957. Fr. Michael Courey, the present rector,
emphasizes that St. Katherine's "was established on the foundation of a
community gathered together to study Holy Scripture," so adult learning is a
core value of the community.[57] Since 1957, St. Katherine's has grown its
facilities—in addition to the church, a recreation hall and cultural centers
were also constructed on the site, and substantial renovations occurred in
2017.[58] Fr. Courey observes that these facilities were designed to cultivate
youth and young adult activities, to stem the trend of young adults disappear-
ing from the Orthodox Church. Fr. Courey has sustained the parish's emphasis on Bible study while devoting his energy to strengthening young adult
ministry, as he cites the disappearance of young adults from the Church as

the single most important topic requiring attention by Greek Orthodox cler-gy.[59]

Liturgical life at St. Katherine's generally follows the patterns we have seen in other parishes. Sunday morning resurrection worship is the focal point, with Orthros followed by the Divine Liturgy. Services are primarily in English; of the four parishes in this study. St. Katherine's has the highest percentage of Greek (or a non-English language) used for liturgical celebra-tion. At the Divine Liturgy, portions of many of the litanies are taken in Greek, along with some of the presider's prayers. The Liturgy of the Word and the homily are in English. The timing of the homily depends on parish activities, so it could take place after the Gospel, during Communion, or at the end of the Liturgy. Portions of the anaphora are recited aloud for the people to hear. The parish observes the liturgical year with vigor. The ser-vices are not long, but the calendar is full, especially during Lent, which reaches a penultimate moment with the Akathistos Hymn and gains new momentum throughout Holy Week. The parish has two Presanctified litur-gies each week of Lent, which offer the people opportunities to receive the mystery of Confession and Communion for strength during a season of fast-ing. The style of these liturgies is special at St. Katherine: most of the liturgy is recited, clearly for the people to hear, but not intoned (with the exception of a few of the hymns). Fr. Courey frequently preaches at these services as well.

St. Katherine's cultivates musical competence: Byzantine chanters and a mixed choir participate in leading the singing. The chanters sing on the *kleiros* next to the bishop's throne and the choir sings from the loft. St. Katherine's also has a children's choir: they participate in most of the litur-gies, and occasionally sing the responses to entire Sunday liturgies, while also performing concerts. The children's choir is an example of Fr. Courey's emphasis on youth and young adult ministry threading through the parish. Like many Greek and Antiochian parish communities, St. Katherine's has organized a ministry of myrrhbearers, girls of all ages who offer liturgical service complementing the male altar servers. The myrrhbearer ministry for girls has traditionally belonged to Holy Week liturgies, with the girls follow-ing the model of the myrrhbearing women at the tomb, and Fr. Courey is attempting to expand this ministry beyond Holy Week and into the rest of the year. Furthermore, St. Katherine's continues to host regular Bible study ses-sions as originally established by its founders. The Bible study functions as a source for studying the entirety of Church tradition, and participants learn about the liturgical life of the Church through the gathering.

St. Katherine's offers unique perspectives on liturgical perspectives among Orthodox people in America. While liturgy is the focal point of parish life, it belongs to a larger enterprise of ministries oriented towards caring for established members and reinvigorating participation among youth and young adults. The parish's devoted effort to involve young people in the choir and young girls in liturgical service mark distinct ways of granting the people access to the Liturgy. Fr. Courey observes that this ministry is necessary to offer spiritual growth for a generation "saturated with the values of the greater Hollywood culture."[60] St. Katherine's does not emphasize any particular component or dimension of the Liturgy, but prepares all of its people to lead it. In other words, forming liturgical leaders at all levels is a priority at St. Katherine's. Fr. Courey accentuates this point by highlighting the quality of the contribution of the parish deacon to pastoral ministry. Fr. Kyriakos Cary, the current parish deacon, is one of the few permanent deacons of the Greek Orthodox Archdiocese, and his service bridges the liturgical and the pastoral, as he anoints the sick, performs visitations, and other duties designated by the rector. Fr. Cary's diaconal ministry is one example of a larger enterprise of preparing men and women to lead.

The four parishes forming the basis for our study represent the diversity of Liturgy in North America. No two parishes are exactly alike: some parishes are more intentional about their approach to liturgical participation and catechesis, while others choose to emphasize other areas of pastoral ministry. Two trends can be gleaned from the liturgical lives of our four parishes that are particularly informative on the trajectory of Liturgy in American Orthodoxy. First, all four of our parishes have received the basic core values of liturgical renewal, manifest in the practice of frequent Communion. The introduction of frequent Communion was one of two changes that had the most impact on liturgical life in America, along with the gradual use of English instead of Greek or Slavonic. Two of our four parishes still use some Greek in the Liturgy, so these parishes are intriguing because their people are still in the midst of the experience of liturgical renewal.

The four parishes fall in different places on the spectrum of liturgical renewal, with Holy Trinity Cathedral experiencing the deepest immersion in the process. In this sense, the parishes provide a good sample for the way liturgical renewal has impacted Orthodox parish life in America as a whole, since no two examples are identical. Second, the pastors of the four parishes use different sources to shape their approach to liturgical presidency and catechesis. Two of our four pastors are products of a deeply ecumenical education. Both Fr. Arida and Fr. Rochelle rely on early Church sources and an array of modern theologians of East and West who encouraged ecclesial renewal by employing the method of *ressourcement*. Arida and Rochelle are certainly unusual examples, as both have experience in higher education that exposed them to a wider variety of theologians. Their peculiarity is most salient in their intentional approach to applying academic education to liturgical catechesis. Despite this, they represent a broader trend of liturgical formation in American Orthodox academies that have been influenced by Western theologians, especially since teachers like Schmemann, Meyendorff, and Rentel were also exposed to the Western liturgical tradition in their studies. The Orthodox who participated in the ecumenical movement introduced some of those features into their scholarship and pedagogy, and a program for liturgical renewal was part of that larger package.

The people's experience of liturgy, then, is akin to a trickle-down effect. Only a handful of people read several books on the Liturgy to deepen their understanding, but all of them have experienced worshiping in distinctly Eastern Orthodox communities living in Western contexts. Orthodox Christians are known to marvel at the challenge of managing a hybrid identity as Eastern Christians living permanently in the West. This hybrid East-West identity is not limited to their self-identification: it is also inscribed on the liturgical lives of their parishes and the ministries executed there.

CONCLUSION

This overview of the primary schools of liturgical theology and parish liturgical praxis in Orthodox America yields three observations. First, diversity characterizes liturgical theology and praxis, and is the result of multiple contributors. Second, liturgical renewal has been a major factor in the changes that mark parish worship experiences. Last, parish liturgy is constantly evolving and changing, a fact that limits the potential effects of liturgical renewal.

The diversity characterizing the present state of Orthodox liturgy in America is attributable to jurisdictional plurality and varying approaches to liturgical celebration. The American jurisdictional situation is a complicated maze. The Orthodox jurisdictions in America have their own distinct histories and experiences, and there is no convenient synthesis explaining it all. There are simple factors that create liturgical diversity, beginning with the fact that most Orthodox parishes were established by immigrants, with their liturgical traditions migrating with them to America. Each jurisdiction's adjustments to parish life in America contributed to the thickening of liturgical diversity. For example, when parishes began to introduce English to liturgical celebration, this marked the most significant change to the worship experience of parishes within a single jurisdiction. This liturgical change was necessitated by the organic process of parish growth in America, as generations of Orthodox born and raised here did not understand the original language of the liturgy brought from the mother Churches. The Orthodox jurisdictions never assembled together to publish a single English translation of liturgical texts for parish usage, resulting in incredible diversity of English texts among parishes. In other words, when the people recite the Creed together in English, a participant from a parish of another jurisdiction cannot follow if she has memorized the Creed in the translation used by her jurisdiction. This is just one example of the way jurisdictional plurality creates liturgical diversity in America.

The introduction of liturgical renewal from our schools of liturgical theology also contributed to diversity. While liturgical renewal originated among intellectuals of the mother Churches, it migrated to the West and was implemented there, outside of its native habitat. When clergy began to recite some of the prayers aloud and encourage people to receive Communion, this changed the worship experience for parishes that received these changes. But not all clergy were shaped in the spirit of liturgical renewal, and not all clergy understand liturgical renewal in the same way. The renewal promoted by Schmemann was primarily Eucharistic, though he certainly encouraged people to participate in the larger liturgical life of the Church by attending services that had been forgotten or lost.

The experience of liturgical renewal differed from one parish to the next. For some parishes, renewal might have been manifest by an increase in the number of services prayed each week and season. For others, the introduction of new music and the encouragement of the people to join in the singing might have evinced renewal. Other parishes read the anaphora aloud, and in some places, general confession was introduced. Liturgical renewal was a major contributor to liturgical diversity within Orthodoxy, and the different ways clergy implemented it enhanced the multiplicity of parish practices. Many parishes maintained the status quo or resisted certain components of liturgical renewal, as the proponents of renewal did not persuade all of the jurisdictions to receive it. Furthermore, for parishes shaped by the legacies of Schmemann and Calivas, the spirit of liturgical renewal is oriented towards local church life in America, and shares much in common with other Christian churches that were part of the liturgical movement.

The parishes that did receive liturgical renewal experienced significant change in their liturgy. Praying in English permitted the people to understand liturgical words. They communed more frequently, and therefore fasted and prepared for Communion more often. The people participated in the singing, they heard more sermons, they were exposed to more Scripture, and they were encouraged to concelebrate Liturgy with the clergy. For some people, these changes were introduced to Liturgy during their lifetimes, so they could remember the times when another language was used and people rarely went to Communion, just as Catholics born in the 1950s remember Latin and the Mass of the Missal of Pius V. For many Orthodox parishes, then, the introduction of liturgical renewal changed the way parishioners experienced the liturgy. For those who experienced change, the liturgy was in a state of transition, as the people adjusted to the change required of their participation in the Liturgy. The introduction of change was designed to vivify the people so the Liturgy would translate to a deeper immersion in Christian living. In short, then, the introduction of liturgical renewal resulted in a significant increase in the people's ritual participation. The introduction of liturgical renewal is also a primary feature of parish liturgy in Orthodox America as the leaders of these schools taught and formed parish clergy who introduced these practices.

While liturgical renewal is a fixture of some parts of Orthodox America, it remains a work in progress. Parish clergy introduced liturgical renewal with diverse methods; for some, it was simply encouraging people to receive Communion more frequently. In other cases, the assignment of new clergy to parishes that had received renewal may have resulted in new areas of pastoral emphasis or the withdrawal of renewal principles. Elsewhere, parish clergy were careful about introducing too much liturgical change to avoid resistance from the people. This dimension of liturgical renewal is crucial, as it is not accurate to assume that renewal occurred because it was taught by Schmemann and Calivas in their respective seminaries. Parish clergy and lay leaders are ultimately responsible for the liturgical lives of their communities. In attempting to assess the degree to which people in parishes lead authentically Eucharistic lives and become capable of participating in the spiritual dimension of cosmic life—two of the theological objectives of Schmemann's and Calivas's schools of liturgical thought—one must account for the people's exposure to liturgical renewal. It is clear that liturgical renewal was not a universal phenomenon in Orthodox America, and parishes experienced it to varying degrees.

The people who participated in our four focus groups belonged to parishes led by educated clergy whose views on Liturgy are motivated by renewal and have been shaped by an ecumenical lineup of theologians. Many participants experienced the stark adjustment created by liturgy in transition, when English, frequent Communion, and encouragement of lay participation were introduced to parish liturgy. Others experienced Orthodox liturgy shaped by renewal either from birth, or from the time they were received into the Orthodox Church. In the next section of this study, we present their experience and understanding of liturgy in their own words. Readers are likely to notice the diversity that characterizes Orthodox liturgy in America, along with the challenges and questions about liturgy and its relationship to life posed by the people themselves.

NOTES

1. See the survey results of Alexei Krindatch, "Usage of English Language, Ethnic Identity and Ethnic Culture in American Orthodox Christian Churches," http://hirr.hartsem.edu/research/UsageOfEnglishLanguageEthnicIdentity.pdf (accessed January 9, 2018).

2. English translations have been published and introduced to parish liturgy at various times, depending on the jurisdiction. An edition of the Divine Liturgy was published by the Greek Orthodox Archdiocese in America in 1928, and another edition in 1950. The publication of these books does not mean that parishes began integrating English into the Liturgy, as the

preface to the 1928 edition states that "this manual will be helpful . . . especially . . . for the American women married to Greek men." There is also evidence from the correspondence between Georges Florovsky and Alexander Schmemann suggesting that English began to be used at some liturgies in the late 1940s. I am grateful to Fr. Anton Vrame for providing the information on the Greek Orthodox English translation, and to Paul Gavrilyuk for sharing his research on the Florovsky-Schmemann correspondence.

3. Robert F. Taft, "The Liturgical Enterprise Twenty-Five Years After Alexander Schmemann (1921–1983): The Man and His Heritage," *St. Vladimir's Theological Quarterly* 53, no. 2 (2009): 149.

4. David Fagerberg, "The Cost of Understanding Schmemann in the West," *St. Vladimir's Theological Quarterly* 53, nos. 2–3 (2009): 179–207. Also see David Bresciani, "La réception de la théologie liturgique du père Alexandre Schmemann dans l'Église catholique romaine," in *La joie du Royaume: Actes du colloque international "l'héritage du père Alexandre Schmemann," Paris, 11–14 décembre 2008* (Paris: YMCA Press, 2012), 196–202.

5. Job Getcha, "From Master to Disciple: The Notion of 'Liturgical Theology' in Fr Kiprian Kern and Fr Alexander Schmemann," *St. Vladimir's Theological Quarterly* 53, nos. 2–3 (2009), 251–72.

6. Nicholas Denysenko, *Liturgical Reform After Vatican II: The Impact on Eastern Orthodoxy* (Minneapolis: Fortress Press, 2015), 83–84.

7. Nicholas Denysenko, *"Ressourcement* or *Aggiornamento*? An Assessment of Modern Liturgical Reforms" (forthcoming, *International Journal of Systematic Theology*).

8. John Meyendorff, "Postscript: A Life Worth Living," in *Liturgy and Tradition: Theological Reflections of Alexander Schmemann*, ed. Thomas Fisch (Crestwood, NY: St. Vladimir's Seminary Press, 1990), 151. Also see Denysenko, *Liturgical Reform After Vatican II*, 110–13.

9. Alexander Schmemann, *For the Life of the World: Sacraments and Orthodoxy* (Crestwood, NY: St. Vladimir's Seminary Press, 1988), 27.

10. Stefanos Alexopoulos, "Did the Work of Fr. Alexander Schmemann Influence Modern Greek Theological Thought? A Preliminary Assessment," *St. Vladimir's Theological Quarterly* 53, nos. 2–3 (2009): 273–99.

11. Alexander Schmemann, "Notes and Comments: On the Question of Liturgical Practices, A Letter to My Bishop," *St. Vladimir's Theological Quarterly* 7, no. 3 (1973), 227–38.

12. Ibid., 238.

13. Thomas Pott, *Byzantine Liturgical Reform: A Study of Liturgical Change in the Byzantine Tradition*, trans. Paul Meyendorff, Orthodox Liturgy Series, 2 (Crestwood, NY: St. Vladimir's Seminary Press, 2010), 66–70.

14. Denysenko, *Liturgical Reform After Vatican II*, 190–94.

15. For a good example of Schmemann's critique of idolizing the fathers and his attempt to synthesize their liturgical spirit, see "Liturgical Theology, Theology of Liturgy, and Liturgical Reform: A Debate," in Fisch, ed., 42–43.

16. See, for example, Rene Bornert, *Les Commentaires byzantins de la divine liturgie du VIIe au XVe siècle*, Archives de l'Orient chrétien, 9 (Paris: Institut français d'études byzantines, 1966). Robert Taft also shows how the fathers witnessed to liturgical development in several seminal essays, especially "The Liturgy of the Great Church: An Initial Synthesis of Structure and Interpretation on the Eve of Iconoclasm," *Dumbarton Oaks Papers* 34 (1980–81), 45–75; "Is the Liturgy Described in the Mystagogia of Maximus Confessor Byzantine, Palestinian, or Neither?" *Bollettino della Badia Greca di Grottaferrata* 7 (2010): 247–95; and *Through Their Own Eyes: Liturgy as the Byzantines Saw It* (Berkeley, CA: InterOrthodox Press, 2005).

17. Alkiviadis Calivas, *Great Week and Pascha in the Greek Orthodox Church* (Brookline, MA: Holy Cross Orthodox Press, 1982); *Essays in Orthodox Theology and Liturgy, vol. 1: Theology: The Conscience of the Church* (Brookline, MA: Holy Cross Orthodox Press, 2001).

18. Alkiviadis Calivas, "Invigorating and Enriching the Liturgical Life of the Parish," *Greek Orthodox Theological Review* 48, nos. 1–4 (2005): 134. See also idem, *Essays in Theology and Liturgy, vol. 2: Challenges and Opportunities: The Church in Her Mission to the World* (Brookline, MA: Holy Cross Orthodox Press, 2001), 69–82.

19. Calivas, "Invigorating and Enriching the Liturgical Life of the Parish," 134.

20. Ibid.

21. Ibid., 131, 135, 137.

22. Ibid., 131.

23. Alkiviadis Calivas, "The Presbyter and the Essential Activities of the Church," *Greek Orthodox Theological Review* 56, nos. 1–4 (2011): 35–46.

24. Ibid., 40–42.

25. Ibid., 37.

26. Calivas, "Invigorating and Enriching the Liturgical Life of the Parish," 138–39.

27. Alkiviadis Calivas, "The Liturgy: The Church's Faith in Motion," *Greek Orthodox Theological Review* 49, nos. 3–4 (2004), 236–38.

28. Ibid., 223–24, 232–34.

29. Ibid., 229–30.

30. Calivas, "The Presbyter and the Essential Activities of the Church," 46.

31. Ibid.

32. Ibid., 49, and Calivas, "Invigorating and Enriching the Liturgical Life of the Parish," 249.

33. Calivas, "The Presbyter and Essential Activities of the Church," 49.

34. Calivas, "Liturgy in Motion," 239–41.

35. See the footnotes in "Invigorating and Enriching the Liturgical Life of the Parish," "Liturgy in Motion," and "The Presbyter and Essential Activities of the Church."

36. From Calivas's syllabi for two courses offered at Holy Cross Greek Orthodox School of Theology in 2002 and 2003: Theology of the Sacraments, and Liturgics (via e-mail exchange, March 16, 2016). My thanks to Fr. Calivas for sharing his syllabi with me.

37. Pott, 95–96.

38. Bishop Alexander (Mileant), "Life and Miracles of St. John Maximovich of Shanghai and San Francisco: One of the Greatest Saints of the 20th Century," http://www.pravoslavie.ru/54575.html (accessed January 19, 2018).

39. Liturgical music is part of the seminary's curriculum and intense training is offered to musicians who are not enrolled in seminary courses of study through the Summer School of Music. See http://sslm.hts.edu/#intro for background.

40. St. Tikhon's emphasizes the symbiotic relationship of the seminary and monastery in its academic bulletin, https://www.stots.edu/academicbulletin.html, pp. 3–5, 7 (accessed January 8, 2018).

41. Juan Mateos, *La célébration de la parole dans la liturgie byzantine: Étude historique*, orientalia christiana analecta 191 (Rome: Pontifical Oriental Institute, 1971); idem, *Le Typicon de la grande Église*, 2 vols (Rome: Pontifical Oriental Institute, 1962); Vassa Larin, "The Opening Formula of the Byzantine Divine Liturgy, 'Blessed Is the Kingdom,' among Other Liturgical Beginnings," *Studia Liturgica* 43, no. 2 (2013): 239–55.

42. Stelyios Muksuris, *Economia and Eschatology: Liturgical Mystagogy in the Byzantine Prothesis Rite* (Boston: Holy Cross Orthodox Press, 2013); Vitaly Permiakov, "Чин освящения храма в восточных традициах" ("Rite of the dedication of a temple in the Eastern Traditions") in Michael Zheltov, ed., *православное учение о церковных таинствах* (Orthodox teaching on Church Mysteries), vol. 3 (Moscow: Synodal Biblical-Theological Committee, 2009): 346–67; Mark Morozowich, *Holy Thursday in Jerusalem and Constantinople: The Liturgical Celebrations from the Fourth to the Fourteenth Centuries* (forthcoming with Orientalia Christiana Analecta); Gabriel Bertonière, *The Historical Development of the Easter Vigil and Related Services in the Greek Church*, Orientalia Christiana Analecta 193 (Rome: Pontifical Oriental Institute, 1972); Daniel Galadza, *Liturgy and Byzantinization in Jerusalem* (Oxford: Oxford University Press, 2018).

43. Robert Taft, "The Authenticity of the Chrysostom Anaphora Revisited. Determining the Authorship of Liturgical Texts by Computer," *Orientalia Christiana Periodica* 56, no. 1 (1990): 5–51.

44. Taft has consistently been the most vocal and enthusiastic proponent of the method of comparative liturgy for several decades. It is also notable that Taft honors Anton Baumstark as the founder of this school of liturgical method, and tends to attribute the pioneering work in

Byzantine liturgy to Juan Mateos, even though Taft has shaped the majority of theologians working in the field of Byzantine liturgy in North America today.

45. http://www.coffeewithsistervassa.com/ (accessed January 9, 2018).

46. See the survey data and analysis of Alexei Krindatch, "The Orthodox Church Today: A National Study of Parishioners and the Realities of Orthodox Parish Life in the USA," http://www.hartfordinstitute.org/research/orthchurchfullreport.pdf (accessed January 19, 2018), pp. 10, 12–14.

47. I know of a handful of priests who use YouTube regularly to learn regional chants they can incorporate into parish practice.

48. Alexei Krindatch, "Usage of English Language, Ethnic Identity and Ethnic Culture in American Orthodox Christian Churches," http://hirr.hartsem.edu/research/UsageOfEnglish LanguageEthnicIdentity.pdf (accessed January 9, 2018).

49. Ibid.

50. Ibid.

51. Thomas Hopko's four-part series, *The Orthodox Faith*, is now published online: https://oca.org/orthodoxy/the-orthodox-faith (accessed January 19, 2018). See Stanley Harakas, *Living the Liturgy: A Practical Guide for Participating in the Divine Liturgy of the Orthodox Church* (Minneapolis: Light and Life, 1974).

52. Krindatch observes that sustenance of ethnic identity and culture remains a high priority for American parishes in "Usage of English Language."

53. The information for Holy Trinity Cathedral is taken from the parish web site and an e-mail exchange with Fr. Robert Arida on October 30, 2017.

54. See Fr. Arida's response to a question posed on Communion in "Practice of Communion and Confession," http://holytrinityorthodox.org/ask_the_priest/index.htm#a8 (accessed October 25, 2017).

55. During my visit to the parish in January 2017, Fr. Rochelle read excerpts from the writings of St. Ignatius of Antioch and preached on those writings.

56. Taken from Fr. Michael Courey, "Walk in the Light: Spiritual Exercises from 1 John, A Lenten Ministry for Young Adults," Doctor of Ministry Thesis, Fuller Theological Seminary (December 6, 2007), 8–9. My thanks to Fr. Courey for sharing his doctoral thesis with me.

57. Ibid., 9.

58. Ibid., 9–10.

59. Ibid., 11.

60. Ibid., 14.

Chapter Three

Parish Focus Groups

What the People Said about Liturgy

Our general sketch of Orthodox liturgical practices in America invites us to explore the ways people experience the Liturgy. We now turn to the words of the people themselves. The introduction to this book provides a detailed description of the four focus groups. The next chapter will engage the information provided by the people in the focus groups and provide a synopsis of its meaning and significance for contemporary Orthodox liturgical theology. Here, we will provide the words of the people themselves. The chapter's structure brings the material from the four focus groups together. The topics covered in the focus groups function as the organizing principles of the chapter. A total of 39 people participated in the four focus groups. Table 3.1 summarizes the participants in the focus groups; the acronyms identify the home parish of each participant.

The presentation of reflections on the liturgy offered by the focus groups follows the course of open-ended questions on the Divine Liturgy, receiving Holy Communion, memories of important holidays, especially the seasons of Lent, Holy Week, and Pascha; methods used to learn about the liturgy; liturgical events that are particularly memorable, and why; and the role of gender in liturgical participation.

PARTICIPATION IN THE DIVINE LITURGY

Each session began with questions asking participants to reflect on the meaning of the Divine Liturgy: What parts of the Divine Liturgy appeal to you the most, and why? In your own words, briefly: what is happening in the Divine

Table 3.1.   Summary List of Focus Group Participants

SG1	65–75, female (convert)
SG2	65–75, male (convert)
SG3	65–75, female
SG4	35–45, male
SG5	65–75, male
SG6	35–45, female
HTC1	45–55, male (convert)
HTC2	45–55, female
HTC3	55–65, male
HTC4	55–65, female
HTC5	55–65, female
HTC6	45–55, female
HTC7	55–65, male
HTC8	25–35, female
HTC9	35–45, male
HTC10	55–65, female
HTC11	35–45, male (convert)
SA1	25–35, male (convert)
SA2	35–45, male (convert)
SA3	35–45, male (convert)
SA4	35–45, male (convert)
SA5	65–75, female (convert)
SA6	65–75, female (convert)
SA7	55–65, female
SK1	55–65, male (convert)
SK2	65–75, male
SK3	75–85, female
SK4	75–85, male
SK5	75–85, male
SK6	75–85, male
SK7	75–85, female
SK8	45–55, female (convert)
SK9	55–65, female (convert)
SK10	45–55, female

SK11	45–55, female
SK12	65–75, female
SK13	65–75, female
SK14	75–85, male
SK15	45–55, male

SG = St. George Greek Orthodox Church, St. Paul (six participants)
HTC = Holy Trinity Cathedral (OCA), Boston (11 participants)
SA = St. Anthony of the Desert Orthodox Mission, Las Cruces, New Mexico (7 participants)
SK = St. Katherine Greek Orthodox Church, Redondo Beach, California (15 participants)

Liturgy? What does it mean? Once respondents became comfortable with the setting, they searched for words to describe the meaning of assembly. Appreciation for community, awareness of a global community, desire to hear the word of God, and lament over their own lack of preparation and enthusiasm for the Liturgy are among the themes elaborated by participants.

Detachment and Centering

Participants depicted the Divine Liturgy as an opportunity to detach from the cares of everyday life and center on God. HTC1 said, "it's the focal point of my liturgical life. It's a culminating experience. There are places where I am struck, but they seem to vary." HTC2 remarked, "there is a pattern to what happens, there is the ability for us to kind of shed whatever we walked in the door with. The sequence of activities, the pace, the length of the litanies everything is really designed for maximum ability for the human person to find a way to step in." HTC1 noted how easy it is to "get lost in your own thoughts and be suddenly pulled out of that at different moments." He expressed his frustration at the inability to attend "the regular services during the week' and to limit participation "here just on Sunday." He mentioned that it is a real effort to come to church, and "even the services, they require effort." The services pull you away from your "self-focus and busy-ness."

SG6 remarked on the liturgy by referring to the challenge of family life: "getting married, having kids, I'm always late and I always feel out of sync, so when I'm actually there, there at the beginning, I get to start and I feel like I'm on track. It's hard to come to liturgy late and get the fullness of it, you're just never really in sync." She expressed her frustration with the obstacles to arriving to church on time and identified the "hymns that begin the liturgy" as helping her settle down. SA7 expressed a similar sentiment: "for me, it's been very centering. I could sing songs in Greek and not tell you a word what they meant. Somehow through the essence of it, the incense, the melodies and architecture, I sensed a presence, something higher than myself . . . a feeling of the whole being in a place of God." SA3 added, "maybe if I'm lucky with kids I'm able to come twice a month. . . . I'm leaving the world behind, being so far away I cherish every minute I have here, in that space." For SA3, this is the closest Orthodox parish to his home. The round trip is 220 miles, to and from church, a four-hour round trip. He lives in a rural area, so there are a few churches in his area—there are no closer Orthodox churches.

For some participants, attending the Divine Liturgy was an opportunity for ascetical detachment from the self, an activity described aptly by SA4: "I'm an opinionated intellectual myself, I have all these ideas, and I come into the Church and have to ascetically put them aside—I have to let the prayers of the Church do their thing . . . because I'm an opinionated intellectual, connecting with other people can be difficult. The fact that it's communal, not just God, but also other people, means a lot to me . . . it checks myself, it checks my tendencies, I have to participate in something that's bigger than my ideas." I asked SA4 if the liturgy challenged him, and he responded affirmatively, adding that "I'm attracted [to the liturgy] the challenge is not the liturgy itself, but the challenge is . . . leaving [behind] the attractions of the world. Once I'm in the liturgy, it's a relief."

One respondent takes refuge in a prayer book, keeping her head in "the little red prayer book," which is the pew book often given to laity, containing prayers for all kinds of occasions, including in preparation for Communion. She observed that you can "just concentrate on yourself," and not pay attention to people around you. "The distraction is the devil who is trying to keep you from doing what you're supposed to be doing (SK10). She says "go away" to the devil, "because you're just trying to get to God, to be filled."

Communion with God and the People

Respondents described the experience of the Divine Liturgy as an act bringing them into the presence of God. "We're being brought from earth into heaven" said SG1. Referring to the aesthetical experience of looking upon the dome in the Church and hearing the music, the format of the Divine Liturgy "transposes you from earth into God's presence." SG5 also commented on the flow of the Divine Liturgy, expressing frustration with the distractions. "Sometimes I think about football or something, and I need to say to the evil spirit, get away from me, you!"

The view of the Liturgy as an opportunity to focus on one's self and avoid distraction of others collides with the Liturgy as a corporate prayer engaged by everyone together. SK9 felt a sense of belonging with the global Orthodox Church when she travelled internationally and worshipped elsewhere. "The liturgy is the liturgy, all across." She mentioned that the service in London was done completely in Greek—she was moved by the liturgy there even though she could not understand it all. "That church was packed and there were different people from all over the world." She found it "revealing" to have such a strong liturgical experience overseas, in a parish where the entire liturgy was in a foreign language.

The sense of sharing worship with others in the local community was strong for SA5: "We're there to worship God together—and nowadays, if I don't go to the Liturgy on a Sunday, I don't feel complete, and I need, I want to be there, I have to be there, because it's so much a part of my soul, I find I begin to drift if I do not come to church. Most of the time I make my communion, sometimes I'm not able to fast so I don't, but I'm still there with everyone else." SA6 noted that the appointed prayers of the Church directed her to look outside of herself. "I really like the repetition of the prayer of the Church because every time we go through the list . . . and when we pray for weather, I'm really aware of how much the weather affects the pecans, the coffee, and the chili here." She added that the liturgy made her aware of people who are suffering: when she first heard prayers for captives, she did not understand the reference, it was opaque to her, but now she has the two Orthodox bishops of Syria who are in captivity in mind, along with other people. "As a church community, I'm disciplined to pray for all of these things I'm not aware of at first. . . . I'm a little more sensitive to one petition or another," noting that the liturgy's repetition engaged her sense of awareness of the world.

SA2 described the liturgy as an ancient timelessness. "We're in a modern world with all our Apple products, and then we're in the Church with the incense, candles, and icons, so it jars me out of my everyday routine." He noted that his everyday life is typified by "adversarial fights with other people" (on account of his profession), an ongoing cycle of maximizing one's position in relation to the other, so "at the liturgy, I can put that aside . . . it's easier said than done because it will wash over me in waves, but I'll try to let it pass. One of my favorite prayers is 'lay aside all earthly cares.' It rings my bell every time I hear it, I look forward to hearing it because I know it's different from what I do."

The Formative Power of Specific Components

Specific liturgical components communicated an encounter with the life of God. HTC6 referred to the Little Entrance and the prayer said by the priest "that calls the angels and all the invisible forces to stand with us. That's a lovely part." Her comment built upon HTC2's reference to the angels announcing Christ's resurrection, and she disclosed the fact that the priest says the prayer of the Little Entrance aloud at HTC. SG3 viewed the Great Entrance and the consecration of the gifts as components demanding the assembly's complete attention. She mentioned the typical rites performed upon arriving at Church: lighting candles and venerating icons, but the environment was one of "agitation among the people, they've come in there with all of their problems. You can almost feel like a nonverbal buzz, but by the time of consecration, they settle down." HTC1 also used a kind of mystagogical interpretation of the Great Entrance to describe the presence of Christ at the Liturgy: "It's awesome when the cup is brought out—the Great Entrance—I have a sense of Christ walking among us." He went on to say that this was meaningful to him, the ability to have access, whereas encountering spaces where barriers prohibit encounter is a negative experience.

SG4 described the meaning of liturgy as "group prayer, it's the whole service a series of prayers, connecting with the Spirit and Jesus and God throughout, and intercessions for the world, and getting the Spirit to come down and consecrate." He emphasized that there is a real connection between all the diverse parts of the Liturgy occurring. HTC5 said, "One of the things I notice is when we say 'Thine own of Thine own' and 'on behalf of all and for all,' to me that's like almost the high point of the whole service because God is giving himself to us and us back to him . . . it's not just what's happening here in this church, but it's for the entire world." She explicitly mentioned that the priest's manner of intoning that part of the anaphora was particularly powerful.

Several respondents aligned Sunday Divine Liturgy with the celebration of Resurrection. HTC2 emphasized that the Resurrection celebration began with the All-Night Vigil, referring to a recent visit of a choir that sang the Rachmaninoff All-Night Vigil, and that it was a genuine experience of the resurrection, even though it was not the Divine Liturgy or Easter. She attributed these words to the cathedral rector (Fr. Arida)—he addressed the people at church that evening, noting that there were many visitors in addition to the cohort of cathedral people who would normally participate. "The sequence of activities, the pace, the length of the litanies everything is really designed for maximum ability for the human person to find a way to step in." SG1 remarked that the liturgy was a celebration of the resurrection and a communal invocation of the Holy Spirit.

The Liturgy of the Word

Some respondents featured the power of the Liturgy of the Word in their descriptions of liturgical meaning. SG5 depicted the entire Liturgy itself as being built on the foundation of the Scriptures. He mentioned that there was a Bible study at his workplace and that people repeatedly asked him about John 3:16.[1] He said, "we sing all of that stuff. It's all in there if you go through Proverbs, all the Scriptures, it's what got me interested in the Scriptures," an elaboration of the entire Liturgy itself as an echo of the Scriptures. SG1 identified the priest's sermon as the highlight. She said, "probably father's sermon appeals to me the most," since it is the one thing that changes from one week to another, while the liturgy itself is "repetitious." She expressed appreciation for the rector's sermons in particular because they are "uplifting," and "you can take that knowledge with you throughout the week." The respondent also said that he "sends it out on e-mail" the following week, which enables those who heard the sermon to "take Orthodoxy out into the public." SG2 expressed agreement, saying that the Epistle and the Gospel were the highlights of the liturgy. In her response, she mentioned that they followed the appointed daily readings throughout the week.

SG4 expressed appreciation for the pastor's homilies ("I like his message") and added that "he's always testing people to see if you're paying attention." He also mentioned that Fr. Andrews is constantly "teaching people the parts of the liturgy," while humbly referring to his own struggle to remember things he has learned from one year to the next, since "there is just so much within the liturgy to learn and understand that it is so hard to take it all in, it's so hard to pay attention to it all." HTC8 also identified the sermon as a high point of the liturgical experience: "The sermon's really important to me. And it's particular to here. Through the years, Fr. Robert (Arida) has done a good job of structuring it more like a discussion, than a lecture. It's been helpful for me for bringing my faith into the rest of my life. . . . Going to church is not just a thing that happens for a couple of hours every week." SK4 highlighted the importance of the Epistle and the Gospel, on a par with the reception of Holy Communion.

Some respondents noted challenges in interpreting the scriptural lessons and mentioned the parish Bible class as the place they were able to find answers to their questions. SK4 noted that he did not know much about the prophets he was hearing about in the liturgy. He observed that Bible class is the way he's learning about Orthodoxy and about the liturgy itself. He was one of many participants who noted the strong biblical foundations of liturgy. SK15 teaches the Bible study at St. Katherine's parish—he observed that he learns from the questions coming from the adult learners. He also observed that the altar servers know the liturgy by doing it, so he watches them.

Liturgical Presidency

In three of the four parish groups, participants referred to particular contributions by their current pastor. This sentiment was especially strong at Holy Trinity Cathedral. HTC1 referred to occasions that Fr. Arida is absent from liturgy and a replacement is necessary. His liturgical style invites people to participate in the prayer—it is a common offering. "He points beyond himself as the one being special, as it were—he points to God." He described it as a space created by the priest where one can find or discover joy.

HTC8 added that "mutual forgiveness is not pro forma." The respondents were attuned to the particular liturgical style promoted by the rector. SK11 referred to the priest's request for the assembly's forgiveness at Liturgy and mused, "It's hard to believe that someone like Fr. Michael (Courey) could be a sinner."

Respondents described their participation in the Divine Liturgy in diverse ways. Many respondents expressed a desire to be in a place and space where they could detach from their cares and passions, and depicted the Divine Liturgy as an office that called upon the assembly to pray for and with others and to become aware of local and global needs. Several respondents noted the significance of the Liturgy of the Word. The imprint of the pastor on the life of the parish was manifest in respondent comments.

HOLY COMMUNION

In general, respondents had much more to say about the meaning and processes of Holy Communion than they did about the Liturgy in general in response to three questions. What does it mean to receive Holy Communion? How often do you receive Holy Communion? How do you prepare for Holy Communion? Comments coalesced around the sobriety of receiving Communion and the responsibility of preparing for it and living up to the expectations for life afterwards. SG6 expressed this sentiment: "don't get mad at your kids, you just had Communion, you don't want to be losing your blessing. You center and focus on what you're supposed to be doing." SG4 mentioned that one should receive even if one has not been perfect, and he questioned the reference to "burning" in the pre-Communion prayers as perhaps prohibiting people from receiving who perhaps should have received.[2] SG3 suggested that no one could ever be worthy of receiving Communion; suggesting that following a procedure would make one worthy was unrealistic.

HTC1 described Communion as evoking the presence of Christ: "it's the most sustaining thing I get out of the services. To once again be physically reminded, reconnected with Christ." He refers to the presence of Christ in his life through Communion. In comparison with his previous Church experience (non-Orthodox), he refers to Communion as "I am brought into Christ, and Christ is brought into me." Communion is a "palpable sense of presence, a physical sense of presence." He also related the presence of Christ to participation of other members of the community in Communion. When someone is absent, he noted that there is a sense that "a part of Christ is absent," because each person represents Christ to one another.

The Participation of Children in Communion

Respondents were sensitive to the participation of children in the process of receiving Communion. HTC4 was particularly attuned to the children's focus on performing the rite: "[It's the] Connection that is there—here we are together, again, for this event. . . . When the children line up for communion. There's something wonderful about that. . . . There's all kinds of issues with behavior in church. But when it comes to Communion, the kids are so focused, they know what to do. My grandson, he's seventeen months old now, he knows what to do. . . . There's something that people experience at a very young age in the liturgy that's so deep." HTC4 mentioned people who were taken to church as small children, but then were completely denied that experience once they started school. "They talk about that experience [as children in church], and it's hard for them to articulate what that was . . . but there's a memory that's there. I see that in our kids."

SA6 noted that she had been Lutheran and that children typically began to receive Communion in fifth grade. "I just love watching. . . . It's so wonderful to see everyone come up. I'm not taking Communion in the same sense as the babies are . . . but we're still together, it's such a community act. . . . Theoretically no one is left out by virtue of age. I love the visual of the kids . . . family meal time, it's a nice feeling." SG5 mused on his recollection of preparing for Communion as a child, and compared the experience to his observation of the present practice: "I knew that I couldn't have milk or anything, it sets the tone for what you're going to do in church, it's very important." He also referred to the time of reflection after Communion, as a moment of the lifting of a burden, of "getting something off your chest." SG5 asserted that fasting was particularly important in "the old days, in the Greek villages. The whole school would attend Divine Liturgy, we would march in for Divine Liturgy. When we fasted, it was important." He added that the requirement of fasting before Communion as a child prepared him for something important: "you knew that the first thing you were going to put into your mouth was Communion." SG5 suggested that fasting is now relaxed, as people might come to Church having "fried eggs" or some other breakfast before liturgy.

Respondents did not hesitate to describe their own challenges of preparing for Holy Communion. SK11 said, "I go into a guilt phase—I have a lot of trouble with fasting." She went on to say that "I am not worthy of Communion," and "I'll show you." In other words, her disagreement with the Church's teachings on fasting are enough for her to sustain a position where she will deny herself Communion. "When I come to church, I feel like a dirty car, and when I leave, I feel like I've gone through a car wash. . . . When it's time to go up for Communion it's almost like, 'run Forrest, run,' I want to leave because I'm not deserving because I haven't fasted." The worst time of year for me when I want to run is the forty days of Lent."[3]

Comparing the Past with the Present

Generational perspectives on Communion were illuminating. SK2 stated that as a child, "it was four times a year." He thought that it was a generational issue—he noted a change at some point, as people were urged to partake frequently. "It's hard to get your head wrapped around that by fasting say on Wednesdays and Fridays, and making that little effort so that you're worthy." He remarked that you can never be worthy, even if you read the appointed prayers beforehand. He raised a problem about the older generation looking at the younger generation, and asking if they are taking Communion seriously since they're receiving so often. "Are eyes on me as I look at others?" SK2 said he heard an elderly lady say about a younger woman, "oh, she must have a lot of sins, she goes every Sunday" (laughter erupted). SK4 mentioned that he and his wife receive every Sunday and try to observe a Wednesday and Friday fast: "they have to take things into consideration that your body needs a certain amount of energy to make it through church." He added that he wonders what people think about his wife and him, that they receive Communion every Sunday. He added that they used to receive once or twice a year: "I appreciate the fact that I can do it every Sunday."

SK12 narrated her story about her experience growing up as Greek Orthodox in Cyprus. In elementary school, she learned the fundamentals of the Bible. On Thursdays, the children had to attend catechism. A woman was teaching them the lives of the saints. The children had to attend church every Sunday; if they were absent, they had to account for it to the principal. "It takes a long time to understand and learn our Orthodox religion." She observed that the clergy were strict in Cyprus—they had to fast at least three days, and the kids were "frightened" to take Communion if they had not observed the austerity of the fast. She observed that "I kind of cringe" when she takes her medication and eats breakfast, as she has a mental block because of her childhood experience. Later, she added that the children were encouraged to read about the faith in secondary school.

Awareness of Others

Several respondents observed the difference between communicants and non-communicants. HTC2 described Communion as "a huge moment of differentiation. There's an intense moment when you see someone who's out of line, you know they're not Orthodox." In reference to non-Orthodox who come forward for Communion, she commented that it's available to everyone "who has made a commitment . . . Communion creates a lot of clarity" on the meaning and significance of the Eucharist as a whole. She referred to her experience in other churches, where she is always invited to receive Communion as a gesture of hospitality, and differentiated this experience with Orthodoxy, which deems Communion to be more than hospitality—"it's available to everyone, but you have to act."

HTC10 was sensitive to the deepening of Communion created among all participants. "I thought that when I had the real body and blood of the Eucharist that it was going to help me. But I've learned from reading Schmemann that you are one with everybody else, too. It's not just my own personal journey; it's sharing in this beautiful thing that you're doing with everyone else at the same time." She was the second respondent to refer to Communion as an experience of elevation, and she described the joy resulting from sharing in the experience with everyone else "in the same room." She initially thought that it was going to be the fulfillment of a personal journey, but "it's become much more theologically complex for me."

Communion and Separation

Many participants feel the pain of intra-Christian division as they are participating in Holy Communion. HTC9 said that Communion "also represents a closed door." He was referring to Communion as something shared only by the people in his Orthodox parish, and he described the knowledge that some are not included as "a heavy cross to bear" and "a painful experience." For him, it's personally painful because he cannot share it with others. HTC10 echoes his pain, saying "I can't take Communion with my own family."

HTC6 described her experience attending an interfaith conference in London, during her first travel abroad (she was living in the USSR). They were present at an Anglican Church, her first time at a non-Orthodox service. "There was liturgy, to take part with everybody, Communion, they are all Christians . . . my priest stopped me . . . I knew that I wasn't supposed to." She was attending this interfaith conference along with Orthodox clergy, and said that the liturgy itself compelled her to stand up and to receive—she referred to this as an impulse to "movement" she was feeling within. Her comments are provocative, contrasting the natural compulsion to respond affirmatively when invited to partake in a sacred meal with the official Church prohibition on receiving Communion in a non-Orthodox Church.

HTC3 said that "it grieves me" to be in the presence of "sincere Christians" who cannot receive Communion in the Orthodox Church. He shared a story of a time when he informed non-Orthodox who stood up to receive that they could not receive, saying "I felt so horrible . . . I wish it could be otherwise . . . It comes out as 'we're better than you,' and I hate saying that." HTC5 responded to the previous comments by saying that her husband was cradle (Russian) Orthodox, and that his bishop instructed her (through him) to receive Confession and Communion before she had been received into the Church.

Many participants reflected on the gifts received from God in Communion, especially forgiveness and freedom. SA3 said that there is "mystery and mercy when you're approaching Communion, and even during the liturgy there are penitential prayers—it's all part of that dynamic process of being saved, approaching Communion and working through your sins." Select respondents took the opportunity to connect the mysteries of Confession and Communion, an unplanned discussion during the course of sessions that yielded profound insights. SA5 said, "I think the deeper I get into Orthodoxy, God doesn't dump all of my sins in front of me and say, 'what a mess!' I can tell God about it, but I need to hear a human being, I need to hear my priest answer me, talk to me and dig something out. It's such a relief, I can go away and find peace." Going to Confession is quietly acknowledging that "this is a problem for me," and fortunately, "God doesn't show me all of my sins at once." SA7 stated that "The reason I like it, I get to verbalize it. When I actually go and sit down, I say 'this is bothering me.'" She observed that there is a "moment in time" when one says "I'm acknowledging this about myself, I'm verbalizing it, okay, let's try this again, fall down, get up, fall down, get up. That's what Confession is, I welcome it."

St. Anthony's discussion on Communion evolved into ecumenical comparisons. SA3 said that there is "mystery and mercy when you're approaching communion, and even during the liturgy there are penitential prayers—it's all part of that dynamic process of being saved, approaching communion and working through your sins." SA7 depicted the Roman approach as a "court of law. . . . To me it's just so freeing. I have permission to be healed." She went on to attempt to define the "Orthodox sense of sin." Sin is a way of "veering off" and repentance means "going back to the target, being guided back to that. . . . I feel free from judgment in the Orthodox Church. . . . The pedestals [from which one will fall] are way high in the Catholic Church," a process that can result in great "hurt."

Changing Paradigms in Rules and Regulations

SA4 said that one side of his family is Roman Catholic, and he suggested that the post-Vatican II generation has shifted on the matter of legalism. SA4 observed that some Orthodox are having "trouble listing the sins" whereas others, specifically those who had been in the Catholic Church, were "having trouble narrowing the list." SA3's conception of Confession was poisoned over time when he was Catholic—he felt that the juridical approach to Confession in the Catholic Church was intimidating. "Am I going to hell? I don't know, maybe," as a typical experience of Confession in the Roman Church.

A bit later, he added that he sensed Roman Catholics were beginning to favor a therapeutic program of Confession over a legalistic one.

Respondents were generally wary of rules and requirements concerning Confession and Communion. SA7 asserted that churches with policies that require the mystery are making an error—she thought Orthodoxy emphasized the notion of "wanting Confession, I want to do this, I desire to do this. . . . Holding it over my head, seeing if I'm fasting or if I ate a hamburger on Wednesday" was an example of forcing the issue, coercing people into participating in the mystery.

Respondents from St. Katherine's identified the changes that had occurred in their lifetimes concerning Communion. SK13 observed that "now they're trying to go back to the beginning of Christianity." She observed that early Christians communed all of the time, and that changed, so that the current practice of frequent Communion is a return to the early Christian model. SK3 observed that the priests at St. Nicholas Ranch consistently encouraged people to receive Communion every time, "because you're invited to a banquet."[4] SK9 verbalized some discomfort with the frequent reception of Communion: "it wasn't an every Sunday event." She referred to specific holidays on which they would receive Communion—the Panagia (the Dormition feast on August 15), Christmas, and Holy Saturday. "Too often, I feel as if I'm not prepared enough to take Communion." She added that the priest is always reminding the people that Communion is the table of Christ, so they should come forward to partake. "I guess I should, but I don't feel like going every Sunday."

SA3 values Communion as a precious opportunity, as "coming to liturgy is really special, being able to receive the Eucharist is really special, I hate leaving the Church on Sundays. . . . Being so far away, you're not connected to that weekly Divine Liturgy. I wish I could be here [more frequently] because I see the value in that." SA3 said that his time on the road to church provided him with an opportunity to pray, to reflect. When she was a Methodist, SK8 did not receive Communion every Sunday. She watched everyone go up for Communion as a catechumen for Orthodoxy—"it was so beautiful. . . . I try to take it every Sunday because I feel this sense of desperation, that I need Christ, And I never feel worthy, never, even if I fast. . . . I feel like I'm also taking it for my family, especially since my husband is not Christian. It's big for me." She observed that there is something special about watching the Church comes forward to receive Christ. SK2 noted the healing power of Communion: "even though we are unworthy, we should receive Communion because it's our medicine, every time." HTC4 related the story of discussing Communion with a child, who defined Communion by using the word "kingdom." She referred to Communion as "the door leading to the kingdom, leading us to fulfillment." She also noted that Communion is not the only door, but one of many.

Respondent reflections on Holy Communion yielded multiple views of the Eucharist. Receiving Communion sheds light on sin, divine mercy, modes of belonging (to God and the local community), concerns about the perceptions of others, and mourning over exclusion. One common theme underlines the mosaic of reflections on Communion: it is a crucial part of participation in Church life that inspires people to reflect.

LITURGICAL SEASONS AND SOLEMNITIES

Lent, Holy Week, Pascha, and Christmas are all staples of Christian worship, so the focus groups devoted some time discussing the liturgical celebrations of these seasons in depth. Respondents discussed their thoughts in response to these questions: "What features of the liturgical year engage you the most? Holy Week and Pascha: how do you understand this week? When you go to Church, what are you remembering? How does the theme of that week speak to you and your life?"

The discussions yielded some convergence on the meaning of prominent solemnities along with profound statements on liturgical events that spoke to individuals with special strength.

There is a brief, but intense preparatory period for Lent in the Byzantine Liturgical tradition, five Sundays devoted to specific themes from the Gospel readings appointed to the Sunday Divine Liturgy. The themes for the preparatory Sundays are Jesus' encounter with Zaccheus, the Publican and the Pharisee, and the Prodigal Son (all from Luke), the Last Judgment (Matthew), and forgiveness (from Jesus' Sermon on the Mount in Matthew 6). Faithful experience a gradual immersion into Lent as a season of repentance and begin the process of fasting, intensifying prayer, and reconciling with their neighbors.[5]

Lent as Training

SA3 said, "I look forward to great Lent, it's something I get excited about, I can't quite put my finger on it. I enjoy the Sundays leading up to Lent, the preparation, the readings. I guess I look at it as a challenge, it's a challenge for myself to change. It's a time to reflect, to evaluate. Not that it shouldn't happen throughout the year, but it's that time of year." He notes how Lent "encapsulates everything." Someone told him that the Orthodox Church is like the "marine corps" for Christians. Returning to the Sundays before Lent, SA5 remarked that "it's a build up, isn't it?" She added that she couldn't fathom how she was going to make it through all of the fasting again, but finds comfort in the services: "By the time I get to Pascha, I find that I'm going to miss this discipline."

SA4 said that he looks forward to the Sunday of the Last Judgment and Mary of Egypt, "because I learned about what Origen and Gregory of Nyssa were saying about universalism and that thread in Orthodoxy, and that really turns me off, to me, that really negates the Christian story in a fundamental way. To me, the Church . . . you can't find a direct refutation of that line." He explains that he comes from Unitarian Universalism and he sees commonality with *apokatastasis*.[6] "I look at the Sunday of the Last Judgment as the Church responding to that in some way, because the Church affirms the judgment." He clarified his statement to say that it is not an affirmation of hell, but an affirmation of judgment.

Special Lenten Services

In the Orthodox Church, Lent begins with Forgiveness Sunday. In many parishes, the season commences with the daily Lenten office of Vespers and a rite of Forgiveness where all of the people of the congregation request forgiveness of the others and impart it in kind, beginning with the pastor. "It's the Forgiveness Vespers. I can't think of a better starting spot for Lent,"[7] said SG6. HTC3 also referred to Forgiveness Vespers, and said that the service is done with bows and prostrations, asking the other congregants for forgiveness at HTC. He said that "it was revealed to me every year that I have something to be sorry for." He mentioned traveling to the cathedral of another city while on a work trip, and considering skipping the Forgiveness Vespers "since I didn't know anyone there and it would be stupid to stay, but I stayed anyway. . . . Going around that group of strangers was a profound experience, to bow before every stranger. It felt like we were doing it on behalf of the whole world . . . it was like we were doing it for everyone, for people you didn't know about." He went on to say that he was away from the Church for several years (because it's a "love-hate relationship, of course"), "during that time I was away—there's a kind of participation that happens, I can't explain it." HTC3 is referring to the sustaining power of liturgical participation—the experience of forgiving and receiving forgiveness remained a part of his life and habit even though he was on hiatus from active church participation.

Two other distinct features of Byzantine Lent are the Liturgy of Presanctified Gifts and the Akathistos Hymn chanted on the fifth Friday evening of Lent. SG4 referred to his childhood when he never attended any of the special Lenten seasonal services. He said that he thought (at the time) that they might be superfluous ("what is Lazarus Saturday for?"). He was impressed especially by "the Presanctified Gifts liturgy, I was really impressed by that, it was something completely different than anything I had seen." His impression did not include immediate understanding: he said, "I didn't get it, but I was completely blown away. I sat there in awe and tried to figure it out.

SG4 also referred to the Friday service (the Akathistos Hymn, or Salutations of the Theotokos) as something "really joyous," since multiple priests would have their own singing parts—he compared the performance of the Akathistos with a "drinking song." SG2 returned to the Akathistos as a poignant moment of Lent, partially because of the special inclusion of children in the service at St. George's. SG1 offered that "we've watched a lot of our church's children grow up doing that service; it's always very special to see them in front of the icons and do the prayers." SG4 noted that "different groups" of children are matched with adults, and those who are able to sing do it well.

Holy Week

The vast majority of comments concerned Holy Week. HTC1 said, "I feel terribly cheated with every service I miss," in reference to Holy Week. "It's almost impossible for me, unless we have vacation set aside." He also noted that the children feel "bitterly disappointed" if they have to miss any of the services. SA1 noted that the hymn appointed for Friday Vespers in Holy Week about "Joseph taking Christ down from the cross and wrapping him in a linen shroud—it struck me as something of pure beauty, I like saw it in front of my face, more than any film could portray, and it just was totally real, as seen from the Bible, brought forth for me." SK11 referred to the ritual performance of the un-nailing of Jesus from the cross. "I'm not sad because I know. I find peace in the death of Christ. I have hope."[8]

The rites of Holy Friday seemed to inspire the respondents more than other aspects of Holy Week. SG5 reflected on the way Holy Friday was celebrated in the village, which he likened to a funeral. He remembered the entire village coming for Holy Friday services, bearing candles, and processing "around the entire perimeter of the village." I asked him to say more, and he said that they stopped in the center because the church was in the center of the village. He said that even though today's conditions are not identical, it offers a "good witness" to the public that asks, "what are they doing? Well, we're celebrating the funeral of Christ."

SG1 picked up on SG5's reference to witness by saying that "Holy Week is a good opportunity for Orthodox Christians to witness to their faith." She echoed SG5's reference to non-Orthodox asking, "what are you doing? Why do you go to Church every night, what are the services about?" She also suggested that Orthodox should invite people to come to Church with them, "to see the services." SA7 reflected on her childhood memories with references to the decoration of the church, the "yayas performing great prostrations, and people—in those days, they crawled under the epitaphios."[9] SK2 had a profound experience on a Good Friday—he felt like he really wanted to be in church. He never had this experience again. He kvetched about taking the epitaphios into the street in Brooklyn. Bishop Isaiah told him that they were taking the epitaphios into the darkness to show the world, to bring the light into the darkness. He added, though, that the particular neighborhood of the church was Jewish, so performing the rite there chafed interreligious sensibilities.

A few respondents identified the office of Lamentations sung at Matins of Holy Saturday (Friday evening in parish practice). SA7 spoke emotionally about this service: "singing the lamentations, because the poetry is on the Mother of God who is lamenting the death of her son, and as a mother, and having lost a child and having to, at a very early age make the *kolyva* for my own first-born . . . when I heard those prayers . . . " (she was overcome by tears and could not finish her sentence—SA5 attempted to finish for her, saying, "they're beautiful," and SA7 said, "yes . . . overtaken with pain . . . but then, Christos anesti (Christ is risen) . . . is the hope. And that sums it up for me."[10] SK4 found meaning in the actions of women narrated in the Gospels appointed toward the end of Holy Week: "Holy Week. The Virgin Mary, Mary Magdalene, and one of the other women really brought women to the forefront. That is so admirable. . . . I think women should appreciate Mary Magdalene, she found the tomb empty and found Christ."

Pascha

Reflections on the Paschal celebrations ranged for participants. As with Communion, a few participants used simple metaphors to describe their experiences of Pascha. SK10 identified "the liturgy after the Anastasi" as the most profound experience for her, "even though it is very difficult to stay . . . he brightness, the hymns, the joy on everyone's face." [11] SK2 identified the "sermon of St. John [Chrysostom]" as a highlight.[12] SA5 described the Pascha service as a "burst of music," since there is much more singing appointed for these services than at other times of the year.

Powerful Paschal Rituals

As with Lent and Holy Week, some respondents identified specific rituals as bearing profound meaning on Pascha. HTC5 mentioned "a transitional moment from purple to white on Pascha . . . and with the doors being opened for Pascha." She was referring to the first resurrection service on Holy Saturday during the chanting of the verses of the Alleluia responsorial psalm, when it is customary to change the vestments from purple to white in anticipation of proclaiming and hearing the resurrection Gospel. HTC5 suggested that the deacon's doors should also be opened for forty days or longer during paschaltide (referring to the tradition of keeping the royal doors open during Bright Week). HTC4 observed the solemnity of the moment when "the gifts are brought out in silence," at the liturgy of Holy Saturday. HTC2 mentioned that the fifteenth reading from the Prophecy of Daniel was particularly moving to her. This is the fifteenth and final Old Testament reading of the Vespers portion of the Holy Saturday office. HTC8 mentioned the power of Paschal Nocturne.[13] She added that she was unsure of the particular Gospel, but looked forward to hearing the story of the angels telling the disciples that "he is not here; he is risen. . . . I get chills every time I hear it" (Mark 16:1–8).

SA3 shared a story about his first Pascha—he had studied Orthodoxy for five years and attended St. Anthony's for four years before he was received. He was out of town and attended Pascha at a small Orthodox mission: the matushka (priest's spouse) asked him, "isn't Pascha beautiful?" and he did not understand the magnitude of the festal liturgy. He said, "I couldn't grasp it all." Once he participated the second time, he said, "I understood it— everything hit me, I'm standing in front of the icon of Christ, the doors open, and it hits me. I understand the meaning of the liturgy, the depth of it. . . . It's amazingly important for my life . . . it takes me out of the world and it brings me closer to God . . . for me it was that one night at Pascha and then continuing after that."

Repetition and Exhaustion

The seasonal services proved difficult for cradle Orthodox Christians to understand as well. SG5 made several editorial comments about the Passion Gospels on Thursday night.[14] "It is the length of the service. Now sometimes there is the same Gospel by John or Matthew, but those are repeated. I don't know if there's anything the Church can do. Now the fathers have done a wonderful job designing the whole Divine Liturgy around Holy Week, but I don't know how they can get around repeating the same section or same verse from Matthew or Luke. . . . I think there's some repetition there. That's the problem with Thursday. When the priest comes out with the cross on Thursday, that is very moving, you know—'he who is hung upon the cross.' You get goose bumps with that one. It's too long; twelve Gospels."[15] SG1 was sure to mention that it had nothing to do with disrespect for the word of God, but was a matter of arriving home very late, and also was difficult for people without facilities in Greek: "for us who do not speak Greek you lose out when the Greek starts, because you're trying to see what's being read in a dim church."

SA5 told the story of participating in the services of Holy Week at a parish in El Paso and having the feeling of "understanding the enormity of Christ's sacrifice." In 2016, she referred to her participation of reading the psalms at Christ's tomb as building up a sense of "the sacrifice and the majesty of Pascha." The key for SA5 was "going through the whole process."

For some respondents, Pascha was the conclusion of a liturgical season that was physically exhausting. SA5 said that she can't fathom how she is going to make it through all of the fasting again, but finds comfort in the services. "By the time I get to Pascha, I find that I'm going to miss this discipline. After Pascha, I'm sort of sad that I've left Lent. Is that weird? It's a worthwhile discipline and endeavor." SA3 said that "everyone in the parish is so involved, their mind is set, they know what's coming, they know what they're preparing for." He observed that he too is sad that it ended. SA5 said, "After Pascha, everything is flat for a while. [During Lent] everyone is making an effort, to do more things, I try to continue, but it's such a special effort during Lent, once it's over, I don't want to give it up." SA6 explained that she and her colleague work hard as the mission choir directors, and it is disheartening to have invested so much work into leading worship during the season to behold people at the Paschal service who were absent from the Lenten services. "You don't know what it's like to do Lent." "When we come to the sermon of [St. John] Chrysostom, 'come one, come all,' that takes me down a notch." SA6 described attending all services despite the fatigue as "a joyous burden being here for every service." SA5 noted that she loses her voice every year once they arrive at Pascha.

SG4 thought that the Church emphasizes the continuation of Pascha through the fifty days of Pentecost. He regarded it as tiring, saying that "you get tired, you get a break, it's not over, it doesn't end, you have to persevere with it." I asked him to elaborate his comment on fatigue, and he said that he had extra duties as an usher this season, stayed up until 4 a.m. on Pascha, and returned the next morning. He joked, "I'm not sure how the priest does it. Lots of coffee?" SG3 referred to the fact that she could no longer attend the midnight Paschal liturgy. "Out of the whole year, these couple of hours are completely different from anything else you've ever experienced." She referred to it as "ecstasy," a "pinnacle experience," and a "release. It's like the completion of a journey. You go through these long forty days and that is it. You have gone up the mountain. So I miss that."

Besides the frank admissions of fatigue, some respondents pointed to a burst of energy accompanying Pascha. HTC1 said, "the joy is so huge, the whole community" attends the Vespers celebrated on Sunday afternoon on Pascha. Several respondents noted that the Sunday Paschal Vespers is short, but compact: "everything is right there." A bit later, HTC1 added "there's some genius behind that," referring to the relative brevity of Paschal Vespers. Respondents reported that HTC yields large attendance for Paschal Vespers. HTC8 shed light on the non-liturgical aspects of Pascha: "After church, everyone is just milling around, talking, and it's okay, that would *never* fly any other time of the year." Interestingly, the respondents at HTC related the joy of Pascha itself to the joy of being together in a less formal, non-liturgical way, yet still in church. It appears that the release from the previous week unleashed a freedom to be joyous, and to laugh with freedom, informally.

HTC1 discussed the children's role in celebrating Pascha, noting that the children feel "bitterly disappointed" if they have to miss any of the services. HTC8 added that "the kids are really into it." HTC4 suggested that the absence of pews from the Church granted the children a freedom they would not otherwise enjoy to fully participate in the services. HTC1 mentioned that Fr. Arida pays attention to the children in a special way. HTC8 said that "it's very theatrical and dramatic when you're a kid, it's the only time of the year that it happens. Nocturnes, the procession, the changing of the covers on Holy Saturday, there's a lot of theatrics involved."

A handful of respondents were sensitive to the relationship between the services and the human condition. SK9 saw the Gospel appointed to the Saturday of Lazarus as disclosing Jesus and the human condition. "He's telling us the story of God as manifested in that day. Jesus wept. That really shows us his humanity. He came to our level, emptying himself, to be with us." SG6 saw the human condition communicated in the services of Palm Sunday: "We have Palm Sunday and Christ enters the city and they're adoring him with the palms, and then they turn around, and all of a sudden they'd rather have a murderer and Christ has to suffer, and it's such an interesting reflection on the human condition. How can people turn like that? How can people be so blinded to all the miracles they attributed to him? And they pick a murderer. It's so hard to comprehend that. The human condition is very scary, and you get reminded to pray for discernment, you know, with that mob mentality."

In summary, respondents were animated in their descriptions of their experiences of Lent, Holy Week, and Pascha. Respondents were attuned to specific Gospel lessons as fundamental to Christian daily living. They described festal rites with great detail, and were typically able to recall specific passages from hymn texts. They were especially attuned to the sheer humanity of the liturgical season: they were disappointed in their inability to participate in the entire cycle of appointed services, and yet admitted feelings of complete physical exhaustion by the time they reached Pascha. Respondents did not point to one specific rite as the primary defining moment of the services: different liturgical rites provided inspiration, although the services occasionally proved to be too esoteric for participants to understand.

THE ROLE OF WOMEN IN LITURGICAL LEADERSHIP

The focus group sessions included a segment on the question of increasing the role of women in the liturgy: "Is gender equality or differentiation important to you in terms of liturgical ministry and participation? If so, why?" I included this topic for two reasons: first, many Orthodox parishes in America embraced certain changes in liturgical practice, and this development included a significant increase in women exercising liturgical leadership. Second, the question of the role of women is controversial in the contemporary Orthodox Church: some are advocating for the restoration of the order of deaconess, whereas others see the topic of women as the entrance of political theology into the Church.[16] Focus group respondents offered diverse views on women and the liturgy.

SG1 referred to a Lenten retreat that had been delivered at the parish on the role of women in the Church as a positive experience. She expressed opposition to the possibility of women's ordination to the priesthood: "things should stay the same as they are because I think that women have a great role in the Church." SG6 expressed agreement on this topic and said that it is a matter of respect of differences. She shared a story of a hospitalization following a miscarriage and the discomfort she felt when a woman priest came in to see her: "this woman came in with a collar and I was like, what it this? This is just not my day." SG1 stated that "we have lots of ways to serve in the Church . . . women have a role in the home with raising their families and raising their children." SG6 referred to "the *Panagia*; the Mother of God, there's your role model."[17] She referred to the female saints, the female martyrs. SG2 said that "women can do anything, except for bishop, priest, or deacon." SG1 referred to her participation in the local Philoptochos chapter, remarked that there was plenty of ministerial work to be done by women, and that any woman who would take on the challenge of doing the work would not have time to be a priest or deacon.[18] SG2 stated that the Christ had established the Church so that men occupied the primary ministerial functions, and that people needed to be more accepting of divine institution. SG1 suggested that the gender issue was generated by the tendency to questioning, and stated that the solution is "to take it on faith" ("it" referring to the appointment of men to orders): "We don't understand everything . . . there are things that you just have to take on faith." SK12 observed that they talk about the issue frequently. She suggested that "from now on, if anybody wants to help, they're welcome, in that capacity," not to say, "from now on, the women are going to take over."

Several respondents at St. Katherine's thought about ways women might perform ministry in the Church. SK2 suggested that women should be ordained to the diaconate to help with baptisms, and to assist adult women preparing for Baptism. SK4 thought it might be fine for Orthodoxy to have deaconesses, but he would be uncomfortable with deaconesses assisting with the distribution of Communion. SK9 stated that the Orthodox Church is patriarchal and she's comfortable with it, but "if [the female diaconate] was historical, if God had it in place for this church, I think it could be helpful, these priests are so overworked sometimes." SK5 observed that a deaconess could go out and give communion to the sick, especially given the universal shortage of priests everywhere. SK1 mentioned that he was raised Episcopalian and that they started to ordain women to the priesthood in the 1970s. "I see that as the start of the downfall of the whole church." He added that there are now women priests with partners—it was a slippery slope that gave way to "a whole wave of radical ideas." SK11 suggested that there is no need to change anything.

SK12 discussed qualifications for ordination to deaconess: "it should be required that she has the same qualifications as a male deacon, not just anybody, because then I think we are getting into a problem that people who don't have anything else to do are going to do it to just pass their time." She observed that a woman who is dedicated to the ministry could contribute much good. Another participant asked about women who receive graduate theological degrees and the opportunities available to them other than youth ministry. SK2 said that "the priest can't be in all places all of the time," and observed that a female diaconate could be helpful to the priest in bereavement ministry and bringing Communion to the sick. SK1 said, "part of life is accepting what you can and cannot do. Part of this is that women cannot accept that they're not men." SK14 added that "nowadays women are trying to compete with men." SK9 observed that maybe "God allowed it to disappear [the female diaconate], that it wasn't meant to be." I added that the male diaconate also fell into deep decline.

SK8 suggested that the Church should appoint nuns to parishes. She added that nuns often function as teachers in the Catholic Church. SK7 disagreed, contending that a monk would not be able to relate to people with families and the presence of young people in the Church. "You don't know what a family goes through." SK5 stated that bringing a monk into the Church would take a monk out of his renunciation of the world, so that he would therefore no longer be a monk.

Ordination of Women as a Sign of the Times

Several respondents viewed the possibility of ordaining women as a sign of the times, and predicted that such a move would cause problems for the Church. SK9 observed that "here, it doesn't seem like it would become that slippery slope," in reference to the Orthodox Church. SK1 said, "In the 70s, would you have thought that gay marriage would become the norm that it is now?" He was concerned that permitting the ordination of women would result in that slippery slope marking the politicization of the Church. SA1 said, "I'm personally convinced of the argument that the churches that have allowed in modern arguments of the twentieth century . . . [things] have declined as a result of letting those things in, so I'd be opposed to doing things like this." SA3 stated that he would like to read more about these issues; he's inclined to agree with SA1, but wants to understand the historical context. SA4 said, "I don't feel the North American Church has enough theological anthropology ingrained in the people to address these issues adequately." He added that he predicts the debate will rage in the Church over the next hundred years or so and he is worried that the Church will divide. He predicted that the Orthodox Church in North America will ordain deaconesses, and that a split will result.

SG5 suggested that questions of gender were worldly and came from political correctness. He referred to Jesus' prayer referring to his disciples as "not of the world" (John 17). SG5 lamented the permeation of worldly affairs into the Church by dismissing the legitimacy of LGBT people: "we're getting worse things now. We're getting two men being Christian kissing each other. Things are getting progressively very bad . . . if you're a little bit conservative and you say that, maybe half the congregation does not like that." SG6 abruptly noted "more than half" of the congregation does not like conservative views. This episode in the discussion provided an important insight into issues on which St. George was divided, although this is a perception gleaned from the group's reflection. SG6 opined that the divisions are a "rejection of God." She expressed frustration on the inability to "talk, to say anything," lest anyone be offended. SG6 was frustrated with the rush to judgment, and pointed to the official Orthodox position that recognizes marriage between a man and woman only as normative, but insisting that conservatives know that they are to be "compassionate" in dialogue with LGBT people in the Church. She also raised the issue of educating children in the Church and addressing their attitudes towards controversial issues. She and her Sunday school co-teacher had assigned an article written by a recognized Church writer explaining the Church pro-life stance and a student took offense. SG6 noted the necessity of considering what children are learning in the public schools to find an effective way of dealing with the same issues in Church school.

SG1 insisted that "we are not to change with the times." The conservative cohort of the St. George focus group expressed frustration with "conservatives being silenced," and noted the difficulty of acting as peacemakers without relinquishing their positions on issues coherent with official Church teaching. Respondent no. 1 stated forcefully that "I'm not going to sit silently and say, well, gee, we can go that way, I guess. We cannot go that way." SG1 agreed with SG6 that conservatives have an obligation to be charitable, that it is never appropriate to "be mean."

The Churching Rite and Gender

The discussion about women covered more than the possibility of restoring the order of deaconess: respondents also discussed the practice of Churching infant boys and girls differently in the rite that occurs 40 days after Baptism.[19] SK12 stated, "We're kind of upset that the female child does not go around the altar at the 40-day blessing." She claimed that they are told to be quiet, to remain silent when this issue emerges. The practice at HTC differs, as boys and girls are churched in the same way. HTC4 referred to the Churching, which is performed in the same manner for all people regardless of gender. "All people are offered at the altar. It's huge. What's the big deal? It's a huge deal." HTC10 said that "sometimes as a woman you say, what's the matter with me? I'm in God's house and not wanted." She referred to the daughter of one of the respondents who helps with preparing the table of bread and wine given to people after they have received Communion. She mentioned that "this is the one thing the girls can do," and that they "take such pride" in performing the task. The girls spend time arranging "the napkins." She said that they do so with great care and attention, "as if there is nothing to do but to fix those napkins. And they want something to do so badly, I watch it every Sunday."

The Ministry of Children and Gender

Much of the discussion on women centered on the opportunities afforded to and denied parish children in participating in rituals. HTC8 said that "it's really important for kids to have a purpose to give them responsibility, it makes a big difference for them to be involved in the service." HTC5 told a story in teaching Sunday school about a group of boys. They were having a discussion about assisting at liturgy, and a girl said she wanted to do something, so one of the boys turned around and said, "you can't, you're a girl." So they arranged for the priest to show the girls the altar, and they all performed the prostration upon entering. The point was to show the boys the meaning of service. "Being a boy does not entitle you to be in the altar. There has to be a reason for you to go in there." These boys and girls were around the age of 7. She expressed a desire for more occasions where girls and boys would not be separated in participating in Church activities. HTC5 told the story of an occasion where the priest allowed two girls to vest and serve in the altar—she prefaced her comments by mentioning that they had expressed a strong desire to serve on a few occasions. Her son's reaction was, "wow, they can serve with me now! He was so excited. . . . We're not born believing in those [gender] divisions. We get used to them, for better or worse."

Some respondents thought that boys should be altar servers because boys tend to favor non-participation in Church. SA5 said, "girls grow up more quickly than boys and they're more outgoing, and I think it's important to keep boys in the Church." She mused that the girls will readily agree to do everything while the boys will hang back; she thought that boys need something to do because "sometimes, boys will be reticent," so they should have something to do.

SA2 said that girls would "rush to be altar servers," while a couple of boys would want to, but that it was lopsided in favor of girls. He observed that the admission of girl altar servers in the Catholic Church resulted in the perception that serving in the altar was only for girls. SA6 said that there are more boys than girls at Sunday school and that more girls hold candles for the Gospel reading than boys. She added that there was a discussion for making garments for the girls to wear when they hold the candles. "I want the girls to feel that they have . . . that holding the candle for the Gospel is an important thing." "I want them to feel equal to an altar server in a way."

The most profound example came from participant HTC6, who spoke of the role of women in a startup parish when she lived in Russia. She was part of a community that was attempting to establish itself, and the women were allowed to serve. They were using a building that did not have the traditional middle Byzantine structure—"there was no altar, we just used a simple table." The priest did not have the assistance of deacons or subdeacons. There was a cohort of girls around the age of 10 or so. "It just happened, naturally. We helped at the liturgy. We were to help with the censer and help to prepare Communion. It was natural. We were just the people, together." She said that the process went on for "a few years." They got used to serving at the altar—she repeatedly said, "it was natural." Once they established a traditional church interior with the iconostasis, "we were gradually kicked out of the process. It was really strange. The main thing is that it felt unnatural." She mentioned that in that particular parish, women continued to help out by reading the Epistle.

HTC8 mentioned her two older brothers. One of them had the opportunity to serve at the altar, tried it out, and decided that he would rather sing in the choir. "I couldn't understand why he wouldn't want to serve." "Knowing from a young age that you are not allowed to participate to the extent that you want to makes it really difficult to want to participate at all. . . . Gender equality, or however you want to put it—I don't think it's limited to gender, quite frankly—those kinds of things that exist in the Orthodox Church made me struggle being Orthodox my entire life. I don't always want to go to church, and I'll go for long periods of time where I don't go to church. Things like that, a patriarchal system that is built in I find so asinine and insulting and archaic and sometimes I want absolutely nothing to do in the Orthodox Church. . . . It's never going to be your turn. . . . It's a huge problem." She went on to say that this is a problem in the Church and that gender division creates just that—division.

HTC6 said that her daughter is learning everything: biology, astronomy, and she is performing science experiments, and "there is no limit. she can do anything. She's so engaged. And then she comes to Church, and it's (like you just said—to HTC3)—a gated community, it just ends for her. She cannot explore and experience things to the full extent that she'd want to. It breaks my heart. I want her to grow up and be part of it." HTC6 described her daughter as very inquisitive, and stated that she asks, "why not? What's wrong with me?" in terms of being prohibited from participating to the same extent that the boys her age are allowed to participate.

SG3 was the only member of the combined cohort of St. George participants who expressed a feeling of exclusion from liturgy based on the liturgy in referring to the translation of the Nicene-Constantinopolitan Creed. "For us men and for our salvation—doesn't apply to me . . . every time they use those words, for us men, for all men, it's like, okay, you don't need me." She said that she could try to rationalize it by thinking "they mean people," but suggested that they should "say 'people'" and not ask participants to imply inclusion. She said that having a different translation would be "helpful for me" and in general. SG5 disagreed, he claimed that other churches were exploiting democracy to make changes in the church, and this was a dangerous precedent for Orthodoxy.

In summary, the conversation about the role of women in the Church was explosive and disclosed the deep divisions among faithful. Participant remarks had a broad range: proponents of increasing women's liturgical leadership were interested in absolute gender equality, including women to share the burden of pastoral liturgy, restoring the order of deaconess to help priests and honor Orthodox history, and encourage girls to participate in Church life. Opponents were wary of confusing lay activity with political democracy, ignoring the honor women enjoy in the Church (e.g., the Theotokos and the Philoptochos society), and tended to view the question of gender equality as exemplifying the kind of change that is both foreign to and in violation of traditional Orthodoxy (same-sex marriage was offered as another example).

An important fact was nearly obscured by the heated debate: women's participation in the liturgy had already experienced change, as women were more involved in choral leadership and the proclamation of the Word, and girls were performing tasks that had previously been performed by adults. Related to the larger umbrella issue of women was the liturgical formation of children: participants were attuned to the ways children responded to liturgy and sought strategies for increasing their involvement, sometimes quite passionately.

"STRONG" MOMENTS: LITURGICAL AND NON-LITURGICAL

Respondents shared memories of particularly strong moments from the liturgy and from their personal lives.[20] Their reflections on this matter are unique because the session had explored the Divine Liturgy and the holy seasons of Lent and Easter in depth. The question sought to disclose liturgical moments that were extraordinary with the hope of parsing out some meaning on the dynamics of liturgy and life from respondent recollections.

A handful of respondents described powerful episodes of participation through the metaphors of being "drawn into" the Liturgy. SA2 described an experience as "a feeling that I was not singing but being sung, it was like the liturgy was going through me like a reed . . . not pursuing it, but being pursued." He had a sense of the liturgy being done unto him and struggled to find the words to describe it. He was "sung." SG3 referred to an extraordinary experience receiving Communion at another parish. At the very moment of Communion, she had the sensation of something "whizzing down" from on high upon her, and it left her hot, so that "I had to be helped back to my seat. I burst into tears, embarrassed in front of the entire congregation, completely humiliated. After that experience, a whole series of events happened in my life that took me on a completely different path." She added, "years later, my husband bought me a picture of a chalice with a dove going into the chalice. I didn't understand that at all." Returning to the original sensory experience, she said, "you can't explain [it]. You can feel it and hear it, but it was so fast, just going up to communion that set up a whole series of events." SG2 referred to the office of burial for a beloved parish rector who had a particularly long tenure in parish ministry. He remembered the funeral because of its length (three to four hours) and the open casket, as opposed to a casket displaying the deceased only from the waist up.

HTC11's first liturgical experience was on Palm Sunday in 2013. "I did not have a religious background. . . . I didn't even understand the language—my English wasn't good enough. . . . I didn't even know what Palm Sunday was. . . . Everything was so aglow, and I felt very, very much drawn into it." He went on to say that his desire to be a part of it was remote from knowledge—it was the liturgy itself, the local liturgy at HTC on that particular day that drew him in, even though "I didn't know what was going on." He said that he felt compelled to try to understand, that he felt "called to be in the presence" of the liturgical community. Here, he is referring to his openness to hearing the invitation to participate. He referred to that particularly strong liturgical moment as "forcing me into this direction."

Several respondents recalled strong liturgical moments that expressed feelings of communal belonging. SG1 referred to her reception into the Church via Chrismation.[21] "Up until that point, I was going to Church every Sunday, but after the Confirmation you became part of that community and after that I always felt like I belonged to the Greek community." She also referred to her first Divine Liturgy where she received Communion "with all of my brothers and sisters. . . . That's really when I became a part of the Orthodox community."

Threshold Rites

Many respondents referred to rites of passage that inaugurate one into a community of belonging: Baptism, Chrismation, marriage, and funerals. Two accounts of funerals suggested transformative experiences for participants. HTC4 told the story of a funeral, and the closeness she felt with the other parishioners around her in the church. The particular moment was so powerful, that she was likewise struck by "going back into the world and being among people who didn't know what had happened. This person died and the universe changed with that death." She was "jarred" by the attempt to transition to life in the world. The experience of the funeral, of the change in the universe on account of the death of a person raised fundamental questions of life for her: "What am I doing here? Where do I belong?" HTC6 repeated a similar experience having the church filled with people who had prayed for the deceased. Her feeling was similar: "the people on the outside of the Church had no idea what had happened." But even more profound was her feeling that "I had no way to describe what had happened." HTC8 affirmed the same comments. He referred to leaving the funeral as "a letdown." HTC1 also agreed, but commented that non-Orthodox who had attended an Orthodox funeral expressed similar sentiments.

Personal Experiences

Not all stories were communal: one respondent interpreted a medical emergency experienced in church as both liturgical and personal. On Holy Monday in 2014, SG5 was sitting in the church, next to a nurse, and before he knew it, he "ended up in the emergency (room), in the hospital. They found a massive hemorrhage, a lot of blood in my head." He said that the timing was an instance of "God working in mysterious ways," as he would certainly have died had the hemorrhage occurred while he was driving to church or home from church. He stated that the event will always be memorable because he was saved by a miracle, and he viewed the occurrence of his illness on Holy Monday as a miracle. His example illustrates the fusion of an epic personal moment with liturgical experience. In this instance, the personal emergency—a fundamental moment of living and dying—erupted while he happened to be at church.

A few respondents identified specific liturgical components as strong, both didactically and morally. HTC5 said, "One of the things I notice is when we say 'Thine own of Thine own' and 'on behalf of all and for all,' to me that's like almost the high point of the whole service because God is giving himself to us and us back to him . . . it's not just what's happening here in this church, but it's for the entire world." She explicitly mentioned that the priest's manner of intoning that part of the anaphora was particularly powerful. HTC respondents discussed among themselves the use of St. Basil's anaphora, with explicit reference to Lent.[22] They stated that Fr. Arida reads the prayers aloud for all to hear. HTC2 described it as "such a span of things. It's everything but the kitchen sink." She described the challenge of being able to sustain her attention for the duration of that particular anaphora—she also described Basil's liturgy as a "journey."

SG1 also mentioned her church wedding (when she was married to SG2). She said that the priest had attempted to prepare her fiancé, but that he did not "get the gist because of the language barrier because there were no vows. He did not know whether we were married or not."[23] An important point emerged from the levity of the moment: the priest had attempted to explain the salient liturgical components of the rites of betrothal and crowning, including the procession with joined hands three times around the table, but the absence of vows with the language barrier left the groom with some uncertainty.

In summary, respondents shared several stories of strong liturgical moments that had meaning for their lives. These stories included customary rites of passage and emotional episodes of human life and death. Two themes threaded through the comments: a sense of other-worldly powers drawing participants more deeply into Communion, and an inability to explain or describe the larger significance of such strong moments.

LEARNING ABOUT LITURGY

The focus group sessions included time devoted to discussing how laity learn about the liturgy.[24] This topic is crucial to this study's enterprise, as strengthening the connection between academic liturgical theology and the laity is a primary objective of the project.

The Liturgy as Teacher

Respondents identified participation in the liturgy as the best way to learn it. SK7 observed that she understands what is going on because she is Greek and because she is in the choir. She described her liturgical participation "as a two-way conversation." She said that the key to learning what the liturgy is about is to "go every Sunday." She also mentioned that people ask too many questions, that one needs to have more faith. "God said to do this, and I'm going to do it." HTC5's remark on learning embellished SK7's comment: "I don't think there is a way to learn about liturgy without being here. You can read about it . . . in the end, it's about worshipping together, standing together, singing together, and being together." She referred back to a comment made earlier in the session by HTC4 that each liturgy is different and said that "it's the 'always different' that keeps you learning." She said that she learns something new from hymns and readings that are quite familiar to her. "The whole liturgy is a conversation between all of us. We're all conversing together."

HTC2 said that learning liturgy is akin to training on a mat, and doing the same movement fifty times; the fifty-first time makes a significant difference. SA6 offered a similar explanation, referring to liturgy as a "participatory sport." "Listening to the liturgy is the way I learn . . . if you listen, . . . you know when to cross yourself." Our liturgy makes me listen to the actual words of the prayers. She said again that the repetition in liturgy makes it easier for her to learn about its purpose: "there is really power and healing in the words . . . 'Stand aright,' they're giving us bodily directions, it is a participatory event, so [it's a matter of] listening to those directions."[25] SA5 also agreed, saying "I think it's just attending the services, and then discussion with other members of the church, and then reading—it's sort of a combination." She observed that academic books do not answer her questions—she wants plainer teaching, but "basically, it's just attending the liturgy, studying the Bible."

Liturgy Outside of the Home Parish

Respondents expressed a desire to learn about liturgy as it is celebrated in sister Orthodox Churches. SG5 stated a desire to know the differences in the Divine Liturgy among Orthodox jurisdictions, such as Ukrainian, Russian, and Greek. His question suggested that he—and perhaps others—were not familiar with the liturgical styles of sister Orthodox jurisdictions.[26] SG3 elaborated the point to say that she received Communion at "the Ukrainian Church on university," and that she did not understand why the priest touched her head with the chalice after communion. She also stated that the choir members escorted her to the chalice, as "we were getting Communion no matter what!"

Respondents discussed cultural variations in liturgy they had noticed among themselves. For example, SG4 mentioned that Ethiopians remove their shoes in church, to honor God's holy ground. SG3 said that she observed women in OCA churches wearing long skirts and standing barefoot in church, which "seems weird to me. They're all converts, where did they get that from? They read it somewhere. We all come together in the same church and are all doing different things." SA1 echoed the sentiment of participating in Orthodox liturgy elsewhere: "going to another Orthodox Church and seeing how they conduct the liturgy is different from ours."

Respondents offered some information on the sources they use to learn about liturgy. SG4 said that the only way to learn is to go to the Internet, to "Fr. Google," to learn more about the various parts of the liturgy. SA1 mentioned that he enjoyed listening to "priests talking to one another on Ancient Faith Radio in a light-hearted way," but he did not like the idea of listening to a lecture on the liturgy on a podcast. SA7 observed that we need to find effective ways to teach the liturgy "in the 21st century," that the way people learn today differs from the past, traditional models of learning. "I'm seeing the phenomenon of youth, people being raised cradle in the Orthodox Church and not understanding," and added that education for youth, with an emphasis on Bible, is much needed.

The Tradition of Learning Liturgy

Some respondents noted that they learned about the liturgy from an elder family member, and expressed admiration for the devotion of converts who study liturgy more vigorously. SK10 mentioned the traditional approach by coining the term "yaya-ology," which we might define loosely as the traditional rituals handed down from one generation to the next without asking questions or seeking understanding. "Whatever the rules are of yaya-ology—it may be ignorance, or what they were taught . . . I married a convert, so I think you become aware of things from a convert's point of view . . . it's such a joy when they learn it . . . I never knew that, that's how I felt, I never learned all of that, being a cradle Orthodox . . . I had to open my mind up to something new." One of the primary ways respondents learned about the liturgy was through Bible study classes offered in the parish. SK10 explained, "The liturgy became clear once I started to attend Bible study." She said that she learned a little bit, usually one small piece about the liturgy at Bible study: "It takes a long time." She said that she began to pay attention to the pamphlets (informational) offered to people in the narthex as they entered church, and realized that she did not know much about the liturgy at all.

A handful of respondents expressed concern about finding effective ways to teach liturgy to children. SK12 observed, "our kids, they come to Sunday school today and they learn for one hour. What can they learn in one hour?" That's why they don't know much about our liturgy." SK8 discussed teaching liturgy through Sunday school—reviewing the Creed for a course of two months is the primary way to relate the tenets of faith to the celebration of the liturgy. SA5 expressed concern about the Church's lack of resources on cultural war issues for young people: "to me, the Church does not speak about the countercultural anthropology . . . it doesn't speak enough about it in a way people can understand. . . . People reduce it to a moralism and reject it, as they should." He deviated from the topic at hand to observe that there needs to be some teaching on these issues for children, so that they could be faithful. SK4 expressed the same concern, observing that the churches are not fighting back against anti-Christian programs in contemporary society. He added that many colleges are becoming more anti-Christian and that young people are becoming radicalized. HTC1 challenged the observation that this was a particularly Orthodox problem. He suggested that the problem of questioning whether or not I want to be a person of faith is common to all Christians, since we all live in a "profoundly secular world." He added that young adults belonging to faith communities will all eventually face the challenge of whether or not they want the secular world to define their identities. He stated that his priority was to keep them in the Church, and that he had given in to the tradition of "bringing our children, so on the way home there would always be ice cream or pizza," as an added incentive for attending church services. He mentioned that the weekend is the time when we all want to "relax" so it can be hard to make a commitment to Sunday mornings.

SK12 shared her experience growing up as Greek Orthodox in Cyprus, a story providing us with a potentially helpful comparison of approaches to teaching liturgy in the parish. In elementary school, SK12 learned the fundamentals of the Bible. On Thursdays, the children had to attend catechism. A woman was teaching them the lives of the saints. The children had to attend church every Sunday; if they were absent, they had to account for it to the principal. She observed, "it takes a long time to understand and learn our Orthodox religion." She noted that the clergy were very strict in Cyprus—faithful had to fast at least three days, and the kids were "frightened" to take Communion if they had not observed the austerity of the fast. She observed that "I kind of cringe" when she took her medication and had breakfast, she has a mental block because of her childhood experience. Later, she added that the children were encouraged to read about the faith in secondary school.

One respondent, SA6, reflected on the opportunity afforded by having a mission Church community in a university setting. She said, "we have to figure out how to introduce it to people with no background, and how do they learn? I'm sensing that . . . they're not really comfortable crossing themselves, or bowing. They're not used to using their body, literally, physically." She mused that there is no easy way to cultivate an environment of learning through bodily practice. She agreed with the others that books are limited in their capacity to instruct, because "Orthodoxy is a physical thing," and "we need to be better role models."

While respondents were confident that they were learning through participation, some participants also expressed a desire to learn more about the liturgy. SG5 expressed a desire for the pastor to offer a sermon based on the various parts of the liturgy, with the understanding that the project would be challenging. SG2 stated that an abridged history of the Divine Liturgy is available in the books placed in the pew. SG3 said that she would like to know more about the prayers recited bv the priest in the liturgy, since "none of the books spell out every prayer. There is a ton of prayer going on, and I'd like to hear more. There's a ton of prayer going on." SG2 said that he did not understand the significance of the eight tones, how the different melodic modes differ from one another.

In summary, focus group respondents reported learning about liturgy primarily through regular participation and Bible studies. While they expressed confidence in the effectiveness of learning through practice, respondents were quite concerned about the need to develop effective strategies for teaching liturgy, especially to children and converts.

LITURGICAL CHANGE

Select remarks from respondents brought up instances of liturgical change in parish life. Change was prevalent in the two Greek Orthodox parishes, and the primary issue of discussion was the transition from Greek to English, and the tensions resulting from the tendency to cling to ethnic identity in parish life.[27]

Language and Ethnic Identity

SK2 was blunt in his appraisal of the language issue: "you don't understand that something mystical is happening?" So said his mother to him when he said he did not understand everything that was going on in the liturgy. "Language to me is the biggest problem. Sometimes I feel very uncomfortable when I have my daughter and my son who don't understand Greek and the liturgy goes on with a lot of Greek, and I see them looking at the watch, getting very uncomfortable . . . the language to me is a very big problem . . . I love the way we do it here at St. Katherine's. There's enough English to satisfy the kids and any non-Greek speaker."

SG3 noted that she had sung in the choir for the entirety of her life, and that the whole liturgy was important to her "because it is sung." She was the first informant to raise the issue of language: "when I grew up there were Greek hymns, and no matter how many times I opened the book, I didn't understand any of it." She said that the transition to using English in the liturgy "was like somebody flipped a switch," "they were electrifying . . . because singing is different from reading."

SG1 noted that she began to attend Orthodox liturgy as a young adult, but was unable to understand it because it was entirely in Greek: "the repetition and hearing the Divine Liturgy over and over and over again, helped." She narrated her method of learning about the liturgy despite the language barrier at her church. Her godmother had an illustrated Divine Liturgy book she used to introduce her to the fundamentals of the Divine Liturgy, and she also had catechism with the parish priest, which was complicated, since the priest did not know English. The priest simply instructed her to "read, read," which she did. Concerning liturgical changes, she opined that things should stay the same.

SG5 recalled a discussion he had with a Greek bishop from South America, who claimed that activities such as the Creed, sermon, and other forms of communication should be in the vernacular, but that the language of the liturgy itself should not change. He recalled the bishop saying, "Pavarotti does not change to Chinese in China or Russian in Russia." SG5 stated that he understood the need to understand the liturgy, but lamented the loss of the "meaning of words in melody in the original Greek." SG5 referred his mother-in-law, who attended a Ukrainian Orthodox parish in Minneapolis, and he asked her how she could understand the liturgy (since it was all in Ukrainian). She said that she simply "memorized it," since the liturgy was the same everywhere, regardless of the language used for its celebration. SG5 worried about "frictions in the Church" and slightly disagreed with SG1, as he viewed bilingual books as adequate and a fair compromise.

SG6 continued the discussion on language and noted that the Greek used for church "wasn't the same" as the Greek spoken at home. She observed that "I missed a lot growing up" because her parents had a lot of religious instruction in school, as they were raised in Greece. She suggested that one cannot overcome "that gap" with "twenty minutes of instruction in Sunday school," and wondered if parents would be forced to do their own teaching of children in the home to compensate for the gap. She thought that the absence of an Orthodox school or a curriculum created a significant change in between the generations of Orthodox who grew up in Greece and America.

SG4 noted that having two languages is not much of an issue when the English translation is on the opposite page of the Greek text, and the text is repeated from the previous week. He did not hold the same opinion for variable liturgical components of the office, such as Orthros: "I was trying to get an idea of what was chanted so when they switch to Greek I could follow it—when they get going on the festival material, chanting out of a different source . . . a little confusing, but it's just something you have to learn." He was referring to using liturgical sources that were published in books used only by the chanters.[28]

The Power of the Vernacular

HTC6 mentioned the service of Great Saturday as a way of illustrating the power of the vernacular in the liturgy. "The beginning, the Vespers part was a revelation here (at HTC)." She was struck by the Old Testament readings appointed to the service; at HTC, it was the first time she had read them in

English, and she had many years of experience of reading in the church. At HTC, fifteen people read the readings. She heard "those wonderful prophetic" passages in English, an "amazing experience of vernacular language, placing it right in front of you, there is no obstacle, no veil . . . " She was comparing this experience to her past when they would read the lessons in Slavonic, and she (as a professional linguist) understood the readings, but the church was full of people who did not. "There was no feeling that they understood a word. . . . Here, everyone is together. Everyone's participation is alive. . . . It made me feel one together with the congregation."

Her point was the unifying power of serving the liturgy in the local, vernacular language. Her perspective is particularly important as an Orthodox woman with vast experience in a traditionally Orthodox place using an ancient language for liturgy. She said, "I don't have to make the historical effort to get to the meaning, it's just right here. . . . With Church Slavonic, it's like you have the symbol of a meaning. In order to get to the meaning, you have to decipher the symbol." She emphasized the connection between the use of modern English at HTC and the sense that the parish is alive.

SG3 noted that the Church survived the language issue. She suggested that it was a major issue, but that they had survived it. She also noted the emergence of "everything must be Byzantine. It's fanatical," referring to the Byzantinization of Americanized Greek Church practices, especially in music and iconography. She also suggested that the people's posture changed: "there was more physical activity in the Church. You're not supposed to just sit in the pews like the Lutherans, you're supposed to do this other thing. People wanted to do lots of *metanoias* and just express themselves physically."[29]

SG3 was unsure of the origins of the emergence of these practices on the North American scene. She observed that worship was more internal in her childhood and transitioned to a more "outward" expression. She also noted that "we did not have converts" in her childhood, but that there were now converts and "they bring with them whatever flavor they got from whoever helped convert them." She viewed the appearance of new practices as "odd things" which would not have been accepted in her childhood. She referred to women covering their heads with scarves and standing up front, and mused that in a previous time, an usher would have removed such a person.

SG3 concluded by saying that the liturgy itself had not changed, but that "the way people participate seems to be changing over the years, maybe they grow, learn something new, a way of perceiving it . . . the liturgy is pretty much written in stone." SG2 added that "ten-fifteen years ago men used to wear a coat and tie and now they don't," though he said this might not have anything to do with liturgy. He added that people tend to complain about the length of the Divine Liturgy, and noted that he had not noticed an increase in its length, but did notice an uptick in the frequency of complaints on the length of the liturgy. He echoed SG3, who said that liturgy was "like a rock," unchanging. SG5 suggested that there are now many more intermarriage converts, and that "now we're more Bible-reading people." He viewed the entrance of new kinds of people into the church as a good development.

In summary, respondents identified language as the primary obstacle to liturgical understanding, at least in the Greek parishes. But respondents also pointed to other subtle changes of liturgical reform. Some of the changes were demographic and cultural, such as shifts in the way people dress for church. Respondent discussions about converts were particularly insightful: they perceived that converts were knowledgeable about Orthodoxy and devoted to studying it, but they also thought that converts brought change with them into the Church. The reference to Byzantinization can be compared to other liturgical changes mentioned earlier in this study, such as reciting certain prayers aloud for the people to hear, or encouraging frequent participation.

CONCLUSION

We have immersed ourselves in a series of examples of how the people talk about liturgy in their own words. The point of this exercise was to collect a usable sample of lay reflections on liturgical participation. Here, we encountered what the people said about the Divine Liturgy, Holy Communion (and Confession), holy seasons, the role of women, methods of learning the liturgy, and liturgical change. The next chapter turns to an analysis of the people's faith.

NOTES

1. He said "John 16," but the context suggested that he meant "John 3:16."

2. Faithful are encouraged to recite the prayers of preparation for Holy Communion, and many of these prayers include language warning of terrifying perils that will visit faithful who partake unworthily. For more on this topic, see Nicholas Denysenko, "Death and Dying in Orthodox Liturgy," *Religions* 8, 25 (2017): 8–11, doi:10.3390/rel8020025.

3. The respondent was referring to the main character of the 1994 feature film *Forrest Gump*, played by Tom Hanks. Throughout his life, his family, friends, and coaches urge Forrest to run, since he is fast.

4. St. Nicholas Ranch hosts summer camps and other church-related events. It is a haven for promoting youth fellowship with its Central California location, near the Sierra Nevada mountains. http://www.stnicholasranch.org/ (accessed January 19, 2018).

5. See Mother Mary and Kallistos Ware, trans., *The Lenten Triodion* (South Canaan, PA: St. Tikhon's Seminary Press, 2002), and Nicholas Denysenko, "Rituals and Prayers of Forgiveness in Byzantine Lent," *Worship* 86 (2012): 140–60.

6. *Apokatastasis* refers to a teaching that God will save all humankind and created beings, because God's love is boundless and no one will be able to resist the love of God for eternity. Theologians such as Origen, Gregory Nyssa, Maximus Confessor, Isaac the Syrian, and Sergius

Bulgakov popularized this teaching, with their own particular emphases. See Kallistos Ware, *The Inner Kingdom* (Crestwood, NY: St. Vladimir's Seminary Press, 2000), 193–216.

7. Forgiveness Vespers begins Lent in the Byzantine Rite. In parish practice, it is celebrated on Cheesefare Sunday, either after Liturgy or in the evening. Penitential Hymns from the Lenten Triodion (the hymnal for Byzantine Lent) are sung at Vespers; after the prokeimenon, all of the vestments and coverings are changed from bright to purple. The prayer of St. Ephraim the Syrian is said in community for the first time. At the end of Vespers, in some places, the people perform a rite of forgiveness, bowing or prostrating before each person in the Church and asking for their forgiveness while forgiving the other of all transgressions, concluded with the exchange of the kiss of peace. See Mother Mary and Kallistos Ware, trans., *The Lenten Triodion*, 180–83.

8. In the Greek Orthodox tradition, the un-nailing of Christ from the cross is mimetic, elaborate, and visually rich.

9. The *epitaphios* (*plashchanitsa* in Slavonic) is an embroidered burial shroud bearing an icon of Jesus, dead in the tomb. See Anna Gonosovà, "epitaphios," in *The Oxford Dictionary of Byzantium*, vol. 1, ed. Alexander Kazhdan (Oxford: Oxford University Press, 1991), 720–21.

10. Robert Taft hypothesizes that the Holy Week customs of the *epitaphios* emerged in the fourteenth century and are related to the *aer*, used to cover the gifts at the Divine Liturgy. See Taft, *A History of the Liturgy of St. John Chrysostom, vol. 2: The Great Entrance, A History of the Transfer of Gifts and Other Pre-anaphral Rites*, 4th ed. (Rome: Pontifical Oriental Institute, 2004), 216–19.

11. In contemporary Greek Orthodox practice, the "first Anastasi" is the resurrection liturgy of Holy Saturday, and the second Anastasi is the Nocturne and Matins at midnight on Pascha honoring Jesus' resurrection from the dead. These two midnight offices are followed by the Paschal liturgy of St. John Chrysostom, a service that occurs rather in the wee hours of Pascha morning.

12. A famous sermon attributed to St. John Chrysostom is one of the highlights of Paschal Matins. The sermon speaks of the joy of the resurrection, the outpouring of God's hospitality to all, and Christ's triumph over death. For an English translation of the text of this oft-quoted sermon, see https://oca.org/fs/sermons/the-paschal-sermon (accessed March 8, 2018).

13. Paschal Nocturne is the short midnight office consisting of a sung canon of hymns reflecting on Christ's descent into Hades and anticipating his resurrection from the dead. In many churches, this office is sung in a dark church to special melodies.

14. In parish practice, Good Friday services begin with Matins and the reading of twelve Gospels on Thursday evening. There is much repetition among the Gospels appointed to this service.

15. SG5 was referring to Antiphon 15 sung at the Matins of Holy Friday, before the sixth Gospel lesson from Mark (15:16–32), as the priest sets up the cross in the middle of the Church: "Today He who hung the earth upon the waters is hung upon the Cross (*three times*). He who is king of the angels is arrayed in a crown of thorns. He who wraps the heaven in clouds is wrapped in the purple of mockery. He who in Jordan set Adam free receives blows upon his face. The Bridegroom of the Church is transfixed with nails, the Son of the Virgin is pierced with a spear. We venerate Thy Passion, o Christ (*three times*). Show us also Thy glorious Resurrection" (Mother Mary and Ware, *The Lenten Triodion*, 587).

16. A conference recently addressed this issue in depth: "Renewing the Male and Female Diaconate in the Orthodox Church," St. Phoebe Center for the Deaconess, St. Paul Church, Irvine, California, October 6–7, 2017, https://orthodoxdeaconess.org/2017-conference/presentation-recordings-and-transcripts/ (accessed January 19, 2018).

17. *Panagia* means "All-holy woman" and is used colloquially among Greek Orthodox people to refer to Mary, mother of Jesus.

18. The National Philoptochos Society is a major organ of the Greek Orthodox Archdiocese of America, an organization of lay women who perform social service. The reputations for the Philoptochos chapters of local parishes as formidable bodies of influential people is well-known among Orthodox people in America.

19. In the Byzantine Rite, Baptism is not distinct from Chrismation (Confirmation), but forms a unified rite. Once one is baptized and anointed, one joins the Eucharistic assembly.

One of the last liturgical components of Baptism is the Churching. When infants are baptized, the priest recites a prayer of Churching and brings a male child into the altar, walking him around and returning him to his parents while reciting the Canticle of Simeon. Girls are not brought into the altar, but are brought in front of the holy gates. The gender differentiation has become controversial in some Orthodox circles. For a brief overview of this topic, see the essay by Carrie Frederick Frost, "The Churching of Mothers in the Orthodox Church," http://orthodoxdeaconess.org/women-church-praxis/ (accessed January 19, 2018).

20. "Tell me about one moment in church that was particularly memorable and important in your life: when did it happen, and why was it memorable? Tell me about one moment outside of church that was particularly memorable in a Christian way: when did it happen and why?"

21. The official title in Orthodoxy is "Chrismation"; the use of "Confirmation" here is notable.

22. Currently, the Liturgy of St. John Chrysostom is celebrated most frequently in Orthodox practice. The Liturgy of St. Basil is celebrated on January 1 (St. Basil's feast day), on the eves of the feasts of Christmas, Theophany, and on Holy Saturday, Lazarus Saturday, and for the Sundays of Great Lent (except for Palm Sunday). Orthodox faithful tend to connect Basil's liturgy with Lent, but Basil was actually the primary liturgy of Constantinople until the tenth century, when Chrysostom began to take precedence. For more on this matter, see Stefanos Alexopoulos, "The Influence of Iconoclasm on Liturgy: A Case Study," in *Worship Traditions in Armenia and the Neighboring Christian East: An International Symposium in Honor of the 40th Anniversary of St. Nersess Seminary*, ed. Roberta Ervine (Crestwood, NY: St. Vladimir's Seminary, St. Nersess Armenian Seminary, 2006), 127–40.

23. At this point, the group erupted into laughter.

24. "How do you learn about the liturgy? What aspects of the Church's liturgy would you like to learn more? What would you like to see changed in the liturgy, and why?"

25. "Stand aright!" is a command chanted by the deacon at various points in the Liturgy, calling the faithful to stand up to hear the Gospel, offer the Eucharistic prayer, and prepare for dismissal.

26. At this point in the session, SG5 posed this question to me.

27. Respondents reflected on change in response to this question: "How has the Liturgy developed since you began going to church? Is it exactly the same as it was? Has it changed? How?" They also brought up change on their own, without the investigator's prompting.

28. In the Byzantine tradition, chanters and choirs sing many of the hymns appointed for all services from special books. Festival material tends to be taken from a book called the *Menaion*, which contains all of the hymns for feast days of the Lord, of Mary Theotokos, and of the saints. For Sundays and weekday services, hymns are taken from a book called the *Octoechos*, referring to a system of eight rotating model melodies (or "tones") governing the weekly cycle. The aforementioned Triodion is used for Lent and Holy Week, and the *Pentecostarion* (sometimes called the *Flowery Triodion*) is used from Pascha through the end of the Pentecost cycle (Sunday of All Saints). So, there is no single book containing all of the hymns appointed to the liturgical year, a system requiring singers to be familiar with the books, the pattern melodies or tones, and the rules governing the appointment of hymns.

29. A *metanoia* is a reverential bow, where the participant bows at the waist and touches the ground or floor with their right hand.

Chapter Four

The People's Faith

A Synthesis

Having heard about the liturgy from the people themselves, we now turn to the task of synthesizing their reflections on the liturgy. This task may seem unnecessary: Why summarize the people's theology? Aren't their words sufficient? Will a synthesis truly represent the people's liturgical theology? The purpose of this chapter is to probe more deeply into the people's liturgical reflections to identify convergences and illuminate new topics and questions emerging from focus group sessions.

The people's reflections occurred during the course of group discussions: their statements were extemporaneous responses to questions, and not prepared statements. The extemporaneous quality of the sessions permitted the people to speak from the heart, to offer reactions. The information in the previous chapter is often raw, and has a keen ring of authenticity, but it is not always complete. During the course of the discussions, respondents would occasionally pause or lose their train of thought. I consider these pauses to be normal: on some occasions, respondents were simply attempting to articulate their feelings on a topic, but couldn't always find the words to describe their thoughts or were unsatisfied with their own descriptions. At other times, respondents paused to think about a topic and returned to it in attempts to clarify their points. Some respondents were terse in their remarks—one respondent even said, "that's all I want to say about that right now" on one of the topics, a clear indication that the respondent was not comfortable saying more.

I do not intend to attempt to complete the incomplete thoughts: attempting to speculate on how a respondent might have elaborated a point would violate the integrity of this project. It is legitimate to illuminate moments of "grasping," points in the narratives when respondents were trying to find a way to articulate their responses. In some instances, grasping indicates the process of attempting to find the words to articulate a profound meaning, and in such episodes, it is appropriate to explore the contours of a discussion on a given topic to attempt to begin the process of parsing out meaning.

In general, we will follow the order of presentation in chapter 3 and compose the people's liturgical theology beginning with the Divine Liturgy and Holy Communion, and followed by holy seasons, strong liturgical moments, women and the liturgy, and liturgical reform. The chapter concludes with a reflection on the relationship between the liturgical and the personal, with references to modes of belonging. I also reflect on an overarching theme communicated consistently by respondents: a desire for experiencing divine and human compassion during the liturgy, or a sense of experiencing a compassionate God whose historical suffering transcends the boundaries of the liturgical and deeply penetrates into the personal.

THE DIVINE LITURGY: A MONUMENTAL TASK

Each focus group session began with a question on the Divine Liturgy, so it took some time for respondents to gain momentum in formulating responses to the open-ended question. The prevalent themes were the significance of the proclamation of the Word and the homily, a sense that the liturgy entailed a movement of entrance into the presence of God, and several comments on the amount of hard work the liturgy requires of its participants. Several respondents also discussed Holy Communion in response to the question about the Divine Liturgy. A few respondents were hesitant to identify a single component as particularly significant since any given element belongs to a larger whole.

Proclamation of the Word

Respondents from three of the four focus groups featured the proclamation of the Word as a highlight of the Liturgy, specifically the Epistle, Gospel, and the homily. This attention to the liturgy of the Word sheds light on the respondents themselves. It is well-known that the laity tend to arrive at the Divine Liturgy quite late. Many faithful arrive after the proclamation of the Epistle and Gospel, a common tendency throughout the history of the Church that has resulted in the homily being offered at a later point in the Liturgy, or to be omitted altogether. Clergy are formed and instructed to deliver the homily immediately following the proclamation of the Gospel, as the homily is a staple component of the proclamation of the Word. Clergy tend to defer the homily to one of two positions later in the Liturgy: before Communion, or at the very end of the Liturgy, right before the dismissal. The objective is to preach to the largest gathering of people attending the Liturgy, so they do not miss the homily. The problem, well-known to pastors everywhere, is the broken connection between the proclamation of the Word and the homily.

In the case of our respondents, their attention to the appointed lessons and the homily exhibits a high level of commitment to and participation in the liturgy. Their discussion of the Epistle and Gospel suggests that their commitment is enough to motivate them to arrive at Liturgy on time and attend to all of its components. Respondents had also mentioned a parallel commitment to the Liturgy of the Word on the part of the priests. At St. George's, respondents highlighted access to the homily after the liturgy via the Church web site, offering participants an opportunity to reflect on it after Sunday. Many participants had also expressed engagement of biblical studies to increase their understanding of their Orthodox faith. Two participants also mentioned the scriptural saturation of the Divine Liturgy itself, observing that the Liturgy is filled with Scripture, and that studying the Bible is a path toward learning about the Liturgy. The proclamation of the Word is a memorable aspect of Sunday worship. Respondents' references to the power of liturgical proclamation suggest that the pastors of their parishes emphasize the proclamation of the Word and good preaching. Respondent attention does not mean that most people of their parishes share the same interest in and devotion to hearing the Bible and its preaching: we can only make this assertion about the respondents. Our study suggests that some Orthodox laity consider the proclamation of the Word and the homily as central to their experience of the Divine Liturgy.

Children Modeling the Liturgical Journey

Respondents tended to describe the Divine Liturgy as a movement or entrance into the presence of God. While there was no convergence on a common word or description of the destiny of the liturgical process, participants described being with God in some way as the destiny, and understood that they were not on this journey alone. In fact, participants were keenly aware of sharing the journey with others—in some cases, the common journey was desirable as a marker of communion, but in other cases, respondents worried about how the others on the journey perceived them. Respondents of all four focus groups mentioned the participation of children in the Divine Liturgy, often repeatedly and emotionally. Their reflections on children did not concern proper behavior in church, but the actual ritual participation of the children in the liturgy. In most cases, this ritual participation was no different from that performed by the adults. [1]

There are a couple of minor exceptions to the norm of common participation of adults and children together, such as the reference to the children's choir singing the responses to the Akathistos Hymn at St. George's and the elongated discussions about boys and girls serving at the altar at Holy Trinity and St. Anthony's. These activities can be performed by adults, too, and this is why the focus groups did not mention special activities designated only for children, but reflected on how the children are integrated into the ritual of the entire congregation. A comment from SA6 exemplified adult awareness of children's participation: she described one small child attempting to venerate an icon in the church and failing because she was too short, so one of the older children picked her up so she could reach the icon. HTC4 shared a comment different in content, but similar in sentiment: "When the children line up for Communion. There's something wonderful about that. There's all kinds of issues with behavior in church. But when it comes to Communion, the kids are so focused, they know what to do. My grandson, he's seventeen months old now, he knows what to do."

HTC4's comment is intriguing because she did not care to dwell on behavioral issues in church: she marveled at the children's focus, their ability to participate in the community's ritual. That the children are able to perform the Communion rite properly should not be a surprise to us: even the youngest children are quite capable of ritual functionality and performance. Children's cognitive and animative capacities are not the issue, either; the adult respondents perceived that the children are responding to God's invitation to partake of the holy meal. Children can become intensely focused on ritual requirements to the point that an unexpected interruption disrupts their understanding of liturgical order.[2] A powerful image of the intense focus of children remains with me from a Divine Liturgy I concelebrated in at a small mission parish in Kyiv, in October 2016. The mission has many young children, and they are always first in line to venerate the cross at the end of the Liturgy (so they can proceed to Sunday school). At the last minute, the pastor invited two guests visiting for an academic symposium to deliver greetings before the veneration of the cross, an activity that disrupted the flow of the customary Sunday order. The children appeared a bit agitated at this disruption and pressed forward towards the cross. This example and instances like it are not remarkable on their own, but they point to a fundamental quality of ritual order and the human tendency to attempt to perfect its performance.

For the respondents of our study, there was something profound happening, greater than performing the assigned ritual correctly. HTC4 attempted to articulate the children's response to divine invitation in words: "There's something that people experience at a very young age in the liturgy that's so deep." What is it that is so deep, beyond following the steps of ritual order appointed by the community? HTC4 prefaced her reflection on children by stating her understanding of the purpose of Liturgy: "[The] connection that is there—here we are together, again, for this event." For HTC4 and other respondents, the Liturgy draws everyone together for this event. Her description of the children lining up to receive Communion discloses Eucharistic inclusivity—everyone is partaking of the gifts. Ironically, her comment cannot be construed as accentuating the unique aspect of including children in receiving Communion. What was new, from the perspective of HTC5, was the inclusion of adults in receiving Communion: "Where I grew up, only kids went to communion . . . there were times when the priest went back into the altar with the chalice full. It's a miracle, to me, every Sunday."[3] These remarks provide multiple perspectives on participation: the children are able to participate in every aspect of the Communion rite, and are included. The adults, who were once excluded from Communion (when it was offered infrequently), are now full participants with the children. The whole congregation participates in the rite: the children and adults both symbolize response to divine invitation and full engagement of the rite.

The respondents marveled at the children's focus and attention to the rite, and suggested that something deeper is happening. Perhaps the key to interpreting the depth of the event is the wonder of the adults at the children's focus and participation. The profundity of children's participation in the rite is their sense of belonging: it is normal for the children to participate because they know they belong to the divine Communion. The adult's marveling at the children's participation could be caused by their desire to capture the faith of children who press forward to venerate the icons, kiss the cross, and receive Holy Communion without pausing at the specter of rejection on account of sin or some other obstacle to belonging. Heeding the invitation to approach and receive Communion goes beyond following instructions: the children come forward to receive Communion because they know they will not be denied. The children are always welcome at Communion even though some of them misbehaved at one point or another during the course of the liturgy. The misbehavior was not an obstacle to receiving Communion.

It's possible that the adults are trying to articulate something they admire in children: the courage to press forward and participate fully without fear of rejection. Misbehavior in God's house will result in an admonition, but it will not result in the denial of the divine food that all members of the household need to live. It may be that the adults see that the children know they will not be denied and will come forward, again and again, to participate in the liturgy.

Distractions, Peace, and Letting Go

Some of the adults would like to capture this spirit of courage belonging to the children and permit it to permeate their participation in the liturgy. Adults are occupied by countless worries and concerns that accompany them to the liturgical assembly. Every detail of personal and professional life can distract a liturgical participant, even a leisure activity like football, as mentioned by SG 5. Respondents viewed the liturgy as an event that liberated them from the distractions of daily life: attending the Divine Liturgy was a true opportunity to lay aside all earthly cares, as the congregation sings in the Cherubikon.[4]

Respondents were occasionally frustrated by the gap between receiving the peace from God given at the Liturgy and struggling to lay those earthly cares aside. Several respondents expressed remorse and guilt at their inability to completely give themselves over to the Liturgy on account of the lingering distractions. For some respondents, the struggle was simply getting everyone in the family dressed, in the car, and out the door to travel to church for the Liturgy. For others, the Liturgy is an ideal event requiring the absolute focus of the attendees. They expressed frustration at their occasional boredom, and often, at their inability to participate fully because they did not fast, recite the proper preparatory prayers, or drive out all unwelcome thoughts. The potential blessings resulting from successfully avoiding distractions was to obtain a spiritual sense of awareness of the needs of others. The Liturgy becomes the place where God teaches the people how to pray: regular participation and hearing, even if it is forced and inconsistent, teaches the participants the hierarchical priorities of the Great Litany. The people are gathered together to pray in peace, they ask for God's peace, they ask for God's peace to be given to the church, the world and its leaders, and in turn they obtain an awareness that the world is afflicted and is in desperate need of God's peace.

Participants commented on the effort required to arrive at the ideal peace of the Liturgy. There was no question that the effort to arrive on time and cast out distractions was worth their time; what was striking was their perception that they were unworthy of participating. The issue of worthiness is an eternal topic because of its relationship to receiving Holy Communion, but the responses seemed to disclose that faithful are in a continuous process of self-examination even as they respond affirmatively to the invitation to participate fully in the Liturgy. Multiple respondents from St. Katherine's voiced concern that other worshippers would disapprove of their frequent participation in Holy Communion. Most of the focus group respondents at St. Katherine's were elderly and had been raised to receive Communion infrequently, a maximum of four times a year. Adults who received Communion more frequently prior to the inauguration of liturgical renewal were stigmatized as people whose sin was grave enough to require sacramental Confession, a process completed by receiving Communion. Therefore, an adult who received Communion outside of the four holy seasons of the liturgical year could be perceived as someone who had committed a serious sin. The older adults who began to receive communion more frequently in the spirit of liturgical renewal continued to adjust to the new liturgical order: as they received, the possibility that they were unworthy because of their sins never completely left them.

Respondents expressed a desire to arrive at a point where they could participate fully in the liturgy without having to be concerned with others' perceptions of them, and without being consumed by their own distractions. The adults seemed to point to an irreconcilable problem of the Liturgy: the Liturgy requires absolute focus and purity, and they are unable to achieve it. The energy required to enter into the Liturgy could explain why some of the adults viewed the children with admiration, as the children are somehow able to focus on the task required by the order, despite the perception that children have limited attention spans. A second obstacle is likely just as powerful: the adults fear that participating fully will result in God rejecting them because they are unworthy. They want access to the confidence the children seem to possess, that all will be well when they approach. For the adults, the Liturgy requires meticulous preparation and perfect attention: therefore, the Liturgy itself requires supererogatory effort on the part of its participants, as only extremely hard work could accompany a journey ending in communion with God.

What, then, is the Divine Liturgy in the voices of this study's respondents? The Divine Liturgy is an event that brings everyone together, with everyone fully participating. It is an event of the Word of God, where the proclamation of the Word and the homily are crucial features for lives of the faithful. The Liturgy is a place where God gives his peace to the participants—to receive that peace, they must lay aside their own earthly cares. The Liturgy is of such a great stature that it requires an enormous effort to prepare properly and give one's self entirely to the Liturgy, hard labor that is both impossible to achieve and worth the effort. The Liturgy is also the place where the laity receive God's acceptance, marked by their reception of Communion, an acceptance epitomized by the children's confidence in coming forward to participate fully. Finally, participants obtain a sense of a Communion transcending the walls of their church: even a wobbly setting aside of distractions can result in receiving God's peace and learning how to pray that divine peace would be given to the global Communion.

HOLY COMMUNION: TWO SIDES OF A WINDOW

In the previous chapter, we mentioned that focus group respondents dwelt at length on the topic of Holy Communion. Most respondents spoke about Communion in response to the general question on the Divine Liturgy, an expected outcome of the exercise. In this section, then, we'll center our discussion on the respondents' view of Communion as a reception of God's mercy, and how participation in Communion contributed to their view of other people.

Preparing for Communion

Like the Divine Liturgy, respondents understood that preparation for Communion is traditionally quite rigorous in the Orthodox Church. The most complete and rigorous observance calls for participants to pray and fast intensely for approximately three days before the Liturgy, receive the sacrament of Confession, attend the services leading up to Liturgy (Vigil, Vespers, or Matins), recite the office of preparation for Holy Communion, and observe a complete fast from the evening prior to the Liturgy. A complete fast technically prohibits food, coffee, and plain water from midnight on. While some communities still appoint a more complete observance, many parishes have adopted a more relaxed process of preparation. At minimum, communicants are expected to have prayed and fasted prior to the Liturgy. The fasting stipulation can be adjusted to accommodate health needs: people who take medication are encouraged to eat modestly, and some priests do not take issue with parishioners having water or coffee before the Liturgy.

Older respondents tended to refer to the requirement of fasting they learned as children, and how challenging it is to observe the canonical rules before receiving Communion. One respondent expressed her disagreement with Church teachings on fasting and stated that she simply does not approach to receive since she takes issue with the fasting requirement. Another respondent suggested that the Church's relaxation of fasting rules has resulted in laziness, as the new freedom grants people license to eat a sumptuous meal prior to breakfast. The prevailing sentiment of the focus group participants was one of perpetual unworthiness: no feat could be achieved that would make one worthy of receiving Christ, and for that reason, faithful should not hesitate to approach to receive Communion, even if their preparation has been lax. There should be no fear of burning on account of a lack of complete observance.

Respondents tended to confirm this sentiment of approaching to receive on the basis of the mercy imparted by God in Confession. This discussion was especially vibrant at St. Anthony of the Desert parish. Participants were grateful for Orthodoxy's therapeutic approach to Confession, and found courage to approach both sacraments as often as needed for the forgiveness of sins. One respondent took the theological dimension of receiving Communion further than the others by describing it as being "brought into Christ, and Christ is brought into me," a "palpable physical presence." For respondents, the discussion on Communion did not go beyond this description: the most notable feature of their theology of Communion is that it is a precious gift no one is worthy of receiving.

Fear of Divine Punishment

A crucial component of having the courage to approach to receive was the casting away of fear of divine punishment: the respondents who commented on this issue were essentially unanimous in rejecting the notion that some deficiency in preparation would result in damnation. They accentuated the pouring out of God's mercy in Communion, and the discussion essentially occurred on this axis of topics, as mercy and healing are what is received, not judgment and condemnation. While respondents shied away from endorsing rigorous preparation for Communion, they did not express any sense that Communion was trite, or that they were entitled to it. The discussion on preparation was essentially an admittance of weakness that prohibits them from observing the full preparation: absolute fasting and intense prayer remain the ideal approach to Communion, but a failure to observe it should not cause one to hesitate from approaching.

Observance of Other Participants

An equally potent theological dimension of Holy Communion articulated by respondents comes from their observance of others. Respondents said that receiving Communion strengthened bonds with the other people of the congregation. SA6 expressed joy at seeing "everyone" come up for Communion, even though her reception was not in the "same sense as the babies." She explained that age was not an obstacle for receiving, a punctuation point on the Eucharist as a celebration that does not discriminate: everyone participates. Orthodox parishes tend to be small enough that people notice when someone is absent from the Divine Liturgy, a nuance picked up by HTC1, who had previously mentioned that Communion is an act of being "brought into Christ." He added that "a part of Christ is absent" when someone is unable to attend the Divine Liturgy. His comments evoke the Eucharistic ecclesiology popularized by Afanasiev and Schmemann in the twentieth century, as Christ is present when the Church is in one place together (*epi to auto*, Acts 2).[5] HTC10 had also emphasized the experience of receiving together with the rest of the congregation, and she added the dimension of this act occurring in the same room together: Communion is truly communal.

Awareness of Non-communicants

Focus group respondents offered remarks that guard against the idealism of a perfect Communion. Several respondents noted their own mourning and discomfort concerning those who are unable to participate in Communion because of canonical impediments and Christian division. HTC9 said it was painful for him to have Communion without being able to share it with others, whereas it was even more personal for HTC10, who cannot receive

Communion with the rest of the family. More than one respondent reflected on Communion as a closed door experience, but it was not a sentiment expressed by everyone.

Nevertheless, the negative feelings that emerged from Eucharistic exclusivity can be placed alongside the view of the Eucharist as fastening the gathering together into one body. The view of Communion emerging from our focus groups, then, can be described as two sides of the same window: on one side, the rite of Communion is an image of a single body partaking of the Lord's banquet together, with no obvious discrimination, as people of all ages dine together. It is the other side of the window that exposes the discrimination: the local assembly is not actually one where everyone is in one place together, because there is an assembly of people on the other side of the glass that cannot participate in Communion, because of canonical impediments and interfaith division.

The people's experience of Communion grants them a vision of Communion on these two sides: some are perfectly content to receive alongside those with them, while Communion evokes the scandal of Christian separation for others. A common element holds the two sides of the window together: for participants, Communion was not an individual act between God and me, but was thoroughly human. In fact, in their remarks, the respondents privileged images of Communion in human and communal terms, an act performed together. There were no references to feelings of Communion with the Triune God, even though the liturgical texts themselves announce the offering and the gifts as participation in the Communion of the Holy Spirit.[6] The absence of explicit references to Communion with the Trinity do not necessarily suggest that respondents do not experience communion with God, but the remarks indicate that people tend to describe their understanding of Liturgy in human terms. Communion involves the human activities of eating and drinking together, so it is not unusual that respondents described the meaning of Communion through the idioms of human life. These expressions do not diminish the meaning of Communion for the people: it is an outpouring of divine mercy that grants participants the courage to let go of their fear and come forward to receive the son of God, even though they are unworthy.

HOLY SEASONS: RAW, RITUAL PARTICIPATION

Historians of the Byzantine liturgy have demonstrated how the offices of Lent and Holy Week have become amalgamations of solemn worship in Jerusalem and Constantinople.[7] For example, there are dozens of lessons appointed for the offices of Good Friday, and many of those readings are repeated on account of the various mergers and adjustments that took place with the Studite-Sabaitic liturgical synthesis.[8] In contemporary celebration, the most popular offices surround the mimetic ritual reenactments of Jesus' crucifixion, death, and burial, especially the venerations and processions with the epitaphios, or burial shroud of Christ. Faithful also look forward to the drama of the Holy Saturday Liturgy, when the vestment colors change from dark to bright, and the priest walks around the temple throwing rose petals. They gather in huge crowds in the darkness of Sunday midnight to keep Vigil at the tomb, process around the church, and receive the light, to proclaim "Christ is Risen!" to and with their fellow worshippers. We have not yet mentioned some of the other popular Lenten offices, such as the Liturgy of Presanctified Gifts and the Akathistos Hymn of the fifth week of Lent. The people testified to the power of these special rites, and they did so with a sense of responsibility in sustaining the tradition they received from the previous generation and passing that tradition on, unsullied, to the next one.

On the topic of holy seasons, two trends emerged among the participants. They identified a fissure between the Lenten cycle and the rest of the year on account of the sheer weight and demand of the requirements for Orthodox Lenten worship. They also referred to certain services as challenging them, because of the degree to which the services expose the frailty of humankind. Also notable in their descriptions was the near absence of reflection on liturgies of the liturgical year outside of Lent and Pascha: no one bothered to mention Christmas at all, and the only other service to be named as significant was Theophany, particularly the experience of participation in the blessing of waters.

Raw Ritual Participation

The primary reference point for the people's liturgical theology of holy seasons were the rituals themselves. In fact, the people essentially confirmed the prevailing narrative about Lenten and Paschal worship: the popular, mimetic rites are the ones that resonate with them, and they look forward to them. The rites of Pascha are by far the most popular. Several respondents spoke glowingly of Pascha and its dramatic rituals. For example, respondents at St. Katherine's referred to the first and second Anastasi services as powerful moments they anticipated each year.[9] The testimony of SG3 on Pascha also referred to the power of that evening: she is no longer able to attend Pascha because of her health, and her inability to participate is a source of sorrow. The joy ushered in by Pascha has the kind of liberating effect respondents hoped for from the regular Sunday Divine Liturgy. Respondents at Holy Trinity Cathedral had reflected on the excitement and anticipation of the children, who hungered to participate in the grueling services. Respondents also referred to the levity of the non-liturgical time following the celebration of Pascha, with the community gathering together, laughing, breaking bread, and feasting. There is no other way to describe this post-liturgical joy: it is a Paschal holiday party. Respondents were self-conscious about laughing and socializing in the sacred space of the church, admitting that Pascha was an exception for a party atmosphere in the church—it "would never fly" on another occasion.

Strong Liturgical Moments and Joy

Respondents had referred to the customary ritual actions of Pascha: the movement from darkness to light, the constant singing, the opening of the royal doors, a visual symbol that all are truly welcome at the Lord's banquet for the resurrection. Pastors are familiar with this festive atmosphere. It has long been a custom for the people to linger after the Paschal liturgy and break the fast with roasted lamb, or in the Slavic traditions, to fill their baskets with their favorite savory foods and libations, sharing a festive meal with one another. A Russian tradition calls for the priest or bishop to throw boiled eggs (representing the resurrection) into the assembly, with the people catching them in a kind of contest, like bridesmaids lined up to catch the bouquet at a wedding.[10] Respondents appeared to cherish this raw joy, the kind of radiance one would like to capture in a bottle for the other times of the year.

This is not to suggest, though, that the dramatic and mimetic ritual actions caused the joy. The joy comes from the reception of the good news of the resurrection, and is a natural release culminating the end of a long process of fasting, prayer, and preparation for the feast. The people's reference to the preparation and inclusion of children in the festal celebration elucidates a strong sense of tradition. The joy they experience is so powerful, they cannot live without it. They desire to pass this joy on to their children because they regard it as lifegiving—in other words, the people are grateful for having received this tradition, and therefore desire to pass it on.

Post-Paschal Letdown

What is passed on is an annual celebration that doesn't sustain its intensity after Pascha Sunday. The celebration is so intense that everyone feels fatigued. This is one of the reasons several respondents referred to the post-Paschal season as a letdown, a time when people feel flat and tired. The resurrection has its own special time of fifty days, up until Pentecost throughout Christian tradition. The season of Pentecost appoints fifty days of rejoicing. People with jobs and families cannot sustain the rigor of Lent, Holy Week, and Pascha beyond that point, and this is a problem that has afflicted the Orthodox Church for some time now.[11] The joy they experience is real, and experienced in all the senses, with others in the community.

Another dimension of the people's faith is at work in their identification of raw, ritual participation as a feature of the Liturgy. They sense that something powerful has happened to them—a major source of their faith is their observation of and engagement with others. One respondent was unable to grasp the meaning of Pascha on his first experience, but he was encouraged by a woman to consider its beauty, and the question she posed resonated with him. He now says that he "can't live without it" (Pascha). People who are relatively new to Orthodoxy have a sense of receiving help in learning how to observe Pascha, to keep trying each year even if the celebration seems foreign.

Tradition and Beloved Elders

For native Orthodox, the models from the past generation are sources of inspiration. They remember the faithful elderly men and women (the "ya-yas") bending backwards to walk underneath the epitaphios at the Matins of Holy Saturday. It is not merely a matter of admiring the piety of elderly faithful. In her description of this ritual, SA7 paired her description of the elderly straining to perform the prostrations with a seemingly unrelated story of a priest who had spilled Holy Communion from the cup, and knelt down to lick it off the floor. Her pairing of the two examples shows that the Holy Week rituals of the epitaphios are not merely requirements to be continued by the succeeding generation of faithful. Her story suggests that these people's engagement of the rituals illuminated the gift imparted to faithful through the rituals. In other words, the succeeding generation is given the capacity to enter into the Paschal bridal chamber of the Lord, much like the hearer of the Haggadah becomes a child of the covenant alongside the others at the table.

The people's observation of others is not always inspiring, and represents the reality of human failure in liturgical celebrations. Fellow worshippers challenge one another with customary annoying behaviors. These can be particularly problematic in the choir, when a core group of people has handled the hard work of singing the responses to the offices for the entire season, and a cohort of newcomers arrive to sing on Pascha. SA6's honest narration of her annoyance with those who joined the bandwagon at the end reminds us of the human element cutting through the euphoria of the resurrection offices.

In summary, respondents identified Holy Week and Pascha as the primary solemn seasons defining their participation in the liturgical year. The core messages of the season challenged them to discern their lives and reflect on the human condition. They value popular ritual traditions and regard them as holy gifts passed on from the previous generation. Respondents consider it their duty to share this tradition with the children of their parishes, and they witness to the power of tradition by observing the children's anticipation of Holy Week and Pascha. The rigorous demands of the season challenge the stamina of Orthodox faithful. Pascha delivers a release from the intensity of Lent. The joy of God-given freedom to humanity is received, but physical and emotional fatigue come with it.

CHALLENGING NARRATIVES

A profound liturgical theology of the people can be gleaned from their descriptions of the meaning of particular commemorations during Lent and Holy Week. A remark about the human wonder at Christ's sacrifice for us on Pascha is somewhat expected. But respondents proved quite receptive to other commemorations and liturgical moments as well. Earlier, we mentioned the mimetic ritual actions of the offices of Good Friday (observed on Thursday evening in most parishes). In the Greek Orthodox tradition, there is a ritual procession of Jesus carrying the cross and being crucified while the singers intone the hymn "Today, He who . . . ," often set to special music.[12] SG 5 had described this moment as generating "goose bumps."

Inspiring Characters of Liturgical Narratives

Several respondents mentioned the narratives of women attending to Christ's anointing and burial at the end of Holy Week. Female respondents in particular found meaning with the privilege given to women to attend to the final moments of burial, and to be the first to discover the empty tomb and hear the news of the resurrection. Several respondents mentioned service of Matins and Lamentations of Holy Saturday, a rite containing numerous poetic stanzas of the Mother of God weeping at the tomb of Christ, even as she anticipated his resurrection. This is a very popular service, perhaps one of the best-attended liturgical offices of Holy Week, again appointing special music for the singing of those poetic verses. One respondent found authentic compassion in her reflection on Mary's lament for her crucified son, as the respondent had also lost and mourned a child.

In addition to the powerful liturgical rites of Holy Week, which are constructed to encourage the people's engagement, a variety of other seasonal services evoked profound responses. One respondent identified the commemoration of St. Mary of Egypt and the intonation of her entire vita in church as a particularly powerful message; the reading of the vita occurs in the context of the chanting of the canon of St. Andrew of Crete and Great Compline, and the respondent felt that St. Mary's story enlivened a hortatory verse from the kontakion of the canon: "arise, my soul, why are you sleeping?"[13] She described the service, which occurs on a Thursday evening toward the end of the fifth week of Lent, as an immersion with "deep theology."

One more example rounds out the capacity of liturgical narratives to challenge congregants. SG6 mentioned Palm Sunday and the irony that the same people who greeted Jesus with palms of victory as he entered Jerusalem shouted for his crucifixion. She mentioned this episode as disclosing the fundamental problem of the human condition, and how easy it is for anyone to be transformed from one who glorifies Christ to one who condemns him.

These examples illustrate how select liturgical narratives have the capacity to challenge participants. Respondents offered these moments as particularly strong and memorable, which means that they have sustained power to transform. From this section, we can conclude that select liturgical components and entire offices challenge participants to confront the dilemma of humankind: the propensity to become stuck in a vicious cycle of sin, and the possibility of receiving liberation from that cycle and becoming human. The respondents' examples are illustrative: they tended to be moved by scriptural lessons that function as the building blocks of Christian identity. In most cases, these scriptural lessons were enlivened by their liturgical context and the surrounding rites. For example, the Markan account of the empty tomb and the announcement of the resurrection occurs at the end of the midnight procession and the beginning of Matins when the people are assembled outdoors. The festal liturgical accents highlight the biblical stories, with hymnographic refrains and poetic stanzas elaborating the story itself. The Liturgy is designed to pay special attention to that moment in time, to garner the people's attention. The people's testimony gives us a precious glimpse into the authentic theology of festal liturgy: we have the impression that people hear an invitation to become transformed, and are in the active process of making that transformation.

THE ROLE OF WOMEN: GENDER WARS AND INDECISION

Heated discussions occurred on the question of the role of women in the Church, which is documented with some detail in chapter 3. This discussion yields the perceptions of the people on questions of liturgical leadership, the nature of the Church, the role of women, and the boundaries of legitimate debate on controversial issues in the Church.

Two Opposing Views on Women and Liturgical Ministry

From a strictly liturgical perspective, two opposing views emerged. One view sustains present Church practice and understands the orders of the Church to be divinely ordained. Several respondents, men and women, do not agree that women should engage in liturgical ministry. These respondents did not elaborate a rationale for men exercising liturgical ministry, but instead argued that the dignity of women is intact in the Church's orders. The primary rationale for the existence of the equal dignity of women in present Church practice is the Church's veneration of the Panagia (Mary, the Mother of God) and the leadership carried out by lay women in the Church, especially the Philoptochos Society of the Greek Orthodox Church. This rationale holds that all is well with the orders of the Church and no change is needed. When asked about the possibility of restoring the order of deaconess, this group questioned the motivation of those who seek a female diaconate in the twenty-first century. Several members of this group expressed concern that feminism is the driving force behind the push for female deacons, and that Orthodoxy would suffer the same fate as Episcopalians if the feminist agenda would result in real ordinations of deaconesses. [14]

The proponents of increasing ministries for women in the Church and restoring the deaconess argued that priests need help in numerous parishes, and that women are often available and wiling to assist. They asserted that the rules of the Orthodox Church prohibiting women from assisting cloak an underlining patriarchal culture that seeks to subjugate women, and thus distort Orthodox theological anthropology. They asserted that ordaining women and blessing girls to serve was not a matter of a contemporary feminist agenda imposed upon the Church, but was an attempt to purify the liturgical orders of the Church so that they bear Orthodoxy's authentic theological anthropology.

The two perspectives appear to be completely irreconcilable. Proponents of each position maintain that the integrity of the church's theological anthropology supports their position. Opponents of the restoration of the order of deaconess seek to defend a theological anthropology they view as present in the liturgy. Proponents of the female diaconate and women assisting at the altar would like to see the restoration of a theological anthropology they believe is consistent with Orthodoxy. The common core of the two opposing views is that the liturgy must represent authentic theological anthropology.

This notion of a dynamic relationship between liturgy and theological anthropology has ramifications for the debate on the relationship and theology that exploded in the twentieth century, with Alexander Schmemann often setting the tone for the discussions. In this case, it is difficult to determine what is *theologia prima*, as a view of the liturgy throughout the entirety of its history discloses a substantial period of time when the order of deaconess exercised a significant ministry. If the entirety of history is consulted, then the disappearance of the deaconess could be interpreted as a consequence of some combination of historical context resulting in the decline of all non-presbyteral clerical orders, and a theological anthropology that permitted only men to exercise liturgical ministry. Some might argue that the process of organic development resulted in a natural disappearance of the deaconess, which raises suspicion about the motivations for restoring this order. However, in the contemporary Church, women have assumed leadership roles that previously belonged to men, presiding over lay organizations, performing choral leadership, and reading and chanting hymns and the appointed lessons for the Liturgy of the Word. It is probably impossible to resolve this particular debate: the point is that the debate will continue to rage as long as the people see the liturgy as an expression of the Church's theological anthropology.

Women's Ministry and Politics

During the course of the focus group discussions, it became clear that opponents of increasing women's roles in the Church viewed the movement for increasing the role of women in the church as one of several attempts at introducing contemporary political theology into the Orthodox Church. A few respondents referred to society's acceptance of LGBT people and gay marriage as a sign of another issue that threatens Orthodoxy. While no one mentioned the possibility of permitting LGBT people to receive Communion or blessing same-sex marriage in the Church, a few respondents opined that the Church has a responsibility to devise new strategies to teach children about the differences between Church teaching and secular influence. More than one respondent suggested that some kind of liturgical catechesis was needed to communicate Orthodoxy's theological anthropology. On the other hand, one respondent elaborated her young daughter's desire to serve at the altar with the boys, and bemoaned her daughter's declining interest in Church on account of her exclusion from serving. She explained that her daughter excels at many things, including math and sciences, but somehow is not qualified to assist at the altar. An adult respondent who had recently become Orthodox said she did so despite instances of excluding women and described her feeling as "what's wrong with me?" Proponents of increasing women's ministry in the Church stated that the current form of Orthodox liturgy essentially teaches women that they must be subject to men, and that the liturgy could be revised to excise this distortion.

The discussion on women and contemporary issues was the most heated of them all during the focus groups. As long as the liturgy is viewed as the symbol of the Church theological anthropology, these debates will only increase. Two items for consideration in anticipation of flaring tempers on women and the Church can be taken from the focus group sessions: first, none of the respondents vocally advocated for the ordination of women to the presbyterate or episcopate, although it's quite possible that some people hold this opinion in private. Second, some of the proponents for the restoration of the order of deaconess also expressed concern that the movement is inspired in part by political theology. Multiple respondents suggested that a candidate for the order of deaconess must have an advanced theology degree commensurate with her ministry, and that women—like men—should be carefully vetted to ensure that they want to serve God and the Church, and not obtain power in a hierarchical structure. This final point demonstrates that there are more than two positions on this complicated and divisive issue confronting the Church.

LITURGICAL CHANGES AND CHALLENGES

Throughout the sessions, respondents occasionally identified specific liturgical changes they had experienced in their lifetimes. A few respondents also suggested some liturgical changes on the basis of their observations and experience. Respondent narratives suggested that some reforms are necessary for the people to be able to access the Liturgy, and the most significant of these was language.

Respondents testified to the power of the liturgy when it is celebrated in the language the people understand. While a small handful of people insisted that not all Greek terms and phrases can be translated adequately, several respondents said that their experience of the liturgy changed dramatically when parishes began to offer it in English. The testimony of respondents who did not know that his marriage ceremony was complete punctuated the difference between confusion and understanding in the liturgy. Respondents made it clear that they were much more capable of engaging and participating in a service they could understand, presupposing that active participation includes attentive listening and observation along with performing animated rituals and singing along. This was particularly true of respondents who were struck by the liturgical narratives of Palm Sunday, St. Mary of Egypt, the Lamentations of Holy Saturday, and other services. The celebration of these services in the vernacular made it possible for those words to permeate their hearts and confront their consciences.

Unveiling "Secret" Liturgical Components

Understanding was not limited to the use of the language of the people, despite that component's primary importance. The people also noted a desire to have greater access to unknown aspects of the liturgy. Several respondents complained about the private, quiet prayers of the priest, exemplified by one remark of "who knows what they're doing back there?" Another respondent from St. Katherine's praised Fr. Courey for explaining the program of iconography in the Church. The respondent suggested that this kind of fundamental catechesis was necessary, even if it were to take place during the course of the liturgy, so the people would understand their purpose for participation. One respondent mentioned Fr. Arida's practice of reciting the prayer of the anaphora of St. Basil aloud for the people to hear. Their ability to hear the petitions that God remember so many kinds of human beings gave the respondent something to ponder in terms of her own prayer life. [15]

Liturgical Understanding

The people's appreciation for understanding the liturgy, and their desire to understand opaque liturgical elements exposed something that should be obvious about liturgy, but often remains unsaid. Understanding is a catalyst for greater engagement of the liturgy, and active participation in it. A precise definition of what we mean by understanding is necessary here. Understanding does not suggest that the people can teach liturgy or articulate its official, textbook definitions by memory. Throughout the sessions, people often struggled to find the words to describe what they were experiencing, but this did not mean they were bereft of understanding. The people's appreciation for understanding discloses the nature of liturgy as primarily dialogical, God speaking to us and revealing himself to us here and now, today. The people's response to God's initiative is an act of dialogue, but response is possible only when the initiator can be clearly understood. Therefore, the verbal and nonverbal liturgical changes mentioned by the people highlight the liturgy's dialogical nature and the *sine qua non* of its expression in the vernacular and through culturally recognizable symbols.

COMPANIONSHIP ON BOTH SIDES OF THE WINDOW

The focus group sessions consisted of a small group dialogue. Unlike a one-on-one private interview, respondents listened to one another, and frequently developed themes established by another participant. Several respondents reported that the experience of reflecting on the liturgy in a group setting was pleasant. One respondent expressed a desire to convene and discuss the Liturgy more frequently. A spirit of camaraderie emerged during the sessions, and on a few occasions, the groups seemed to forget that I was among them, and continued the discussion amongst themselves.

In comparison to large Catholic or evangelical congregations, Orthodox parishes in America tend to be quite small. The congregations in our study range in size, from 50 to 600. Even the largest parish of the study (St. Katherine's) is small enough for people to know one another, to recognize each other's faces during Liturgy. In each focus group, respondents knew one another. Some respondents sang in the choir together, others served on a committee or parish council, and others had experienced the process of becoming Orthodox together. But there was also diversity in each group: respondents tended to be older, but some had young children, and women and men were represented equally. Several respondents were born in countries other than America, and not only in the Greek parishes—there were participants from places like Russia and Germany as well.

The occasional disagreements that emerged from the sessions countered the periods of camaraderie. The diversity of opinions expressed by respondents illustrated the absence of one-mindedness. The divergence of perspectives was powerful even at St. Katherine's, since the focus group consisted of select people who participate in the parish Bible study.

Life in smaller American congregations was traditionally shaped by location. People of a town would gather at the local church. In many cases, people also worked together, intermarried, and went to the same schools. The commonalities shared by the people did not equate to a peaceful congregational life. Every congregation has a story about infighting and internal divisions. Camaraderie and one-mindedness are neither guaranteed nor perpetual.

Our contemporary situation has changed. Mobility, education, and demographics create shifts in many locations, so congregations often have to accept shifts and can no longer rely on families remaining in one place for several generations.[16] Congregations also have to learn how to welcome and integrate newcomers into parish life. For Orthodox parishes in America, the process of welcoming newcomers consists mostly of receiving converts into the Church, and in some places, welcoming immigrants from the Middle East and Central and Eastern Europe.

The person standing next to you in the pew can either be familiar or a complete stranger, and the process for truly accepting someone new is not easy. Mark Searle touches upon the tendency for people to seek companionship in a parish setting, to make friends, and share like-minded interests with people of similar backgrounds.[17] On the surface, there is nothing unusual about this pattern. Drawing closer to one's fellow worshippers in the same congregation is one of the patterns yielded by this study, and the objective of strengthening communion with the people of one's congregation was certainly a feature of twentieth century sacramental theology.

As we have seen, the matter of building communion with people occurs on two sides of a window. Orthodox parishes in America have emphasized strengthening intra-parish Communion, often as a method to allow new life to rise from the ashes of parishes that were in the process of dying. Schmemann himself pointed to the Eucharist as the only solution to mitigate the internal bickering and infighting afflicting many parishes in a lecture he delivered in Boston in 1970.[18] A realization of the Eucharist uniting the local parish into the body of Christ would result in authentic companionship among the people in the parish, assuming the people wanted to share bread with one another.[19] Creating authentic companionship on the other side of the window, with those who do not belong to the parish for reasons of

Christian division or canonical impediment, is a task the Orthodox Church has yet to undertake in postmodernity, with a few notable exceptions. [20] Despite measurable progress on building companionship on the other side of the window in the global Church, participants in our focus groups expressed both remorse for the failures and a desire to share bread with those who do not belong.

DIVINE COMPASSION AND THE UTTER HUMANITY OF LITURGY

The final theme to be explored in this chapter is one that participants did not explicate at length: divine compassion. There is no doubt that the Byzantine liturgy is saturated with images of divine compassion. Usually, the liturgy communicates these themes through hymns, especially with exhortations that conclude select festal hymns of the liturgical year: "glory to your condescension, o Lord."[21] The hymns communicate the paradox of the Incarnation of Christ: the creator of all voluntarily takes on human nature, receives Baptism from the hand of John, is beaten, mocked, crucified, and dies. [22] The Liturgy pairs this image of the God who came to dwell among the people with hundreds of narratives of Mary and the saints witnessing, suffering, and receiving the gift of glorification for picking up their crosses and following Christ.

The people did not use the phrase "divine condescension" in the focus group sessions, but there was a strong sentiment that the people believe God, Mary, and the saints suffer with them in the Liturgy. Participants expressed this sentiment in two ways. A few respondents referred to the examples established by Christ, Mary, and the saints as inspirational. SG5 gets "goose bumps" every year when he hears the hymn about the Lord hanging from the cross. HTC8 gets "chills" every Pascha, at the proclamation that the tomb is empty and Christ is risen. SA5 marvels at the "enormity of Christ's sacrifice." SA7 finds comfort in Mary's lamentation at the tomb of Christ in a very personal way.

These examples offer enough testimony to demonstrate that respondents relate to the narratives of Christ, Mary, and the saints. The sessions yielded a crucial pattern of reflection that identifies the liturgy with an outpouring of divine compassion even more powerful than the individual examples. In their responses to questions on the Liturgy and Holy Communion, respondents were generally hard on themselves. The pattern of reflection was one of self-examination. Respondents said that no matter how hard they tried, they were falling short of the demands of the Liturgy. Despite falling short, many of them opted to approach the Lord's Table and participate fully, over and over again. As they participated in the Liturgy, they had conflicting feelings about their relations with others. Some of them felt like they belonged with the rest of their community; some lamented the prohibitions preventing others from belonging; some were worried that their participation would expose them as sinners.

Underlying this pattern is a general desire for acceptance. Respondents marveled at the participation of children in the Liturgy because it is a symbol that God accepts them, and they long for the same confirmation of divine love as they are aware of their own deficiencies and sins. Respondents want the others in the community to accept them, and some participants want to extend acceptance to those on the other side of the window. The desire for acceptance in community is a fundamental to humankind and a staple feature of Liturgy. When respondents hear the narratives of Christ's suffering and rejection, of St. Mary of Egypt's conversion and isolation, of Mary's weeping at the tomb, they see the entirety of their own woes echoes by these stories. When respondents said that they approached God's banquet table despite their awareness of unworthiness, they were unveiling their fear of rejection and isolation, and demonstrating how participating in the ritual was an act of courage to receive divine acceptance.

A theme threads through these narratives: Christ's sacrifice and Mary's lamentation show that they, too, experienced the utter humanity of isolation, rejection, and fear. When the people marveled at the holy models presented to them, they found courage to approach in spite of their fear because of divine compassion. Liturgical participation in the sacrifice of Christ is a living experience of divine compassion, Christ co-suffering with us in the woes of our daily lives. Therefore, the Liturgy is a living experience of divine compassion in the present.

CONCLUSION

In this chapter, I have created a synthesis of the people's faith, the laity's liturgical theology. The people view the Liturgy as a monumental task requiring excruciating effort and energy. The Liturgy is an experience of Communion with Christ and the community that provides liberation from life's daily worries, yet causes some to mourn for those who do not have access to Christ. The people experience Holy Communion on two sides of a window: they feel one with Christ and his body, which is a source of joy and a privilege, but they are aware of those on the other side of the window, sometimes painfully. The holy seasons are a gift they received through tradition, one they have a responsibility to pass on to the next generation. The epic stories told in the Liturgy lead them to ponder the human condition and work on their own salvation. The Liturgy is the primary bearer and communicator of the Orthodox Church's theological anthropology; most of all, the

Liturgy is utterly human, an outpouring of divine compassion, and the assurance that Christ, Mary, and the saints continue to dwell, walk, and suffer with us in this world.

The main points of the people's faith have been established, but not everything is resolved. One aspect of this chapter carries special significance: the people's understanding of the liturgy depends on their access to hearing it in their language and experiencing it in forms and idioms of their cultural contexts. We address the relationship of Orthodox academic theology to the people's faith in the next chapter, and offer a proposal for the agenda of liturgical theology on the basis of this contribution from the people's faith.

NOTES

1. For scholarship on the ritual formation of children, see Gertrude Mueller Nelson, "Christian Formation of Children: the Role of Ritual and Celebration," in *Liturgy and Spirituality in Context*, ed. Elanor Bernstein (Collegeville, MN: Liturgical Press, 1990), 114–35.

2. Kimberly Hope Belcher, *Efficacious Engagement: Sacramental Participation in the Trinitarian Mystery* (Collegeville, MN: Liturgical Press, 2011).

3. The clergy invite the laity to Holy Communion when the deacon (or priest, if no deacon is serving) walks through the holy gates to the ambon and chants the command, "With the fear of God, faith [and love], draw near!" When there are communicants, the clergy take positions around the ambon and the people come forward and receive Communion from a spoon. In the era of infrequent Communion, clergy would emerge from the sanctuary in the same way, inviting the people to "draw near," and would immediately turn around and place the gifts on the altar. In these common occurrences, Communion was essentially prepared only for the clergy, often one priest in most parishes, since no one else came forward for Communion.

4. The *Cherubikon*, or Cherubic Hymn, is the song chanted as the Church prepares for the Great Entrance, the ritual transfer of the gifts from the table of preparation to the altar. The text of the song: "Let us, who mystically represent the Cherubim and who sing the thrice-holy hymn to the life-creating Trinity, now lay aside every worldly care. So that we may receive the King of all Who is invisibly escorted by the angelic hosts. Alleluia. Alleluia. Alleluia." Text taken from https://www.goarch.org/-/the-divine-liturgy-of-saint-john-chrysostom (accessed March 15, 2018).

5. Nicholas Afanasiev, *The Church of the Holy Spirit*, trans. Vitaly Permiakov, ed. Michael Plekon, foreword by Rowan Williams (South Bend, IN: University of Notre Dame Press, 2007), 238.

6. The anaphora of St. John Chrysostom includes this passage concerning the consecrated gifts, towards the end: "So that they may be for those who partake of them for vigilance of soul, remission of sins, communion of Your Holy Spirit, fullness of the Kingdom of Heaven, boldness before You, not for judgment or condemnation." Before the Lord's prayer, the deacons bid the people to pray: "Having asked for the unity of the faith and for the communion of the Holy Spirit, let us commend ourselves and one another and our whole life to Christ our God," and the priest again prays that the people would be granted the gift of the communion of the Holy Spirit. Texts taken from https://www.goarch.org/-/the-divine-liturgy-of-saint-john-chrysostom (accessed February 27, 2018).

7. See Robert F. Taft, "A Tale of Two Cities: The Byzantine Holy Week Triduum as a Paradigm of Liturgical History," in *Time and Community, in Honor of Thomas Julian Talley*, ed. J. Alexander, NPM Studies in Church Music and Liturgy (Washington, DC: National Pastoral Musicians, 1990), 21–41; idem, "In the Bridegroom's Absence: The Paschal Triduum in the Byzantine Church," in La celebrazione del Triduo pasquale: anamnesis e mimesis. Atti del III Congresso Internazionale di Liturgia, Roma, Pontificio Istituto Liturgico, 9–13 maggio 1988 Studia Anselmiana 102 (1990): 71–97. Thomas Pott, *Byzantine Liturgical Reform: A*

Study of Liturgical Change in the Byzantine Tradition, trans. Paul Meyendorff, preface by Robert F. Taft, Orthodox Liturgy Series 2 (Crestwood, NY: St. Vladimir's Seminary Press, 2010), 153–95.

8. Pott, 169–73.

9. The respondents are referring to a series of resurrection (Paschal, or Easter) services, as "Anastasi" means resurrection. In this scheme, the "first anastasi" refers to the Vesperal Liturgy of Holy Saturday. In parish practice, this liturgy is celebrated on Saturday morning. Historically, this is the ancient Paschal Vigil of the Byzantine rite, with the resurrection lesson from the Gospel of Matthew announcing Jesus' resurrection. In the fusion of cathedral and monastic services, the Paschal vigil was moved up as the midnight offices became popular among the people. The "second Anastasi" is the midnight service of Pascha. This service begins in a dark church, when the priest lights the people's candles and everyone proceeds outdoors chanting a paschal hymn. This is a festive service with singing and the priest greeting the people with "Christ is Risen!" repeatedly.

10. PriestOVCHA, "Архиерей поздравляет мирян и разбрасывает пасхальные яйца," YouTube video, posted 14 April 2015, https://youtu.be/WA_ku8l5VvY (accessed February 27, 2018).

11. Writing in the 1930s, Fr. Alexander Elchaninov echoes the sentiments of the respondents of our focus groups: "I always feel sad about the slow ebb of spiritual life after Easter. First, there is an increase in spiritual forces as we enter deeper into Lent. Everything inward becomes considerably easier; our soul is purer and more at peace; our love is greater and our prayer better. Then come the days of Holy Week which are always so remarkable; and after that the joy of Easter. I do not know how to thank God for letting me participate in all this so fully as a priest. But then comes Saturday of Easter week, the doors into the sanctuary are closed as if the gates of heaven had been locked, and everything becomes more difficult, the soul grows weaker, becomes faint-hearted and lazy, every spiritual effort is hard." Alexander Elchaninov, *The Diary of a Russian Priest*, trans. Helen Iswolsky, ed. Kallistos Ware, introduction by Tamara Elchaninov, foreword by Dimitri Obolensky (London: Faber and Faber, 1967), 57.

12. "Today He who hung the earth upon the waters is hung upon the Cross," in Mother Mary and Kallistos Ware, *The Lenten Triodion* (South Canaan, PA: St. Tikhon's Seminary Press, 2002), 587. See entire text in chapter 2, n. 16.

13. "My soul, o my soul, rise up! Why art thou sleeping? The end draws near and soon thou shalt be troubled. Watch, then, that Christ thy God may spare thee, for he is everywhere present fills all things." Kontakion (hymn) of the canon of St. Andrew of Crete, sung the first and fifth weeks of Lent. From Mother Mary and Ware, *The Lenten Triodion*, 205.

14. The primary documents representing opposing views on the order of deaconess are "Orthodox Liturgists issued a statement of support for the revival of the order of deaconess by the Patriarchate of Alexandria," https://panorthodoxcemes.blogspot.ca/2017/10/orthodox-liturgists-issued-statement-of.html?m=1 (accessed February 22, 2018). See the rebuttal of this statement signed by dozens of scholars, clergy, and laity in "A Public Statement on Orthodox Deaconesses by Concerned Clergy and Laity," http://www.aoiusa.org/a-public-statement-on-orthodox-deaconesses-by-concerned-clergy-and-laity/ (accessed February 22, 2018). For a detailed study of the ordination of deaconesses in the Orthodox Church, see Petros Vassiliadis, Niki Papageorgiou, and Eleni Kasselouri-Hatzivassiliadi, eds., *Deaconesses, the Ordination of Women, and Orthodox Theology* (Cambridge: Cambridge University Press, 2017).

15. A passage from the anaphora of St. Basil offers a sample of the mosaic of humanity the assembly commends to God's memory. In addition to remembering saints, the dead, rulers and civil authorities, the petition to remember stretches ecclesial boundaries by calling upon God to remember people absent from the Liturgy, those who live in diverse conditions, and those who are not friendly to Christianity "Remember, Lord, the people here presented and those who are absent with good cause. Have mercy on them and on us according to the multitude of Your mercy. Fill their treasuries with every good thing; preserve their marriages in peace and harmony; nurture the infants; instruct the youth; strengthen the aged; give courage to the faint hearted; reunite those separated; bring back those in error and unite them to Your holy, catholic, and apostolic Church. Free those who are held captive by unclean spirits; sail with those who sail; travel with those who travel; defend the widows; protect the orphans; liberate the captives; heal

the sick. Remember, Lord, those who are in mines, in exile, in harsh labor, and those in every kind of affliction, necessity, or distress; those who entreat your loving kindness; those who love us and those who hate us; those who have asked us to pray for them, unworthy though we may be." Taken from Divine Liturgy of St. Basil, Greek Orthodox Archdiocese of America Web site, http://www.goarch.org/chapel/liturgical_texts/basil (accessed February 27, 2018).

16. Michael Plekon, "Belonging to the Christian Community in the Twenty-first Century, When 'The Church Has Left the Building,'" in *The Church Has Left the Building: Faith, Parish and Ministry in the Twenty-first Century,* ed. Michael Plekon, Maria Gwyn McDowell, and Elizabeth Schroeder (Eugene, OR: Cascade, 2016), 3–10.

17. Mark Searle, *Called to Participate: Theological, Ritual, and Social Perspectives,* ed. Barbara Searle and Anne Y. Koester (Collegeville, MN: Liturgical Press, 2006), 71–75.

18. Alexander Schmemann, "Transformation of the Parish," Lecture at St. Andrew's parish, 1971, cited from Nicholas Denysenko, *Liturgical Reform After Vatican II: The Impact on Eastern Orthodoxy* (Minneapolis: Fortress Press, 2015), 130–33.

19. See Searle, 75–80.

20. "It is still not the case, even in the modern period, that an absolute division between the two communions has ever existed. Under communist rule in Russia, for instance, Orthodox and Catholic communicants sometimes received from the same chalice, with tacit episcopal consent, and there are parts of Syria and Lebanon today where this fluidity of boundaries is an open secret and intercommunion a simple fact of life. In fact, I know of two Syrian parishes in the United States that have passed from the jurisdiction of an Orthodox to a Catholic bishop or in the opposite direction where communicants who consider themselves either Catholic or Orthodox belong to one church and one altar. To put it simply, there has never been a time when a perfect and impermeable wall has stood between the sacramental orders of East and West." David Bentley Hart, "The Myth of Schism," cited from *Clarion: Journal of Spirituality and Justice,* http://www.clarion-journal.com/clarion_journal_of_spirit/2014/06/the-myth-of-schism-david-bentley-hart.html (accessed February 28, 2018). Print article in *Ecumenism Today: The Universal Church in the Twenty-first Century,* ed. Francesca Aran Murphy and Christopher Asprey (New York: Routledge, 2016), 95–106.

21. This doxology concludes the hymns appointed to the Aposticha at Vespers on Good Friday. The translation in Mother Mary and Ware (*The Lenten Triodion*) is less obtuse: "glory to Thy self-abasement, o Thou who lovest mankind" (615).

22. The following hymn from the Vespers of Theophany (January 6) sums up the paradox of God becoming human and living among us: "The streams of the Jordan received Thee who art the fountain, and the Comforter descended in the form of a dove. He who bowed the heavens, bowed his head, and the clay cried aloud to him that formed him: 'why dost Thou command of me what lies beyond my power? For I have need to be baptized of Thee'. O sinless Christ our God, glory to Thee!" Mother Mary and Kallistos Ware, *The Festal Menaion,* intro. Georges Florovsky (South Canaan, PA: St. Tikhon's Seminary Press, 1990), 338.

Chapter Five

Common Ground

Liturgy in the Academy and in the Church

Our working hypothesis is that liturgical theologians working in the academy need to hear the reflections of the people on their experience of liturgy. Our focus group sessions have delivered several foundations for further research on the meaning of the Divine Liturgy, Holy Communion, the liturgical year, extraordinary moments in the liturgy, the liturgy and theological anthropology, and liturgical reform. Our final task is to bring the liturgical academy into a more engaged dialogue with the people's faith, to determine how our initial assessment might contribute to the agenda of the liturgical academy, and to suggest the next steps for the work of the theologians.

THE PEOPLE'S PERSPECTIVE: A NEW VIEW
FROM "MRS. MURPHY"

Orthodox liturgical theologians have reshaped the liturgical environment in enough American parishes to open the doors widely for the people to engage and understand the liturgy. That people receive Communion more frequently and are able and willing to reflect on its significance is possible only because of the Eucharistic revival. A commitment to the proclamation of the Word and quality preaching has resonated with the people. The people's engagement of the sermon on podcasts and general enthusiasm to understand the Bible, and the Liturgy through biblical studies demonstrates a restoration of the proclamation of the Word in American Orthodoxy. A respondent's expression of wonder and an examination of conscience from participating in the canon of St. Andrew with the reading of the life of St. Mary of Egypt shows that the method of adding liturgical offices has also had an impact on the people.

In short, there is plenty of evidence demonstrating that the efforts of renewal from liturgical theologians are bearing fruit in the Church. We can also assert that engagement of the science of *Liturgiewissenschaft* has played an important role in fomenting fruitful liturgical reform. The study of liturgical history illuminated aspects of liturgical life that had been neglected, especially how the structure of the Divine Liturgy points to its culmination in participating in Holy Communion, resulting in the transfiguration of people, and not only the transformation of the gifts offered at the table. It would be unwise, however, to approach the liturgical enterprise from a unilateral perspective, in which the theologian's work is to impart information to the people. The liturgical enterprise is much more potent when the process is reciprocal and bilateral, with the people informing the theologians.

Reception and *Sensus Fidelium*

Throughout history, Orthodox teaching has depended on the people's reception of a given idea or practice. The Orthodox notion of reception is similar to the Roman Catholic teaching on the *sensus fidelium*, the existence of articles of faith and devotion among the people.[1] Orthodoxy does not subscribe to the Roman Catholic process of establishing magisterial teaching on the basis of the *sensus fidelium*, as in the case of the formation of the Catholic dogma on the Assumption of Mary.[2] But Orthodoxy does honor the *sensus fidelium* of the laity even if it never comes to be inscribed on official conciliar teachings or theological handbooks, and this is particularly true for lay witness to theophanies in the life of the Church.

We can refer the dependence of the Church and the theological academy on lay witness, or *sensus fidelium*, as a confirmation that laypeople are theologians. Laypeople are not professional theologians, but they are authentic theologians in the spirit of the famous maxim of Evagrius Pontus: the theologian is the one who prays. The praying theologian is the ordinary person participating in the worship of the Christian assembly. This person does not need to own a small library of theological books, or claim some kind of expertise about a given liturgical tradition or topic. The theologian is the one who joins in the corporate prayer of the local assembly and sustains a life of prayer in ordinary daily life. This theologian received a name from the Benedictine liturgist Aidan Kavanagh in the twentieth century: Mrs. Murphy.[3] Kavanagh popularized the idea that Mrs. Murphy is the authentic liturgical theologian to show how liturgical participation can result in the transformation of the ordinary layperson. Kavanagh does not define Mrs. Murphy as someone who should lead liturgical catechesis or write a book on the Liturgy, or even lead an informed tour of the church building. Mrs. Murphy might not be able to articulate liturgical theology with precision, but she is a theologian because she prays and lives the Liturgy. Kavanagh's imaginary Mrs. Murphy symbolizes the kind of human being envisioned by select pioneers of the liturgical movement: one whose theology is incarnate in daily life. She can't explain the Mass, but she may know it better than the liturgical expert. She cannot offer a textbook definition of the meaning of the feast, but her observance of the feast is lived theology, embodied, vibrant, and in motion.

This study presents several Mrs. Murphys, ordinary people who participate in Liturgy and shared their reflections on it. Our focus group participants are theologians in the spirit of Mrs. Murphy, but I am demanding more of them than Kavanagh or Fagerberg could have imagined. To this point in the study, I have asked our theologians to articulate their reflections in words, and they have obliged. Their statements are worthy of the attention of the professional liturgists, who have the requisite training to inform the Church on what is possible for liturgical reform. The rest of this chapter will strengthen the dialogue of the people with the academy, to confirm what the people have actually received from the enterprise of liturgical reform, and to draw from their *sensus fidelium* to update the agenda of Orthodox liturgical renewal.

THE ACADEMY: RECEIVING THE PEOPLE'S CONTRIBUTION

The people can enrich the academy's work on liturgical theology by encouraging liturgists to research and reflect on the people's actual experience of the liturgy. This study has identified several potential areas for further research and reflection. We will explore most of those areas below in a revised SWOT analysis, which identifies areas of strength, weakness, opportunity, and threat. Our scheme will not identify areas of weakness or threat, but will populate all of the categories enumerated by the people under strengths or opportunities. Strengths are areas of convergence between liturgists and the people, including Eucharistic ecclesiology, the sobriety of the Liturgy, the experience of Liturgy as dying with Christ and rising to new life, the power of the proclamation of God's word, and the epic stories communicated through the feasts and commemorations of the liturgical year. Our discussion of strengths will explore ways that liturgical theologians might expand these areas of convergence with the people's faith. Opportunities are expressions of faith articulated by the people that have not been explored consistently by liturgical theologians. Identifying opportunities permits us to encourage liturgists to study and pray the Liturgy in new or different ways, not to test or correct the people's faith, but to find and expand images of God that might have been implicit or understated for some reason. Before turning to strengths and weaknesses, two issues emerging from this study of the people's faith must be examined because they are fundamental to one's participation in the Liturgy.

BIG ISSUES: UNDERSTANDING AND PARTICIPATION

The people are not always able to articulate their understanding of the Liturgy with many words, but the focus group sessions suggest that many respondents understood what was happening in the Liturgy and happening to them. Since the end of the nineteenth century up until today, liturgists have lamented the people's deficiencies in understanding the Liturgy.[4] The lack of understanding is usually attributed to the obtuse nature of liturgical symbols that ceased to develop and evolve in the aftermath of the collapse of the Byzantine empire in 1453. The Byzantine Liturgy evolved after the fifteenth century, but the invention of the printing press permitted official versions of the liturgy to be distributed on a larger scale. In other words, an earlier medieval version of the Liturgy was passed on to succeeding generations. The people of each generation evolved alongside their cultures and demographics with technological, demographic, and linguistic changes, but the Liturgy did not change with the people, retaining the symbols and linguistic idioms from decades and then centuries earlier. The twentieth century witnessed to efforts to teach the people on the meaning of the Liturgy by removing the obtuseness of ritual actions, symbols, and texts from a different era. If revising the Liturgy was not possible, then offering some catechesis on the historical development and meaning of the Liturgy was necessary.

Orthodox liturgists were certainly not alone in promoting understanding. All of the Christian churches belonging to the liturgical movement promoted a new need for participation and understanding, culminating in the canonization of Vatican II's famous teaching on the conscious and active participation of the people in the Liturgy, a teaching that was inseparable from the council's persistent emphasis on the need to teach the people about the Liturgy.[5] Liturgical catechesis is a part of most Christian churches, and this study also suggests that the people have not only learned much about the Liturgy, but hunger to learn more.

Concluding that understanding is a matter of obtaining knowledge about the Liturgy is missing the boat. Employing this approach of assessing understanding is a reduction of comprehension to possessing information. Obtaining knowledge about the historical development of the Liturgy, or receiving a fundamental explanation of its meaning is one step of a larger process of arriving at understanding. The point of deepening, expanding, and promoting liturgical understanding is to introduce the people to the telos of the Liturgy: communion with God and one another. All Liturgies have multiple symbols the people encounter and engage. Learning the historical development of a symbol is helpful as part of the process of demystifying the symbol, in the sense of permitting people to approach it with some knowledge of its function and purpose.

A good example of helpful teaching about the Liturgy and its symbols is in the Great Entrance of the Divine Liturgy. When people learn that the Great Entrance originated as the procession bringing the gifts to be offered into the church, to place them on the altar so they can be offered to God, it is helpful for people to understand that the contemporary movement is a vestige of the process of gathering and preparing bread and wine in a *skeuophylakion* or *pastophorion*, and bringing that food and drink into the church.[6] In plain terms, the Great Entrance is akin to a dinner when the host arranges for the servers to bring the food and drink into the dining room. The process requires setting the table, and the imperial heritage of the Church made that simple function of setting the table into a solemn, decorated liturgical moment. The next level of understanding would occur if the people are able to see how the process of setting the table (the Great Entrance) is connected to the main event: to express their thanksgiving to God for providing the food (i.e., to "say grace" as a community), to share the meal with one another, and to praise God, as a community, for providing the gift of his son in the food. When respondents marveled at the way people were coming together and all partook of the same meal, they were expressing this second level of understanding. It was good that some respondents had an awareness of the historical origins of the procession, but that was only the first step of the larger process.

The first level of understanding is essentially informational. The participant obtains information about the rite that was previously unknown. A participant might learn that Jesus shared a festive Jewish meal with his disciples, an occasion that included breaking bread, giving thanks, and drinking from a cup.[7] One may also learn that laity once received the body and blood of Christ separately in liturgical history, and came to receive both at the same time from a spoon around the eleventh century.[8] The respondents of our focus group sessions provided a few hints at the information they had about the Liturgy and its historical development. Most of them expressed understanding at the second level, an acknowledgment of encounter and experience in the personal and relational dimensions. Their attention to a sense of partaking in a solemn event together, a gift received from their parents and the elders of their parishes, and shared with their children highlights their attention to the personal and relational. Many of them spoke of a sense of belonging to something larger than them and their personal concerns in the moment, an informal conversational way of relating ritual experience to church as community.[9] The people were able to articulate their sense of belonging to community clearly, with reference to participating in the community's ritual together with the others who had gathered for the same purpose. When describing their understanding of the Liturgy through personal and relational references, the people were actually referring to the telos of the Liturgy itself: creating, building, and sustaining Communion with human-kind and with God. The people's lament on the exclusion of some people from the assembly sheds light on the same meaning of Liturgy: they sensed that something is not right when there are people who are unable or not allowed to partake.

The prevailing tendency of the liturgical academy is to teach Liturgy with the first level of understanding in mind. Attending to the first level of under-standing by providing the people with a clear picture of how the Liturgy has developed throughout the course of history is a necessary and valiant task. The people have confirmed the need for this genre of liturgical theology by requesting more information on liturgical history. The process of researching and writing liturgical history is laborious and time consuming, and liturgical theologians are expected to publish their research for specialists in the field, and to offer counsel to the Church in the publication of liturgical books. This kind of work does not leave much time or space to devote to the second level of understanding, reflecting on the personal and relational aspects of the Liturgy. For the Mrs. Murphys of the typical Orthodox parish, Liturgy is experienced as a personal and relational event, and the Liturgy contributes to the development of the second level of understanding. The people's revela-tion of the Liturgy as an event of belonging to the Church as community provides the liturgical academy with an opportunity to adopt a new approach to liturgical studies. The task is to explore the Liturgy as an utterly human event involving bodies in motion, dialogue, and an environment producing keen perceptions of the others participating in the event. The people have produced a vision of the Liturgy that occasions this new approach. The task is not to correct the people's perceptions of the liturgy as a human event, but to enrich them by reflecting on the rites and their capacity to build and sustain community within and outside of the parish.

Dynamics of Understanding and Participation

An essential aspect of this enrichment is the dynamic relationship between understanding and participation. The people testified to increasing participa-tion on the basis of understanding. Increasing participation has been an ob-jective of liturgical renewal in Orthodoxy for over a century.[10] The primary rationale for increasing participation is the nature of the church itself. The entire church participates in offering the gift to God and receiving Christ in return, just as children participate in a meal prepared and presided over by adults. The bulk of discussion on active participation in the liturgy occurs on the surface and concerns the visible and audial dimensions of ritual. Theolo-gians across Christian traditions have proposed liturgical adjustments to in-

crease the people's participation, especially in the composition and performance of liturgical music. In Orthodoxy, musicians and liturgical historians
have demonstrated that several liturgical components are to be sung by all of
the people, especially responses to litanies, acclamations like "Alleluia," and
common refrains threaded throughout the liturgical offices. When the people
join in the singing, they are participating in the ritual along with the appointed liturgical leaders.

Like the discussion on understanding above, participation has several
levels. Mark Searle, the late Roman Catholic expert on liturgical and ritual
studies, asserted that Vatican II's teaching on the full active and conscious
participation of the people in the Liturgy had a telos beyond the people
singing the parts appointed to them.[11] Ritual participation was the first of
three levels. The second level of participation is communion with the Church
by joining in the Liturgy with Christ, the head of the body. The third level of
participation is to partake of the life of God, through Christ. Stephen Wilbricht and Gabriel Pivarnik are two Roman Catholic theologians who have
further developed Searle's thesis on liturgical participation as strengthening
the bonds of Communion with God and the Church.[12]

Patristic Mystagogy and Understanding

Orthodoxy honors this same sense of participation, especially in its Greek
patristic heritage of sacramental theosis epitomized by the mystagogies of
Cyril of Jerusalem, Maximus Confessor, and Nicholas Cabasilas in particular. In the middle to late medieval eras, the popular mystagogies of Byzantine
liturgy were occasionally published in liturgical books as quasi-official explanations of the Divine Liturgy.[13] The mystagogy of the Liturgy authored
by Patriarch Germanos of Constantinople in the eighth century (early eighth
century) was particularly popular because of his explanation of the Liturgy as
a mimesis of the events in the life of Christ, an allegorical presentation of the
Liturgy akin to the earlier mystagogy of Theodore of Mopsuestia.[14] Paul
Meyendorff explains that Germanos's mystagogy was likely inspired by the
iconoclastic crisis, so his description of the liturgy invites the worshipper to
create a mental image of Christ's life in relation to liturgical components.[15]
An outcome of this mystagogical approach was to follow this allegorical
pattern and explain participation in the Liturgy as a way of remembering the
life of Christ. Alexander Schmemann was outspoken in his public expression
of distaste for the "illustrative symbolism" of the classical Byzantine mystagogies, reserving respect only for the liturgical treatise of Maximus Confessor, who viewed the Liturgy itself as an ascent to God resulting in Communion.[16] Schmemann laments the reduction of the Liturgy to a dramatic representation of the life of Christ and interprets Maximus's treatise, suggesting
that the liturgical symbols "make present and active the ascension of the

human soul to God and communion with him."[17] Schmemann also says that the symbols enable "theoria," which he describes as "knowledge and contemplation of these saving mysteries."[18]

Schmemann's reading of Maximus's mystagogy distinguishes Liturgy as dramatic representation from Liturgy as encounter with the living God. Schmemann is not alone in this regard: Taft also views the liturgy as the place of encounter between God and humankind, and uses the image of the creation of Adam painted by Michelangelo in the Sistine Chapel as a powerful illustration of this point.[19] Taft's approach differs from Schmemann's as Taft accounts for the entire historical development of Byzantine liturgical commentary as necessary for understanding how the Liturgy came to be interpreted as both a dramatic representation and communion with God.[20]

Is Byzantinism Necessary?

Schmemann questions the need to continue to retain Byzantinism in Orthodox liturgy.[21] Schmemann offered his own mystagogical reflection on the Divine Liturgy, posthumously published as *The Eucharist*.[22] In this book, Schmemann suggests that the Liturgy itself reveals the authentic personal and relational given to humankind by God. He develops the renewed personal and relational aspects of liturgy through the rite of the kiss of peace (a sacred rite of love):[23]

> I really don't know the man who is standing across from me in church. I can neither love him nor not love him, for he is a stranger to me and thus no one. And we are so afraid of this hollow form, so utterly sincere in our individualism and egocentrism that we forget the chief thing. We forget that in our call to "greet one another with a holy kiss," we are talking not of our personal, natural, human love, through which we cannot in fact love someone who is a stranger, but of the love of Christ, the eternal wonder of which consists precisely in the fact that it transforms the stranger (and each stranger, in his depths, is an enemy) into a brother, irrespective of whether he has or does not have relevance for me and for my life; that it is the very purpose of the Church to overcome the horrible alienation that was introduced into the world by the devil and proved to be its undoing. And we forget that we come to the church for this love, which is always granted to us in the gathering of the brethren.

Schmemann's passage coheres nicely with the reflections on the Liturgy offered by the people of our focus groups. His passage reveals the process of liturgical participation as an authentic struggle. Many of the people confessed their alienation from others in church in expressing their anxiety about people's perceptions of their receiving Holy Communion, or annoyance with people who decided to sing in the choir even though they had been absent for much of Lent and Holy Week. The people's personal responses to their relations with others are real, regardless of one's attempt to rationalize or dismiss them. Schmemann suggests that participating in the kiss of peace appointed by the Liturgy capacitates the participant to receive the love of God that permits one to see the same suspicious people as authentic brothers and sisters.[24] One could argue that it is the same gift of God that removes the scales from the eyes of the people so they are able to lament the conditions that cause others to be excluded from the Eucharistic assembly.

Understanding *through* Participation

I have privileged Schmemann's passage from his book on the Eucharist because he attends to the utterly human characteristic of the liturgical assembly. His passage is also a strong example of the dynamic and reciprocal relationship between understanding and participation. Simply doing one's part by engaging the appointed rite opens a door to receive the gift of God. The exchange of the kiss of peace ushers one into the possibility to participate in God's life of love, and to share that love with the strangers one encounters in the assembly—and also in the world. Schmemann's example is particularly potent because he fuses participation in the life of God with strengthening communion with one's fellow brothers and sisters. There is no doubt that faithful who learn about the origins of the kiss of peace will understand its place in the liturgy and perhaps feel compelled about engaging it, which is one way understanding and participation cooperate. When participation in the rite permits one to receive God's gift and thus to see other people in a new and different way, authentic understanding is the outcome of this process.

One of the lessons the liturgical academy can learn from the people's testimony on liturgical understanding is to leave ample space for reflection on the deep layers of what happens when one participates in the Liturgy. Liturgical theologians do not need to attempt to formalize or canonize the vocabulary for these levels of understanding. The exercise can be more reflective than formal, as the canonization of a particular theological interpretation of a rite can result in rigidity. The people's difficulty in finding the words to describe the deeper layers of understanding is instructive: it may be that a core feature of what is happening in rite evades sure words, outside of expressions of wonder and gratitude. The task for the liturgical theologian is essentially the same as it is when liturgists take on the hard scientific work of liturgical history: ultimately, the objective is to show the Church how liturgy developed, and what is possible on the basis of solid historical research. The professional theologian's reflection joins the chorus of the people's uncertain words about understanding: the theologian does not need to correct the people's theology, but to act like an informed tour guide as the people make their way through the liturgy. In other words, the professional theologian performs his or her work alongside the people, who are also theologians.

UNVEILING THE COMPASSIONATE GOD

The second major issue presented to us by the people is theological: their testimony points to a desire for an encounter with a compassionate God, one who walks through this life in solidarity with the people. Going on a journey with God means that the experiences of this life, its joys, sorrows, triumphs, defeats, and doubts all find a place in the Liturgy. This assertion is not an appeal to transform the Liturgy into a series of petitions for help or to reduce liturgical participation to the emotional. It is an acknowledgment that the people bring the entirety of their lives with them into liturgical prayer, for better or worse. They testified that they try hard to lay aside their earthly cares and focus on God, yet take comfort in the great stories of enduring temptation, suffering loss, and witnessing to sacrifice communicated to us in the Liturgy. The people discover sympathetic saints such as Mary of Egypt, Mary Theotokos, and Christ himself through their liturgical participation.

Divine Compassion in Liturgical Texts

One might be tempted to reject the notion that liturgical theologians should labor at disclosing the compassionate God through the liturgical experience. Christ's Pascha is the entire foundation of the liturgical experience. Countless liturgical services call upon the people to wonder at God's love for humankind, manifest in his willingness to take on human nature, live and dwell among us, receive Baptism for the remission of sins from the hand of the prophet, suffer the indignity of mocking, shame, and crucifixion, to die among thieves and be buried in the same ground he created. In Byzantine liturgy, participants are constantly recalling Christ's Passion: hymns exhort the people to glorify Christ, to praise Him for all that he has done for us. Christ's condescension to be with humanity is expressed seasonally, as the hymns of Christmas and the feast of the Cross call upon the people to marvel that Jesus' birth and death have removed the flaming sword guarding the gate of paradise.[25] The same theme is evoked at each Divine Liturgy, offered in memory of Christ's death and resurrection. The primary service of Good Friday is the Matins with the Twelve Gospel readings, and many focus group participants mentioned this service during sessions. Each Gospel reading is bracketed by two acclamations. "Glory to the Passion, o Lord" is the acclamation beginning each reading, and "Glory to your longsuffering, o Lord" concludes it. The act of singing these hymns is one of thanksgiving to God for suffering as a human being, a suffering that was lifegiving, done for all of us. The thanksgiving is not limited to the wonder that God would suffer as a human: the people give thanks because Christ's suffering has removed the cherubim with the flaming sword guarding that gate at paradise. In plain terms, this means that Christians now have the privilege of living together in Communion with God as their Father.

It is easy to demonstrate that the Byzantine Liturgy not only discloses the incarnate God who became flesh, suffered, died, was buried, and rose from the dead. The Liturgy is quite explicit in communicating Christ's passion and suffering, and the Liturgy connects his suffering with the resurrection and ascension into heaven, to grant holy confidence to the worshipping assembly that human life will be lived with God with no end. The Liturgy is saturated with words and images of Christ's passion and his victory over death.

Divine and Human Companionship

The Eucharistic revival of the twentieth century was an occasion to renew the Liturgy as an experience of companionship. This companionship was to be experienced both horizontally and vertically by the people. The horizontal experience of companionship is to participate in the Eucharistic Liturgy with the other members of the community; the vertical dimension is to break bread with Christ, who presides at the Liturgy and is present among us. Companionship draws from the metaphor of sharing bread (com-panis), a potent ritual vibrant in both religious and domestic traditions that refers to strengthening the bonds holding communities together.[26] The primary biblical source for companionship was the story of the disciples in Emmaus (Luke 24), who journey with a stranger that explains Christ's Paschal mystery to them, only to recognize that Christ himself was the stranger when he took bread, broke it, and gave thanks. The sensation of the burning heart served as the impetus to enliven discipleship among the laity in the twentieth century, as participation in the Eucharist could capacitate the laity's service to the world, and even make social transformation possible.

In the Christian context, companionship can have the capacity to end divisions in communities of all sizes. Mark Searle suggested that companionship could become a "company of strangers" in parish life.[27] Approaching the Eucharistic assembly as a company of strangers is a way of reducing emphasis on the formation of exclusive and like-minded cohorts within a parish, and to recognize the assembly as a gathering of strangers. Sharing a holy meal with a stranger is an initial step toward breaking down the divisions afflicting communities, a way to build an experienced communion that exists not only at the eschatological level, but also in the present, so that the present is an icon of the future life to be shared by all in God. Schmemann's exposition on the kiss of peace and its potential to transform a stranger into a brother echoes Searle here.[28]

The respondents in our study seemed to recognize the experience of companionship during liturgical participation. They expressed joy that all had come together for the Liturgy, and the inclusion of children enhanced a sense of sharing bread with everyone. The lament of some on the obstacles to sharing bread with those on the other side of the window also refers to the strong sense of companionship in the Liturgy.

Authentic Compassion

Companionship, however, does not always translate into a strong sense of compassion. Expressions of the joy in sharing the Eucharist with the community were accompanied by fear that others disapproved of their participation. Several respondents noted that they felt as if others in the assembly were judging them and questioning their worthiness to participate. The joy of companionship is mitigated by the stench of the fear of rejection. It is difficult to disentangle the fear of rejection from the strong sense of acceptance: why does this fear persist amidst the joy of partaking with others in a community?

Fear as an Obstacle to Receiving Compassion

The vast majority of respondents who volunteered remarks on their experience of Holy Communion said that they partake frequently, some of them regularly. Many older respondents noted that frequent reception of Holy Communion began when they were older, as the prevalent pattern of their childhood was to partake infrequently. Many of the older respondents expressed this tension of approaching Communion (because one should) while worrying that perhaps they were unworthy. Only a few respondents referred to the possibility of damnation resulting from unworthy reception of Communion in the focus groups, but we know that the fear of damnation was prevalent with Communion, especially during the period before the Eucharistic revival, when people received only a few times in the liturgical year.

Respondents who reported frequent reception of Communion also reflected on their desire to be more adequately prepared to receive. They expressed some relief that the Church now permits people to receive, as there is really no act or rite one can perform that makes one truly worthy of the gift. The relief at the Church's mercy was contradicted by their own regret that they are not as adequately prepared as they should be. When older respondents said that they sensed other people appraising them with disapproval, they are articulating an underlying desire for acceptance. In other cases, respondents asserted that they are accepted and belong to the community, but this sentiment is not threaded consistently throughout the stream of conversation.

Tangible Symbols of Compassion

The utter humanity of the liturgical experience is shaping the expression of sentiments by the people in this case. Even though they are admitted to the assembly and able to participate in its liturgical rituals, they still long for tangible signs of acceptance from the other people gathered to worship. In this sense, the liturgical ritual is akin to other daily rituals. When someone buys lunch and goes to a communal seating area, they hope to sit with others who will affirm their presence and engage them in conversation, signs of acceptance and belonging. It is an utterly human experience, and in the liturgical ritual, the other humans present are the ones who communicate acceptance and affirmation of belonging through all idioms of communication, verbal, nonverbal, and bodily. Any action that does not communicate acceptance can raise doubt in a participant, even if it is unintended. In this case, the humans are the ones who communicate divine acceptance or rejection as well. If a given parishioner senses that I have not prepared adequately, perhaps I am unworthy—not only of receiving Communion, but of belonging to the body of Christ altogether.

Liturgical participants seek signals of divine affirmation and acceptance, and this is why they find comfort in the liturgical offices that narrate stories of saints whose experiences are utterly human. Mary of Egypt endured sexual passion and temptation, and navigated the memory of past sin, just like everyone else does.[29] Mary the mother of God raised a son, worried for him, and had to confront his untimely and unjust death, a human experience that people have to occasionally confront. When liturgical stories communicate real human experiences one can recognize, it creates a sense of suffering together for the liturgical participant.

The Byzantine Liturgy presents countless messages of Christ's passion and suffering, especially in liturgical seasons calling on the assembly to immerse themselves in the biblical accounts of Christ's life. The assembly's collective anamnesis of Christ's suffering and passion is not the same activity as having a sense of Christ walking with us in the present life, and suffering with us as we navigate crises of our own creation, or those that have come to us. The people tended to identify liturgical offices that communicated tangible presence clearly, as we have seen with the examples of Mary, Mother of God and Mary of Egypt. Mary's lament at Christ's tomb evokes the image of a mother weeping over her son; because she suffered from the shock of Jesus' death in the past, it is a small step to petition her to weep and lament with us in the present. Hilda Graef observed that Christian devotion to Mary exploded in the fifth century, not only because of the Council of Ephesus and the Mariology that developed as a by-product of conciliar Christology, but because the emphasis on Christ's divinity had become so accentuated that Mary filled the gap by becoming the holy person who was both approachable and of sufficient stature that God would hear her prayers.[30]

The Byzantine lectionary's lessons appointed to Sundays depict Jesus among the people, talking with them, healing, praying, and feeding them. The lessons unveil the Incarnate God in our midst, and also reveal the God whom the feeble, ill, and sinful dared to approach. The lessons tend to say that Jesus had compassion on the multitude, especially when they had been with him for a long day of hearing his teaching, and were hungry and thirsty. These lessons are threaded throughout the liturgical year, especially during the Sundays after Pascha.[31] On these Sundays, Jesus has compassion on the paralytic, and the blind man and his parents, healing them despite the fierce quality of their infirmities. Jesus encounters the Samaritan woman at Jacob's well, and not only does he converse with her, but he promises her the gift of living water, even as he exposes her sin. On Thomas Sunday, Jesus has compassion on the doubting disciple, healing his deficiency of faith. In addition to the Sundays after Pascha, the final and fifteenth reading from Daniel (3:1–57) appointed to the Holy Saturday liturgy recalled by one of our respondents recalls the three holy youths praising God after being cast in the fiery furnace by the Babylonian King Nebuchadnezzar. Instead of being burned to death, they sang their hymn to God and were joined by a fourth mysterious person identified as Christ in Christian tradition. A special place is reserved for Lazarus Saturday (the day before Palm Sunday), when the people hear how Jesus was deeply moved by the grief of the community, and himself wept. All of these images of compassion are communicated by the Liturgy of the Word—and perhaps this is why a grieving daughter requested that the Johannine lesson of the raising of Lazarus be proclaimed at her father's funeral.

Liturgical theologians have not hidden the image of the suffering Christ from the Byzantine Liturgy. A significant achievement of the Eucharistic revival and the ecclesiology accompanying it was the recovery of the presence of the living, risen Christ with his people at the Liturgy. Christ himself presides at the Divine Liturgy, as stated by the end of the prayer of apology recited by the presider in preparation for the anaphora, "for you are the one who both offers and is offered . . . ."[32] In his magisterial exposition on the Divine Liturgy of St. John Chrysostom and its Paschal foundation, Robert Taft asserts that the people are receiving the living Christ in Holy Communion, and not merely a dead cadaver.[33] Taft is talking about the multiple epicleses that occur during the Liturgy: when the Holy Spirit descends upon the gifts during the anaphora, the Spirit makes the living Christ present. The pouring of the *zeon* (hot water) into the cup likewise signifies the Spirit's descent, enabling the faithful to partake of the blood of the living Christ. Christ is present throughout the Liturgy: Christ is the one who offers peace when the presider intones, "peace be unto all!" Christ is the one who draws all to the assembly to pray together. Christ establishes the laity's priesthood that enables them to join in his offering to the Father and sing the thrice-holy hymn. The singing of the thrice-holy hymn, which occurs at two different times in the Divine Liturgy, is a priestly act: the people praise God without angelic mediation, a doxology made possible by Christ's presence and gift of priesthood to them. These examples do not exhaust the images of Christ's presence in the Liturgy with the people: the customary greeting for each Sunday is "Christ is in our midst! He is and always shall be!", another affirmation that Liturgy is a gathering of the holy people of God with the living Christ among them, leading them, offering petitions and gifts for the life of the world with them.

Because the Orthodox Church has retained a substantial portion of its Byzantine legacy, the Liturgy is saturated with numerous images of Christ and God. The hymns, especially the "Monogenes" or Only-Begotten Son (the Troparion, or hymn-refrain of the second antiphon), accentuate the Christology of the conciliar tradition.[34] Christ is the eternal God who took on human flesh and he is to be glorified with the Father and the Spirit, as the Nicene-Constantinopolitan Creed recited or sung at each Liturgy exhorts. Dozens of hymns honor holy theologians who contributed to the formation of the Christological tradition, a legacy that safeguards Christ's divinity and proclaims his substantial equality with the Father, without diminishing his human nature. The anaphora prayers also proclaim this Christology.

When paired with the human images of Christ presented to the people in the Liturgy, his divinity tends to take precedence. The Church does not privilege Christ's divine nature intentionally; this is a perception of how people hear the Liturgy, which contains several refrains exhorting the people to praise "Christ our God." Theologians would call upon the people to marvel that the one exalted as "Christ our God" makes himself present to the people at each Liturgy, inviting them to co-offer the Liturgy and receive him as the gift.

Liturgy resists reduction to personal experience because it is a communal gathering consisting of corporate prayer. There is no space in Byzantine Liturgy for a participant to offer his or her personal prayer: one could argue that the Church's prayer is objective, and that liturgical structures call people to adjust their minds, hearts, and souls to offer the prayer to God and seal it with their Amen.[35] The prayer is the Church's offering, not an individual's. We observed earlier that the Liturgy calls people to attention, to set aside their personal cares in preparation for the encounter with the living God. The Liturgy does not dismiss personal concerns such as illness, disaster, or war: it calls upon the community to pray for God's mercy upon those afflicted at the appointed times.

The combination of Liturgy as a communal event in which Christ is present as the lover of humankind and yet distant as the only-begotten Son of

God does not appoint a tangible liturgical component for people to reflect on Christ journeying with them and confronting the particular challenges posed to them on a daily basis. Christ's presence with the people is implied on a daily basis: Christ is with the people throughout the week following the Liturgy through the Communion they received, he is with them if they assemble for the Liturgy of the Hours, and when they recite the Church's prayers at the appointed times of the day, since the Church is still praying together, even if it is not assembled in one space.

These images promise the presence of Christ among his people, but there is no tangible liturgical rite, unit, or component from which one can glean that "He is here, now, embracing you as you fret about your job, holding your hand as you grieve the loss of a loved one, shedding tears with you as you weep because of loneliness, or on account of guilt." Though the Liturgy seems to discourage this kind of personal extrapolation, there can be no doubt that people want to sense that Christ is with them when they bring their anxieties into the holy assembly, and remains with them when they depart the assembly and return to the grind of daily life. The people's desire to be close to Christ in his humanity is the reason they flock to venerate the wood of the cross on the appointed feasts, rush to fill their jars with water on Theophany, and set the text of the Jesus Prayer to music, singing it as a Koinonikon at the liturgy, even though its appointed place is in private prayer. The practice in Chile of enormous crowds gathered for long festivals carrying huge statues of Jesús Nazareno provides an ecumenical affirmation of the desire for divine compassion.[36] Such practices and explosions of devotion evidence the people's relentless pursuit of divine compassion: if the official Liturgy doesn't make space for it, they'll find a way to ritualize divine compassion by venerating a tangible Christ.

The people's testimony of communal belonging, experiences of joy through praying and dining with others, relief of comfort that the two Marys are suffering with them show that the Liturgy communicates and affirms shared compassion by members of the entire holy assembly, those in the world together with the saints who are alive in Christ. There is no need for the liturgical academy to discourage people from tuning into the utter humanity of the liturgical event—it is their natural inclination to seek human companionship and compassion. The Liturgy's saturation with images of Christ our God protect and honor Christ's divine nature, equal to and shared with the Father. Christ's divinity is a hallmark of Byzantine Liturgy, and it need not change. Liturgical theologians can use the arrangement of the Lectionary as a foundation for presenting the image of Jesus in the midst of his people, touching them, eating and drinking with them, sensing them reaching out to him for a glimpse of his divine power, and weeping with them. The lectionary provides a teaching tool for liturgists to assure the people that Liturgy is not limited to glorifying Christ for his suffering in the past, but also assures that he is truly co-passionate with them in the present.[37] The most crucial task for the liturgical theologian is to articulate how the experience of joining Christ's offering at Liturgy assures us that he is present and suffering, lamenting, and weeping with us in the present grind of daily life. The people will continue to find ways to ritualize divine compassion: the experience of the Church's Liturgy will be enriched when liturgical theologians explore this dimension of Liturgy with the same vigor with which they honor Christ as God. The Liturgy exhorts Christians to fall down and worship Christ our God: the Liturgy also presents an image of Christ as the Incarnate God who was seen, heard, touched, smelled, ate and drank, born and raised, and buried.

Searching for a Holy Advocate

People are in a constant search for a holy advocate to bring their prayers and intercessions before the throne of God. The popular cult of Mary Theotokos is fervent throughout the world, and perhaps especially so among Latinos in Mexico, and Central and South America.[38] Mary's appearance to Juan Diego has resulted in an explosion of daily, seasonal, and annual entreaties made to Mary, bearing her image, singing songs in her honor, and often offered on bended knees. The image of our Lady of Guadalupe adorns churches, homes, car fenders, and human bodies. The memory of her appearance in the flesh inspires hope that she will continue to hear and present the people's prayers to God.

This kind of popular piety remains alive and well throughout the world. More than one million people stood in a cold November line in Moscow (2014) for a chance to venerate Mary's belt, brought to Christ the Savior Cathedral by the monks of Vatopedi Monastery.[39] In Russia, people have also turned to Tsar Nicholas II, the Passion-Bearer, to advocate for them before God's throne with the reproduction and distribution of his icon.[40] People flock to monasteries to pray and entreat at the graves of holy men and women; they organize solemn liturgies to honor holy presence when an icon begins to stream myrrh; they make pilgrimages to holy temples to ask a saint for their holy prayers.[41] They stand before icons in their private homes, intoning the names of loved ones and friends, and ask for God's compassion. The piety surrounding relics of Jesus himself is well known—almost every divine service of the Byzantine tradition calls for the people to kiss his icon and his cross, and nothing could be more personal and human than to receive Communion, the co-mingling of his body with ours, his blood running through our veins. Christians throughout the world continue to gather in Jerusalem to be near his place of burial and resurrection, and one of the most powerful religious experiences occurs when a crowd keeping vigil at the Church of the Holy Sepulchre exclaims joy and wonder at the appearance of the annual "holy fire," which is then distributed to churches to light the first tapers proclaiming Christ's resurrection.

Academics have analyzed the people's pious traditions in venerating the saints and ritualizing the relics belonging to Mary and Christ. These cases are significant because they testify to an enormous swell of desire to be in the physical presence of the holy people who pray to God for us. In the absence of the living saints, people turn to the material items they left behind—their human remains, clothing, possessions, and the icons depicting them. The desire for holy compassion is inexorably affixed to human need, that God would comfort the afflicted, cure diseases, make the barren fertile, and mend relationships. The prayers and petitions offered to the saints and Mary are sent up in the hope that they would plead our case before God. It is possible that the force of the people's faith to ritualize holy compassion, even converting it into actual liturgical rites, is an organic response within the Church to a deficit of expressions of holy compassion. One could argue that the people are doing what they have always done by providing the only adequate response to liturgical imbalances. I submit that the examples provided here belong to seasons or exceptional rites; there is ample space for a more robust expression of holy compassion in the ordinary liturgical cycles, an opportunity ripe for exploration by the liturgical academy.

STRENGTHS OF THE LITURGICAL ACADEMY

Many of the testimonies offered by the people cohere strongly with the legacy of the Orthodox liturgical academy over the last century. I have identified them as strengths because the people's ability to refer to particular practices and their effects testifies to the positive contributions made by the liturgical academy for the life of the Church. When academics make contributions to the life of the Church, they are manifestations of the value of studying theology for informing the Church. Academic contributions also confirm that many academics are of the Church, and work within the Church for its building up. In addition to identifying the strengths of the liturgical academy in this section, I will also elaborate on areas that liturgical theologians might expand or clarify.

Eucharistic Ecclesiology

A sense of joy in sharing Communion with others was a sentiment threading the four focus group sessions. The sessions were essentially bereft of interpretations of Communion or prayer as a private matter. A number of people commented on their joy to come together with everyone else for all of the occasions in church. The sense of community was neither simple nor idealistic. Anxiety on the way others appraised their participation along with annoyance about those who joined the assembly for the penultimate service of Pascha exposed the realities of community life. People assemble together to pray, but they also bicker and complain, and worry about others' perceptions of them. The annoyance and anxiety expressed about other people in the liturgical assembly manifests a reality of Orthodox parish life in North America: people tend to know one another. A parish of 300 or more people is considered to be large, and most importantly, there is only one Divine Liturgy served in most Sunday parishes. There are a few exceptions in larger parishes, especially if there is a pastoral need to serve Liturgy in more than one language, in which case there could be a second Divine Liturgy. The prevalent pattern for parishes is to have one Sunday assembly.

The typical Orthodox parish, then, is smaller than a medium-sized Catholic parish, and the experience of sharing Liturgy together on a regular basis differs from congregations that schedule several services on weekends. The smaller size of the typical Orthodox parish lends itself to familiarity with the other people. Most parishes in America now have a social hour following the Liturgy on Sunday, and it is common for visitors to be invited to join the community at this informal gathering. These coffee hours are often unofficial ways for people unfamiliar with the Orthodox Church to become acquainted with it, through the people.

Familiarity is shaped primarily through the Sunday assembly. The Eucharistic ecclesiology of the twentieth century attained theological prominence through the theological contributions of pioneers such as John Zizioulas, Nicholas Afanasiev, and Henri de Lubac. De Lubac canonized the ascension of Eucharistic ecclesiology by coining the comparison of "The Church makes the Eucharist," in reference to the medieval synthesis on the transformation of the gifts, to "The Eucharist makes the Church," referring to the transformation of the people through liturgical participation.[42] Afanasiev's theology elucidates the local assembly as the one bearing the fullness of the Church.[43] In his magisterial work on the Church of the Holy Spirit, Afanasiev uses the phrase "epi to auto" from Acts 2, describing the gathering of the apostles in one place. The gathering of the apostles in one place becomes an image of the gathering of the local church. This image is powerful because it is tangible: one can literally see the Church gathered together to offer the Liturgy in a particular place. The Eucharist is the event that gathers the people together in this one place, and the descent of the Spirit on the people manifests the local church as bearing the fullness of the one, holy, catholic, and apostolic Church. Christ is fully present among his people by the descent of the Spirit at each local gathering, so it is in the local church where one receives the divine commission to serve Christ in the world.

The people did not use words like these to express the Eucharistic ecclesiology of Afanasiev, but I believe there is considerable convergence between the people's theology of the local Eucharist and Eucharistic ecclesiology. The people's experience of the Liturgy is shaped by the local quality of the Church. They meet in a tangible, identifiable place, and have a sense that they are all members of a diverse body that has assembled for the same purpose. Remarks about the older and younger generations of the Church speak to the diversity of the local body of the Church. Many of the older people were keenly attuned to the experiences of the children in Liturgy. Some of them expressed joy over the children's full participation, whereas others were worried that the children might not be adequately instructed about the meaning of the Liturgy. A strong sense of tradition prevailed: respondents expressed gratitude and wonder about the elders who had partaken piously of the Liturgy all their lives, and many of them had a grave sense of responsibility of passing the tradition on to the children. The convergence of the liturgical academy with the people is most noticeable in the people's observation that they were all gathered together for the event, and the Liturgy presumes that all will participate completely in the event. The people's testimony seems to confirm Schmemann's oft-repeated description of the Liturgy as a corporate event, one involving the entire body.[44]

The academy's contribution to the liturgical experience is not limited to teaching: many of the actual ritual revisions shaped by theologians have been part of the people's formation. The first one is obvious, namely the Eucharistic revival attributed to Schmemann. A handful of respondents recalled their liturgical participation prior to the opening of more frequent participation in Communion. Corporate participation in Communion reveals a unity of assembly in performing a ritual action. Before the Eucharistic revival, in many cases, the people bore the appearance of passive spectators at Liturgy, as the priest said the prayers and performed the main ritual actions, while a chanter or choir sang the responses. The primary function of the people was to sit (or stand), observe, and listen. The paradigm shifted with liturgical attention to the people's part of the Liturgy. The opening up of Communion for the regular participation was the primary component, but it was not the only one. The people were also invited to sing parts of the liturgy originally appointed to them, especially responses like Litanies, common refrains, and certain hymns. This description of the people's participation resembles the images of active and conscious participation in the Liturgy associated with the teachings of Vatican II, and the shifts in practice have common roots in the liturgical movement. Teachers like Schmemann and Calivas shaped generations of clergy who found ways to implement these practices in parishes, to varying degrees. The convergence of Eucharistic ecclesiology with the people's expression of Liturgy as a communal event was therefore intentional. The people notice that everyone is doing the same thing because all of the people are engaging the appointed rites. When a respondent observed that only the children had lined up for Communion a generation ago, she implied a major shift in practice: presently, the adults join the children so that all receive Communion together. Communities that engage rite as a unified body are able to glean the theology from the ritual, an outcome of the Liturgy illustrated when the adults felt a deeper connection to the children because they were participating together. That's one of the points of Eucharistic ecclesiology, that all have a sense of connecting with one another and deepening the bonds of communion.

EXTENDING COMMUNION TO THE OTHER SIDE OF THE WINDOW

If Eucharistic ecclesiology has confirmed the local assembly as a place of gathering that generates and strengthens bonds of belonging, it has not had a significant impact on healing the divisions that exclude non-Orthodox from Eucharistic participation. This does not mean that scholars have not imagined the universal, united Church through the Eucharist. Many Orthodox theologians capitalized on twentieth-century events to work towards the restoration of broken Communion. Sergius Bulgakov's efforts at rapprochement through the brotherhood of Saints Sergius and Alban is the best example, and he was motivated by the urgency generated from the human catastrophe of the twentieth century.[45] Afanasiev's name appears again, as one whose ecclesiological work brought him to desire the restoration of the *Una Sancta*.[46] Michael Plekon has narrated the stories of Eastern Orthodox theologians who not only labored in the West, but worked with Western Christians to mend fences: Paul Evdokimov, Maria Skobtsova, Lev Gillet, Antoine Arjakovsky, and Plekon himself exemplify a school of theologians that ceased viewing the Western Church as adversarial, and envisioned a Eucharistic Communion beyond the bonds forged by common projects.[47]

The Anti-ecumenical Turn in Orthodoxy

In reality, the Orthodox Church has taken a clear turn away from the table of ecumenical dialogue.[48] Orthodoxy still appoints representatives to carry on the dialogue, but internal disagreement on how to address controversial issues has motivated local Orthodox Churches to approach ecumenism with caution. The Ecumenical Patriarchate remains committed to ecumenism, especially in its longstanding dialogue with the Roman Catholic Church, and other individual churches promote dialogue.[49] Concern about the permeation of radical ideologies through the Church is the most likely reason for Orthodoxy's cautious approach. Many Orthodox refer to the decision of mainline Protestant Churches to ordain women to the priesthood as a symbol of change, but concern about radicalism is not limited to fear of feminism. Most Orthodox Churches hold conservative views on the emergence of new social patterns such as toleration of cohabitation without marriage, premarital sex, and inclusion of LGBT people in the life of the Church. Orthodox theologians tend to hold "the West" responsible for permitting the toleration of new social movements in the world, a development in the mindset of Orthodoxy that only enhanced its already unfavorable view of other Christian Churches.[50]

Orthodoxy's hesitance to engage the West in anything more than polite dialogue perpetuates the canonical separation of the Churches that prohibits Western Christians from receiving Communion in Orthodox parishes. One could counter that plenty of Orthodox leaders and theologians not only engage Western Christians, but pray with them. The ecumenical patriarch's semi-annual common appearances with the Pope include some element of common prayer in addition to warm gestures of embracing and the kiss of peace.[51] On the official level, Orthodox leaders have more recently made public gestures illustrating their growing alienation from the West. Russian Orthodox Patriarch Kirill's renowned Havana encounter with Pope Francis produced a common declaration, but the Pope and Patriarch did not pray together, a demand presented by the Russian contingent prior to agreeing to the meeting. Orthodoxy's withdrawal from ecumenical dialogue was manifest at the Holy and Great Council that convened in Crete in June 2016. The bishops' discussion on the correct words to use in reference to non-Orthodox Christian Churches stirred the most controversy at the assembly. After stating that the Orthodox Church is the One, Holy, Catholic and Apostolic Church, the bishops agreed that non-Orthodox communities could be called "Church" only because these communities identify themselves as Church, referring to the literal use of the word "Church" in their "historical names."[52] The council also decreed that "marriage between Orthodox and non-Orthodox Christians is forbidden according to canonical *akrebeia*."[53] While the council deferred enforcement of canons to the synods of local autocephalous churches, the conciliar position on marriage reflects Orthodoxy's current unease with Christian ecumenism. The conciliar rejection of accepting civil marriages without ritual celebration and prohibition of same-sex marriages in the Church ties all the issues together: privileging marriages between two Orthodox Christians will protect the Church's values relating to marriage, sexual orientation, and ecumenism. The decrees of the Council in Crete are widely viewed as representing mainstream, progressive Orthodox thought on the Church, the world, contemporary issues, and relations with other Christians. There is no shortage of critics of the Council of Crete within the Orthodox Church, represented by the withdrawal of four autocephalous Churches from the Council itself (Antioch, Georgia, Russia, and Bulgaria).

An analysis of Orthodoxy's alienation from the rest of Christianity is a worthy topic to be developed elsewhere. I have documented these select examples from recent Orthodox events to show how opposition to ecumenism is gaining momentum within churches that have historically adopted progressive approaches. It is difficult to envision non-Orthodox Christians receiving Communion in the Orthodox Church when its patriarchs won't pray with other Christian leaders in public. Pastors have been blessing marriages between Orthodox and non-Orthodox Christians for decades, and performing the rites of crowning. The conciliar statement confirming such marriages to be uncanonical was a tepid rejection of the longstanding practice, with the possibility for the application of *oikonomia* a consolation for pastors called upon to bless such marriages. [54]

The conciliar decrees represent the official teaching of most of the Orthodox churches. One cannot presume that local clergy will adopt the decrees and enforce all of their components. Parish policies on Holy Communion have some variants. It has become customary in many parishes to publish an announcement on receiving Holy Communion. Normally, the announcement states that only Orthodox Christians can receive Holy Communion. The pastor may invite non-Orthodox Christians to come forward for a blessing during Communion, or to receive some of the antidoron, the remainder of the bread that had been baked for the Eucharist given to the people after Communion or at the end of Liturgy. The pastor or a delegate might make a verbal announcement on the Church's policy on Holy Communion immediately prior to distribution. Pastors trust that visitors will respect the Church's policy. Occasionally, pastors will inquire if a communicant is Orthodox, and will give a blessing or direct the communicant away if he or she is not Orthodox. In some places, Orthodox pastors will permit non-Orthodox Christians participating in the Divine Liturgy to receive Communion. In these cases of pastors knowingly imparting Communion to non-Orthodox Christians, Communion is offered on the basis of a "don't ask, don't tell" policy. In one way or another, all of these approaches revolve around the official Church policy of communing only Orthodox Christians at the Divine Liturgy. The anti-ecumenical turn within the Church may make it more difficult for clergy sympathetic to the ecumenical movement to continue a policy of asking for forgiveness instead of permission.

The sorrow experienced by some of our focus group respondents on the exclusion of people from participating in Communion clashes with the anti-ecumenical turn and its inevitable effect on Communion policies. Their own participation in Communion rendered them thankful, but wishing they could share the gift with others. The people's joy at receiving Holy Communion with the whole assembly fits the twentieth-century Eucharistic ecclesiology of all assembling in one place, but the view of those on the other side of the window casts a shadow of doubt on whether or not all are included.

On Behalf of . . . All? Or Just Some?

An image of the local Church embracing all of the people of the community is established here. The people's testimony invites theologians to consider who belongs to the "all" of the local community, and why some abstain from partaking. Theologians can help clarify why the Eucharist is a gathering of some and not all by bringing the causes of abstaining from Communion or attendance as a whole into dialogue with the language the Church uses to define belonging. The focus group sessions have already yielded information on why people refrain from Communion: some are concerned about their own preparation, and others will not observe the required fast. A rigorous examination of impediments to Communion can result in an assessment of decisions leading a potential communicant to abstain. While repenting of a serious sin is probably the most likely reason that comes to mind, it is not sufficient for theologians to simply affirm repentance as a legitimate reason for one to refrain from partaking. The Orthodox penitential tradition has established that excommunication or abstinence from Communion are legitimate practices that assist the penitent Christian to return to the Church community, with the confidence that penance is leading to the penitent's separation from sin and full participation in the assembly.[55] Desire for Communion is healthy in this view, as one who wants to return will be motivated to mend their ways.

Penance, Confession, Worthiness, and Communion

With the partial restoration of frequent Communion by the entire assembly, contemporary Eucharistic ecclesiology has moved away from the idea that one can attain worthiness. The removal of a rigorous process resulting in worthiness has emboldened faithful to respond to the invitation to approach and receive. This shift in Eucharistic discipline came from a new approach to the relationship between worthiness and communion. Observing the strict requirements of preparing for Communion created a situation in the local assembly where those who observed the preparatory rites were somehow more worthy than the other faithful. Confessing that no one is worthy of God's gift of Communion facilitated the corporate reception of Communion—in other words, worthiness could no longer be a good reason for abstaining from Communion, especially when the faithful truly desire it. Not all theologians have embraced this shift in Eucharistic discipline: some believe that the Church has compromised the gravity of the Eucharist and the necessity of responding to the call to holiness that comes with the privilege of Eucharistic belonging.

I submit that pastors should encourage laity to embrace repentance and seek Confession: the movement to renew participation in penance is valid and requires attention from theologians and pastors. The pastoral desire to strengthen confession and repentance should likewise motivate theologians to consider the role of Holy Communion in remitting sins and bringing imperfect Christians back to Communion with God from a different perspective. The faithful who respond affirmatively to the invitation for Communion have an opportunity to receive the gift of the Holy Spirit yet again, a gift that cleanses them of sin and draws them closer to God. Communion is an imparting of the remission of sins received at Baptism. Theologians might explore how encouraging faithful struggling with sins to receive Communion might contribute to their healing, with the gift of the Holy Spirit breathing life into their process of becoming like Christ. Considering this view is not a concession to spiritual laxity or an attempt to relativize sin. It is an acknowledgment that the sinner needs the healing medicine provided by God in Communion, a perspective that coheres well with the acknowledgment that faithful are not to proclaim their worthiness when approaching, but rather to accept the invitation with confidence, and to ask God to make the unworthy worthy.

Theologians should adopt a similar approach to the question of offering Communion to non-Orthodox Christians, keeping in mind that the existence of the "don't ask, don't tell" policy among pastors reveals that Communion of non-Orthodox takes place in some places. The anti-ecumenical turn in contemporary Orthodoxy will not permit a public discussion on allowing non-Orthodox to receive Communion at Liturgy. The vast majority of Orthodox clergy and theologians would insist on the resolution of divisive theological issues first, and for Christians who worship at an Orthodox Church but remain in their own denomination, a decisive commitment to the Orthodox Church alone through Chrismation or Baptism.[56] This approach upholds the conciliar definition of the Orthodox Church as THE one, holy, catholic, and apostolic Church. In this approach, ritual participation in Communion must manifest complete unity and fidelity to the Church, so that those who commune would presumably share the "oneness of mind" the Liturgy exhorts them to profess in the Creed.

This view of Communion and Church division accounts for trajectories in doctrinal development and historical definitions of separations symbolized by Eucharistic exclusivity. Ignored are many other potential circumstances such as non-Orthodox Christians who faithfully participate in all facets of Church life because of marriage, or the presence of other Christians who have made the parish their permanent place of worship without converting. Refusing to grant Communion to one who approaches places the onus of responsibility on both parties. Theologians need to reexamine the language of belonging to the Orthodox Church and consider the factors that might cause one to pause at an insistence on converting. For some, it may be a matter of the Church's insistence that they sever the relationship with their native church. Theologians can consider the benefits of Christians who would like to become Orthodox without forsaking their native church. Insisting upon the renunciation of one's native church, which is required in most versions of the rite of Chrismation, is akin to defining that church as an opponent, enemy, or illegitimate representative of Christ's Church.[57] While this view is indeed consistent with the ecclesiology of the council of Crete, theologians need to examine the legitimacy of this view in light of the realities of the people in their parishes. Theologians also need to examine the role Communion might play in contributing to healing the divisions separating Christians. The Church is neither a text nor a set of principles that can be debated: it is an assembly of people. The ritual rehearsal of sharing a holy meal with those who have been estranged may have the capacity to do what official dialogues have been unable to, that is to show that living together in one body is not only possible, but good. One way of promoting awareness of and encouraging encounter with the estranged other is through prayer. The anaphora of St. Basil has a series of beautiful commemorations at its conclusion in which the assembly commends all of humanity to God's merciful care.[58] This prayer is quite powerful since the assembly prays for people in almost every imaginable state: prisoners, heretics, those who hate us, and those who are absent, among many others.

The people's experience of the Liturgy leads them to long for a deeper connection with those who are outside of the Church, those who do not participate in the Liturgy. Liturgy facilitates encounters with God and humankind, and sends the people from the Liturgy back into the world where they will encounter and live among those whom they saw on the other side of the window. As part of the process of sending the people into the world to witness and serve, the liturgical ordo can equip and shape the people to pray for and love all others. The liturgical texts handed down from late antiquity to the present do not speak to all of the circumstances navigated by the present generation. Orthodox tradition permits the pastors and theologians of today to compose new prayers to glorify God in the language and idioms of the present day. In the spirit of this tradition, I present a new Eucharistic Prayer in appendix A that depends on the traditional Eucharistic themes of humility, worthiness, and thanksgiving while calling upon God to remember a mosaic of humanity representing the twenty-first century. As with all prayer, this anaphora glorifies God primarily, and calls upon the assembly to commend all of creation and the entirety of humankind to God, including people of other churches, non-Christians religions, and atheists. The prayer has the capacity to form people to learn how to see and love all of the world's people.

This chapter has commenced the process of analyzing the primary issues emerging from the focus group sessions. We have discussed the meaning of authentic liturgical understanding, the people's thirst for divine compassion, the accomplishments of the liturgical renewal inspired by Eucharistic ecclesiology, and the opportunity for the Church to meet, greet, and engage the world and all of humankind by considering how to extend hospitality to and pray with non-Orthodox people. The review of opportunities for the people's perspective to shape the liturgical enterprise continues in chapter 6.

NOTES

1. See International Theological Consultation, *Sensus Fidei in the Life of the Church*, http://www.vatican.va/roman_curia/congregations/cfaith/cti_documents/rc_cti_20140610_sensus-fidei_en.html (accessed February 14, 2018).

2. For infallible Catholic teaching on the Assumption, see Pope Pius XII, "Munificentissi-mus Deus" *Acta Apostolicae Sedis* 42 (1950). The English text of the Encyclical is available online at http://www.vatican.va/holy_father/pius_xii/apost_constitutions/documents/hf_p-xii_apc_19501101_munificentissimus-deus_en.html (accessed February 26, 2018). For the classical secondary study of popular belief in Mary's assumption exemplifying the *sensus fidelium*, see Martin Jugie, *La mort et l'assomption de la sainte vierge: étude historic-doctrinale*, Studi e testi 114 (Vatican City: Biblioteca apostolic vaticana, 1944).

3. Aidan Kavanagh, "Primary Theology and Liturgical Act: Response," *Worship* 57 (1983): 321–24. See also David Fagerberg, *Theologia Prima: What Is Liturgical Theology?* 2d ed. (Chicago: Hillenbrand, 2004), 133–56, and Robert F. Taft, "Mrs Murphy Goes to Moscow: Kavanagh, Schmemann, and the 'Byzantine Synthesis'," *Worship* 85 (2011): 386–407.

4. See Frank Senn, "The Constitution on Sacred Liturgy and Lutheran Book of Worship: What Was Renewed?" in *Liturgy in a New Millennium*, ed. R. Schuler (Valparaiso, IN: Institute of Liturgical Studies, 2006), 211–13.

5. "With zeal and patience, pastors of souls must promote the liturgical instruction of the faithful, and also their active participation in the liturgy both internally and externally, taking into account their age and condition, their way of life, and standard of religious culture," no. 19 from *Sacrosanctum Concilium,* http://www.vatican.va/archive/hist_councils/ii_vatican_council/documents/vat-ii_const_19631204_sacrosanctum-concilium_en.html (accessed February 21, 2018).

6. In the Constantinopolitan cathedral tradition, the deacons collected the bread and wine brought by the laity for the Liturgy in the skeuophylakion, a building attached to the church, but not within it. The deacons sorted through the gifts and selected those to be used as part of the offering. When the time arrived to bring the gifts from the skeuophylakion into the church, an ornate procession took place, with the deacons bearing the gifts through the church, and presenting them to the patriarch, who placed them on the table for the actual offering. The Constantinopolitan cathedral entrance established the pattern for what is now known as the Great Entrance in Byzantine Liturgy. See Robert F. Taft, *A History of the Liturgy of St. John Chrysostom, vol. 2: The Great Entrance, A History of the Transfer of Gifts and Other Pre-anaphral Rites*, 4th ed. (Rome: Pontifical Oriental Institute, 2004), 185–91.

7. Jerome Kodell argues that the last supper was a festive meal with Passover overtones. See Kodell, *The Eucharist in the New Testament* (Collegeville, MN: Liturgical Press, 1991), 53–67.

8. Taft's scholarship suggests that evidence of the use of spoons for clergy Communion appears as early as the seventh century (in Palestine) and became a general practice in the Byzantine rite—though not universal—by the eleventh century. See Taft, "Byzantine Communion Spoons: A Review of the Evidence," *Dumbarton Oaks Papers* 50 (1996): 238.

9. For more on people engaging one another in conversation as a way of fortifying communion, see Michael Plekon, *Uncommon Prayer: Prayer in Everyday Experience* (South Bend, IN: University of Notre Dame Press, 2017), 177–82.

10. See Pott's taxonomy of liturgical reform, 85-109, and Denysenko, *Liturgical Reform After Vatican II*, 12–33.

11. Mark Searle, *Called to Participate: Theological, Ritual, and Social Perspectives*, ed. Barbara Searle and Anne Y. Koester (Collegeville, MN: Liturgical Press, 2006).

12. Stephen Wilbricht, *Rehearsing God's Just Kingdom: The Eucharistic Vision of Mark Searle*, foreword by Kevin Irwin (Collegeville, MN: Liturgical Press, 2013); Gabriel Pivarnik, *Toward a Trinitarian Theology of Liturgical Participation*, foreword by Kevin Irwin (Collegeville, MN: Liturgical Press, 2013), and Kimberly Belcher, *Efficacious Engagement: Sacramental Participation in the Trinitarian Mystery* (Collegeville, MN: Liturgical Press, 2011).

13. For an English translation of the mystagogy, see Patriarch Germanos, *On the Divine Liturgy*, trans. Paul Meyendorff (Crestwood, NY: St. Vladimir's Seminary Press, 1984); Robert F. Taft, "The Liturgy of the Great Church: An Initial Synthesis of Structure and Interpretation on the Eve of Iconoclasm," *Dumbarton Oaks Papers* 34 (1980–81): 47–75.

14. See Taft's discussion of mystagogy as an adaptation of the patristic method of scriptural exegesis in "Liturgy of the Great Church," 59–61.

15. Germanos, in Meyendorff, trans., 10, 48–53.

16. See Alexander Schmemann, "Symbols and Symbolism: Liturgical Symbols and Their Theological Interpretation," in idem, *Liturgy and Tradition: Theological Reflections of Alexander Schmemann*, ed. Thomas Fisch (Crestwood, NY: St. Vladimir's Seminary Press, 1990), 117–21.

17. Ibid., 123.

18. Ibid.

19. Robert F. Taft, "What Does Liturgy Do? Toward A Soteriology of Liturgical Celebration: Some Theses," in idem, *Beyond East and West: Problems in Liturgical Understanding*, 2d ed., Edizioni Orientalia Christiana (Rome: Pontifical Oriental Institute, 2001), 240.

20. Taft, "The Liturgy of the Great Church," 45–75.

21. "Once more, I am convinced that I am quite alienated from Byzantium, and even hostile to it. In the Bible, there is space and air; in Byzantium, the air is always stuffy. . . . The drama of Orthodoxy: we did not have a Renaissance, sinful but liberating from the sacred. So we live in nonexistent worlds: in Byzantium, in Rus, wherever, but not in our own time." Alexander Schmemann, *The Journals of Father Alexander Schmemann, 1973–1983*, trans. Juliana Schmemann (Crestwood, NY: St. Vladimir's Seminary Press, 2000), 213.

22. Alexander Schmemann, *The Eucharist: Sacrament of the Kingdom*, trans. Paul Kachur (Crestwood, NY: St. Vladimir's Seminary Press, 1984).

23. Ibid., 138–39.

24. See the provocative and insightful essay by Maria Skobtsova on the sacrament of the brother and sister in *Mother Maria Skobtsova: Essential Writings,* trans. Richard Pevear and Larissa Volokhonsky, introduction by Jim Forest, Modern Spiritual Master Series (Maryknoll, NY: Orbis, 2003), 75–83.

25. "Come, let us greatly rejoice in the lord as we tell of this present mystery. The middle wall of partition has been destroyed; the flaming sword turns back, the cherubim withdraw from the tree of life, and I partake of the delight of Paradise from which I was cast out through disobedience First hymn at Vespers of Christmas, *The Festal Menaion*, trans. Mother Mary and Kallistos Ware (South Canaan, PA: St. Tikhon's Seminary Press 1990), 253. "The fiery sword no longer guards the gate of Eden, for in a strange and glorious way the wood of the Cross has quenched its flames." Kontakion (hymn) for the third Sunday of Lent, *The Lenten Triodion*, trans. Mother Mary and Kallistos Ware (South Canaan, PA: St. Tikhon's Seminary Press, 2002), 342.

26. Searle, 75–76.

27. Ibid., 71–76.

28. Schmemann, *The Eucharist*, 133–58.

29. For the best English translation of Mary's vita, see Maria Kouli, trans., "Life of St. Mary of Egypt," in *Holy Women of Byzantium*, ed. Alice-Mary Talbot (Washington, DC: Dumbarton Oaks, 1996), 65–95.

30. Hilda Graef, *Mary: A History of Doctrine and Devotion,* vol. 1: *From the Beginnings to the Eve of the Reformation* (New York: Sheed and Ward, 1963), 111–12.

31. In order: Antipascha, or St. Thomas Sunday (John 20), the Myrrhbearing Women (Mark 16), the Paralytic (John 5), the Samaritan Woman (John 5), the Blind Man (John 9).

32. "For you are the one who both offers and is offered, the one who is received and is distributed, o Christ our god, and to you we offer up glory . . . ," the prayer recited by the

presider before the great entrance quietly. Translation taken from *The Liturgy of St. John Chrysostom*, priest edition (Brookline, MA: Holy Cross Orthodox Press, 2015), 33–35.

33. Robert F. Taft, *A History of the Liturgy of St. John Chrysostom*, vol. 5: *The Precommunion Rites*, Orientalia Christiana Analecta 261 (Rome: Pontifical Oriental Institute, 2000), 485.

34. Robert F. Taft, "Monogenes," in *The Oxford Dictionary of Byzantium*, vol. 2, ed. Alexander Kazhdan (New York: Oxford University Press, 1991), 1397.

35. Robert F. Taft, *The Liturgy of the Hours in East and West: The Origins of the Divine Office and Its Meaning for Today*, 2d ed. (Collegeville, MN: Liturgical Press, 1993), 369.

36. Dorian Llywelyn, "From Trent to Tierra del Fuego," in *Icons and the Liturgy, East and West*, ed. Nicholas Denysenko (South Bend, IN: University of Notre Dame Press, 2017), 128–44.

37. See Paul Evdokimov's profound description of God as the lover of humankind who is the true compassionate companion of people in all states of life in Michael Plekon, *The World as Sacrament: An Ecumenical Path toward a Worldly Spirituality* (Collegeville, MN: Liturgical Press, 2017), 113–19.

38. Stafford Poole, *Our Lady of Guadalupe: The Origins and Sources of a Mexican National Symbol, 1591–1797* (Tucson: University of Arizona Press, 1995).

39. See "Святейший Патриарх Кирилл: Пусть пребывание в России Пояса Пресвятой Богородицы многим поможет понять силу Божественной благодати" (His Holiness Patriarch Kyrill: May the Visit of the Belt of the Immaculate Theotokos in Russia Help Many Understand the Power of Divine Grace") Moscow Patriarchate web site, http://www.patriarchia.ru/db/text/1650148.html (accessed July 11, 2013).

40. The idea that the Tsar-martyr Nicholas intercedes for Russia gained popularity in 1998 when his icon began to produce myrrh, and forty-four thousand copies were printed for distribution in Russia, a testimony to the phenomenology of royal intercession. See Richard Betts, "From America to Russia: The Myrrh-Streaming Icon of Tsar Nicholas II," *Road to Emmaus: A Journal of Orthodox Faith and Culture* (2000), accessed November 15, 2013, http://www.roadtoemmaus.net/back_issue_articles/RTE_01/From_America_to_Russia.pdf, and Wendy Slater, "Relics, Remains, and Revisionism: Narratives of Nicholas II in Contemporary Russia," *Rethinking History: The Journal of Theory and Practice* 9, no. 1 (2005): 53–70.

41. I made a pilgrimage to Holy Virgin Cathedral of the Russian Orthodox Church Outside of Russia in San Francisco in 2014, to study the church's architecture for a project. The Cathedral is home to the shrine of St. John Maximovich, whose tenure as archbishop of San Francisco was brief (1962–66), but memorable. During my brief visit, people streamed into the church on a weekday. My strongest memory was of several young women who came to the shrine bearing bags with children's clothing, removing the clothing and touching it all over the shrine. I do not know the prayer intentions of these women; I express wonder at their approach to touch, to bring themselves and the clothes belonging to unnamed children into contact with St. John.

42. Paul McPartlan, *Sacrament of Salvation: An Introduction to Eucharistic Ecclesiology* (Edinburgh: T & T Clark, 1995), 30–31.

43. Nicholas Afanasiev, *The Church of the Holy Spirit*, trans. Vitaly Permiakov, ed. Michael Plekon, foreword by Rowan Williams (South Bend, IN: University of Notre Dame Press, 2007), 238.

44. Alexander Schmemann, "Problems of Orthodoxy in America," *St. Vladimir's Seminary Quarterly* 9, no. 4 (1964): 170, 179.

45. See Brandon Gallaher, "Great and Full of Grace," in *Church and World: Essays in Honor of Michael Plekon*, ed. William Mills (Rollinsford, NH: Orthodox Research Institute, 2013), 69–122.

46. Nicholas Afanasiev, "Una Sancta," in *Tradition Alive: On the Church and the Christian Life in Our Time*, ed. Michael Plekon, foreword by John Erickson (New York: Rowman & Littlefield, 2003), 3–53.

47. Michael Plekon, *Living Icons: Persons of Faith in the Eastern Church*, foreword by Lawrence Cunningham (South Bend, IN: University of Notre Dame Press, 2002).

48. Brandon Gallaher, "Ecumenism as Civilizational Dialogue: Eastern Orthodox Anti-Ecumenism and Eastern Orthodox Ecumenism: A Creative or Sterile Antinomy," Keynote lecture

for "Questioning Ecumenism in the 20th Century: Who, When, Why," "The Desire for Christian Unity Research Program—2017 Research Conference," Fondazione per le Scienze Religiose Giovanni XXIII, Bologna, 13–15 November 2017. Convener: Prof Alberto Melloni. Nicholas Denysenko, "Steps on the Path to Unity: Courage to Pray Together," forthcoming in *Liturgy* (2018).

49. Noteworthy for their commitment to ecumenical dialogue are the Romanian Patriarchate and the Orthodox Church in Finland.

50. See Vasilios Makrides, "'The Barbarian West': A Form of Orthodox Christian Anti-Western Critique," in *Eastern Orthodox Encounters of Identity and Otherness: Values, Self-reflection, Dialogue,* ed. Andrii Krawchuk and Thomas Bremer (New York: Palgrave Macmillan, 2014), 141–58; George Demacopoulos and Aristotle Papanikolaou, eds., *Orthodox Constructions of the West* (New York: Fordham University Press, 2013).

51. The Pope and Ecumenical Patriarch continue the tradition of participating in the solemnities of the Western and Eastern Churches on the Solemnity of Saints Peter and Paul (June 29, for the West) and St. Andrew (November 30, for the East).

52. The following excerpt from the Council of Crete provides a larger context of Orthodoxy's position on the ecclesial fullness of non-Orthodox Churches: "the Orthodox Church accepts the historical name of other non-Orthodox Christian Churches and Confessions that are not in communion with her, and believes that her relations with them should be based on the most speedy and objective clarification possible of the whole ecclesiological question, and most especially of their more general teachings on sacraments, grace, priesthood, and apostolic succession," No. 6, Relations of the Orthodox Church with the Rest of the Christian World, https://www.holycouncil.org/-/rest-of-christian-world (accessed October 3, 2017). See no. 1 for the conciliar definition of the Orthodox Church "as" the Church.

53. The Sacrament of Marriage and Its Impediments, https://www.holycouncil.org/-/marriage (accessed October 3, 2017).

54. *Oikonomia* is a canonical principle permitting the bishop to apply a canon with much more flexibility depending on the circumstances surrounding a situation. For example, While the letter of canon law stipulates the defrocking of clergy who divorce, *oikonomia* could be applied to allow clergy to remain active, or to even remarry, all depending on the circumstances.

55. See Claudia Rapp, "Spiritual Guarantors at Penance, Baptism, and Ordination in the Late Antique East," *A New History of Penance*, ed. Abigail Firey (Boston, MA: Brill 2008); Alexis Torrance, *Repentance in Late Antiquity: Eastern Asceticism and the Framing of the Christian Life c. 400–650 CE* (Oxford: Oxford University Press, 2012).

56. "True Christian unity cannot be founded upon falsehood on a cosmetic agreement, which pretends that there is agreement on essential issues," in Thomas FitzGerald, "How to Understand Christian Unity (Ecumenism) in Relation to Orthodox Identity: A First Theological Approach," in *Orthodox Handbook on Ecumenism: Resources for Theological Education*, ed. Pantelis Kalaitzidis et al. (Volos: Volos Academy Publications, 2014), 12. Robert Taft presents an original proposal for realizing Eucharistic unity between Catholics and Orthodox in "In Faith and Worship Can Orthodox and Catholics Ever Be One? Communion, Not Reunion, in a Future Church of Sister Churches," *Worship* 89, no. 1 (2015): 2–20.

57. Nicholas Denysenko, *Chrismation: A Primer for Catholics* (Collegeville, MN: Liturgical Press, 2014), 51–69.

58. For an analysis of St. Basil's anaphora and the host of different others commended to God, see Nicholas Denysenko, "Retrieving a Theology of Belonging: Eucharist and Church in Postmodernity, Part 2," *Worship* 89, no. 1 (2015): 30–37.

Chapter Six

Hearing the Word, Penance, and Communion

This chapter proceeds from the general to the particular by drawing from the people's reflections at the focus groups to weigh the current status of the Liturgy of the Word and the relationship between penance and Communion in the Church's Liturgy. The chapter includes a proposal for revising the Gospels appointed for the Sundays of Lent, as the current lectionary emphasizes commemoration of monastic heroes. We also include a proposal for fine-tuning penance by presenting a rite of communal penance that could begin each Divine Liturgy and distinguishing the mystery of Confession from spiritual direction. We also discuss how the Church should approach the thorny and difficult topic of the potential service of women in the Church, with a reminder that voices on both sides of the debate understand liturgy as bearing and communicating the Church's teaching on theological anthropology.

WORD AND SACRAMENT: HEARING GOD SPEAK

If Orthodox theologians like Schmemann led the way in reviving the Eucharist in the liturgical renewal of the twentieth century, the Orthodox Church did not keep pace with the revisions in the Liturgy of the Word implemented in the Western churches. In the West, the twentieth century witnessed to a new epoch in the Reformation. The permission granted to celebrate Liturgy in the vernacular by Vatican II resulted in the Roman Church catching up to Protestants. Vatican II fused the proclamation of the Word to the sacrament and defined it as a single action, hearing the Word leading to participation in the table.[1] When Vatican II authorized a substantial revision of the liturgical lectionary, the Roman Church took the lead among the churches when it introduced a three-year lectionary and expanded the portions of the Bible read aloud for the people to hear.[2] The result was simply more Bible: the Old Testament returned to the Sunday Mass and each year focused on one of the three synoptic Gospels. In the year of Mark, portions of John are included, given Mark's brevity. The Protestant churches adopted the three-year cycle of the Romans and revised it, resulting in a common lectionary for mainline Protestant churches called the Revised Common Lectionary (RCL).[3] The Western churches also devoted themselves to reinvigorating preaching, a liturgical act that was particularly needed in the Roman Church, given the absence of homilies at many celebrations of Mass.

The Orthodox Churches did not join the Protestants in adopting a revised lectionary. Currently, Orthodoxy observes the one-year lectionary it has inherited over the course of thousands of years. The current lectionary contains some repetition and the principle of *lectio selecta* tends to dominate, given the number of feasts requiring the interpolation of second sets of readings throughout the year. The Church has not restored the practice of reading an Old Testament lesson at Sunday Liturgy, despite evidence that the lectionary once contained such a reading through about the seventh century.[4]

Apologists for retaining the received lectionary refer to the practice of appointing three readings proclaimed during Vespers on feasts of the liturgical year as evidence of biblical richness in the liturgy. The most solemn feasts such as Christmas, Theophany, and the Dormition of the Theotokos appoint several Old Testament readings to the Vigil office, with Holy Saturday the most biblical of them all with 15 readings. The rest of Holy Week is saturated with the Bible, especially Good Friday, which begins with a Matins service centered on twelve Gospel readings. In practice, though, parishes often abbreviate the readings appointed to these feasts. For example, for decades, many parishes have only taken three readings for Holy Saturday, adopting the pattern of festal Vespers with its three readings. Apologists also point to the power of the eleven Sunday *eothina* readings, a solemn chanting of one of the resurrection accounts that occurs each Sunday morning on a rotating basis. For the people who faithfully attend Sunday Matins, the resurrection is proclaimed through the Gospel, to be followed by the appointed reading that takes place later during the Liturgy.

Changes in the Liturgy of the Word

In parish practice, there have been some positive changes. The most significant change is the recommitment to preaching that has taken root in many Orthodox Churches of the world. As in the Roman Church, a sermon would simply be omitted from the Liturgy in many Orthodox parishes. Sermons might be delivered on special occasions. For solemn feasts, the rector would read a message from the bishop to the people instead of the sermon. The liturgical renewal movement called for sermons to be offered every Sunday, to be rooted in the appointed Bible lessons for that day, and to be an instance of God speaking to the people. Many churches have attempted to restore the sermon in its proper place, as part of the Liturgy of the Word, after the reading of the Gospel. Seminaries are devoting more energy to training students in biblical languages and in the arts and methods of preaching.

In addition to preaching, Orthodoxy has also witnessed to a revival of psalmody and the singing of biblical canticles in the church. Two examples illustrate the people's experience of this revival. In the Greek churches, the first antiphon was often reduced to the practice of singing the refrain three times, without the appointed psalm verses ("Through the prayers of the Theotokos, Savior, save us").[5] In contemporary Greek practice, the cantor intones the appointed verses, an act that restored the integrity of the liturgical unit by calling upon the people to sing the refrain on the verse. A similar restoration has occurred in other parts of the Church with the psalmody appointed to the Alleluia. The prevailing practice has been to simply sing Alleluia three times after the Gospel, with no psalmody. Now, in many places, the psalmody has been restored, and the Alleluia has returned to its original function as an acclamation sung by all.

Respondents also proved to be receptive to the proclamation of epic stories communicated in the liturgical year. Holy Week provides the most prominent examples, as the Passion, death, and resurrection of Jesus are compacted into one intense week of liturgical celebration. Holy Week has always been a feature of the Church's seasonal celebration, due largely to its public celebration in the main metropolises of late antiquity (Rome, Jerusalem, and Constantinople in particular). Some of the other commemorations of the liturgical year are also breaking through today. The Lenten commemoration of St. Mary's of Egypt is a good example. Respondents from HTC remarked about the power of that evening, to hear her story and be challenged by its message despite the physical demands of staying in church for a long time on a week night. A few other references to liturgical narratives that aroused an examination of conscience in respondents were Palm Sunday and its reflection on the human condition, the lament of Mary at Christ's tomb, and the witness of the myrrhbearing women, who were transformed from those who anointed Jesus' body to the first witnesses of his resurrection. These stories are proclaimed to the people by the liturgy—in most cases, the people hear the stories through the Gospel, and the message is supported by the retelling of the story in the hymns of the Church, especially at Vespers and Matins. The commemoration of St. Mary's of Egypt is special since her vita is read aloud at Thursday evening Lenten service.

These epic stories are integral to the power of the proclamation of the Word for two reasons. First, it is clear that the people are actually able to hear and comprehend the narratives. This is remarkable given the liturgical legacy of the Orthodox Church, as many of the proclaimed words were incomprehensible to the people because of arcane liturgical languages, poor delivery by the clergy and the singers, the tendency to either omit liturgical components or say them quietly to finish the office faster, and the problem of having the choir's singing and the leader's chanting happening simultaneously.[6] Improving the delivery of liturgical proclamation was a primary objective of the Orthodox liturgical renewal movement, with recommendations for polishing the chanting and singing skills of clergy and chanters a top priority. The respondents' remarks on these feasts indicate that the narratives are proclaimed with a reasonable degree of competence, at least in the parishes profiled for this study. Second, the proclamation of these stories tends to introduce complete profiles of secondary characters in the Church's liturgical year, ordinary humans who played important roles in the economy of salvation. The people are challenged by a saint like Mary of Egypt because her struggle with passions is one shared by many human beings. The people's affirmation of the power of the epic stories in liturgy reveals this positive outcome of liturgical renewal.

The renewal of the Liturgy of the Word has occurred with preaching and psalmody in the Orthodox Churches, along with the proclamation of epic stories, but this platform is not a universal one. The process of reviving the Liturgy of the Word is, at best, in-progress, and at worst, stagnant. The lectionary has also been essentially untouched. But even this modest and limited project of renewal has contributed to the life of the Church. Focus group respondents remarked on the significance of preaching, so that the Word was one of Sunday's focal points. Technology has aided this renewal, since pastors are now able to publish their sermons online and make the Word available to the people, wherever they are. But there is much work that can still be done to promote the liturgy of the Word and demonstrate the Word is indeed sacrament in Orthodoxy. In this sense, the liturgy of the Word is both a strength and an opportunity.

LECTIONARY REVISION: RESTORING CHRIST AS THE CENTER OF LENT

The opportunity for theologians to build up the Liturgy of the Word has four components. Revision of the lectionary is the most urgent matter. The myth of unchanging liturgy is the only obstacle to revising the current version of the lectionary, which is an amalgamation of practices from multiple regions. The first task would be a study of the lectionary systems of other churches, so that Christian faithful participating in worship might experience some continuity in the order of the proclamation of the Word. There are few revised lectionaries in Orthodoxy available for study, but the one implemented and used by New Skete Monastery in Cambridge, New York, is worthy of consideration.[7]

If lectionary reform begins from scratch, the Sundays of Pentecost constitute the lessons requiring the most attention, as this season takes up the majority of the liturgical year, and is interrupted only by the pre-Lenten, Lenten, and Paschal periods. These Sundays tend to feature Luke and Matthew, with some Mark, and contain many repetitions. Adding an Old Testament reading to all liturgies is another area of enhancement, to confirm the sanctity of the Old Testament and proclaim more of God's word publicly, to the people. The pre-Lenten Sundays and the Sundays of Pascha are the strongest portions of the Byzantine lectionary. In the Byzantine tradition, the Sundays of Lent retained the old Constantinopolitan stratum of gospel readings from Mark.[8] The themes for the Sundays do not correspond to the primary readings, as the Sundays commemorate, in order, the Triumph of Orthodoxy, St. Gregory Palamas, the veneration of the Cross, St. John of the Ladder, and St. Mary of Egypt.[9] Four of the five Sundays symbolize the monastic hegemony of Orthodox liturgy, which began in the ninth century following the defeat of iconoclasm: the Sundays celebrate either historical victory over heretics or monastic triumph over the passions. The assignment of these commemorations to the Sundays of Lent elucidates a kind of ranking within the most solemn season of the year: in successive Sundays, the monks honor their heroes in descending order. The two themes connecting the Sundays are victory over heresies and passions, and a sense of progress in fasting and prayer, as the fourth and fifth Sundays present models of ascetical feat to the Church. It is a stretch to point to the veneration of the Cross as the heart that pumps blood through the season.

Adjusting the lectionary for the Sundays of Lent would challenge theologians because it would require changing the most solemn event of the year. The Sunday of Orthodoxy and Veneration of the Cross are essentially unchangeable, as the people would be unlikely to receive changes here, since the Sunday of Orthodoxy has local parish traditions of icon processions. These Sundays also provide fertile theological soil: the Sunday of Orthodoxy celebrates the incarnate Christ who can be seen, which leads naturally to beholding the Son of God crucified on the cross. The Lenten schedule is often interrupted by the Annunciation feast on March 25, which tends to take place later in Lent and thus reintroduces the Incarnation yet again. When Lent begins earlier, the feast of the Meeting of the Lord (February 2) tends to add another layer of Incarnation to the cycle of readings. Therefore, the people hear stories of Incarnation and Cross, along with the defeat of heretics and passions in monastic victories. The Sundays of Lent, with the Annunciation feast, represent the whole lectionary, as they communicate the entire economy of salvation and the history of Orthodox theology in one season.

The typical pastoral approach to explaining this amalgamation of themes is to celebrate the opportunity to learn it all at once, with the back and forth of Incarnation and Cross simply an instance of grace upon grace.

New Skete's Gospel Lectionary for the Sundays of Lent

Since New Skete stands alone in lectionary reform in the Byzantine rite, their lectionary for the Sundays of Lent could be adopted. New Skete retained the cycle of readings for the Sundays before Lent and added an Old Testament reading to the Sunday Liturgy for each of those Sundays. For many Sundays, New Skete has drawn from an older stratum of the Jerusalem lectionary based on Bertoniere's research. For some Sundays, the readings alternate between Years A and B. As for the actual Sundays of Lent, table 6.1 presents New Skete's scheme.

Table 6.1.   New Skete's Gospels for the Sundays of Lent

Sunday 1	(Year A) Mt 4:1–11; (Year B) Lk 4:1–13 (Jesus sojourn in the desert)
Sunday 2	(Years A and B) Mk:5:24b–34 (Woman with the flow of blood)
Sunday 3	(Year A) Mk 8:34–9:1; (Year B) Lk 9:18–27 (synoptic appeals to take up the cross)
Sunday 4	(Years A and B) Lk 10:25–37 (The good Samaritan)
Sunday 5	(Years A and B) Lk 16:19–31 (The Rich Man and Lazarus)

New Skete's gospels for the Sundays of Lent are traditional in two ways. First, they draw from the Jerusalem heritage of the Church's liturgical tradition. Second, the gospel themes align closely with Lenten practices. The Church remembers Jesus' fast in the desert on the first Sunday. Jesus as the source of healing for those who seek him is the periscope for Sunday 2. Almsgiving as a pillar of Lenten action is the theme of Sunday 4, and the Lukan parable of the rich man and Lazarus reminds hearers of the relationship between fasting and investing treasures in heaven, a theme from Cheesefare Sunday. New Skete's restoration emphasizes the core values and practices of Lent and renders the commemoration of monastic heroes secondary.

Another Proposal for the Gospels of the Sundays of Lent

Another approach to lectionary reform would be to use the two pillars of Incarnation (Orthodoxy) and the Cross (veneration) as Sundays revealing Christ as the savior of humankind. The remaining Sundays could guide the people through a process of revelation. One example of such a process is illustrated in table 6.2.

Table 6.2.   Gospels on Sundays of Lent, Alternative Proposal

1st Sunday of Lent	Sunday of Orthodoxy—revelation of the Incarnate Christ (Jn. 1:43–51)
2nd Sunday of Lent	Transfiguration of Christ—revelation of divine Christ (Mt. 17:1–13)
3rd Sunday of Lent	Sunday of the Cross—midpoint (Mk. 8:34–9:1)
4th Sunday of Lent	(John 17:1–26)—unity of the godhead, and Christian unity
5th Sunday of Lent	Christ in the Garden of Gethsemane—anticipating Christ's passion (Mt. 26:36–46)

This sequence of readings would develop the Incarnation mystery by folding the central stories of Christ's two natures into the Sundays of Lent. After beholding the Incarnate God with Nathaniel on the Sunday of Orthodoxy, the people would join the disciples in averting their eyes from Christ's uncreated light at the Transfiguration, which provides a natural step on the way to the cross as the midpoint. The inclusion of Christ's prayer to the Father on the fourth Sunday features both the unity of Christ with God, and the eternal human crisis of division, which can only be resolved by joining Christ's prayer to the Father that "they would be one." Christ's prayer in the garden of Gethsemane would function like the cross as a midpoint: this lesson emphasizes his humanity, but it also provides a natural step to the point of Holy Week, which is the cross. This revised sequence would also restore Christ as the center of Lent, a complement to the renewed frequency of the celebration of the Liturgy of Presanctified Gifts, as the people depend on Christ for the sustenance through the season.

Critics might suggest that removing the stories of saints Gregory Palamas, John of the Ladder, and Mary of Egypt from the calendar creates a deficiency by removing secondary stories highlighted above. The Church could either retain these saints on each Sunday as secondary commemorations, or move St. Gregory and St. John to other places in the liturgical year, since Mary of Egypt's commemoration on the fifth week of Lent is already well-established. I offer this outline as a potential revision of the lectionaries on the Sundays of Lent for further discussion among theologians. My objective is to reveal divine compassion in Christ, and the people tend to attend church more faithfully during Lent. This proposed sequence illuminates Christ's divine and human natures and the fullness of his person. Furthermore, the proposed revision replaces commemorations of key victories in Church history with the revelation of the mystery of Christ: pondering his mystery should always be primary, with Church events and secondary figures being just that: secondary.

The secondary task for building up the Liturgy of the Word is to continue to refine and improve the methods of delivery, especially in preaching, intoning prayers and petitions, and liturgical singing. Establishing balance is a crucial objective for the Liturgy of the Word. The restoration of the liturgy occasionally results in singing everything appointed for a feast. A balance in the quantity of content mitigates both maximalism and minimalism. Excessively long sermons and hymns offer more content, but the length of these liturgical components could cause the people's minds to stray and make it more difficult for them to retain the main points that were communicated. One way of infusing balance into the services is to focus on developing the primary theme of the Liturgy, as opposed to mentioning each theme present in the amalgamation of feasts and commemorations. It is clear that the small steps taken in renewing the Liturgy of the Word have contributed positively to the people's engagement of the Liturgy. The Liturgy of the Word is an instance of God speaking to the people and challenging them. The people want to understand the liturgy: the next step is to sharpen precision in delivery and clarify the themes of the events for the people to hear Christ and behold him incarnate, crucified, and risen.

THE ACADEMY AND THE CHURCH: OPPORTUNITIES

The focus groups permitted questions and reflections on aspects of the Liturgy to emerge that are not emphasized in practice and catechesis. I have titled the following topics as opportunities for the liturgical academy to explore. In most of these cases, the people are picking up on issues of serious consequence for the Church. I have already noted the people's sensitivity to the children's participation in the Liturgy. My sense was that these remarks were much more than the momentary appreciation for cute kids: the people beheld citizens of the kingdom of God when they saw the children lined up to receive God's gift. In this next section, I list the insights of the people as a way to urge the liturgical academy to explore these issues and enhance the people's liturgical experience.

A Cosmic Eucharist and Inclusion

The people exhibited sensitivity to children and to all others on the other side of the window. We acknowledged the achievements of the academy in promoting Eucharistic ecclesiology and corporate participation in Communion, so that the Eucharist would make the Church. The people honor the privilege of sharing the Liturgy with the rest of the assembly, but they were also bothered by those who were absent, on the other side of the window.

Like the renewal of the Liturgy of the Word, the Eucharistic revival in Orthodoxy is a work-in-progress. Encouragement of more frequent participation in Communion originated in the mother Churches, migrated abroad, and has now returned to the mother Churches.[10] While encouragement of Eucharistic participation should continue, it is not enough for Orthodox to continue to limit the Eucharistic revival to an intrachurch discussion.

Mercy and Justice in the Eucharist

Several respondents reported feelings of relief that came with their participation in the Eucharist. They acknowledged that the guidelines for preparation are rigorous and communicated a sense that the liturgy itself set a high moral bar for participation, one that no communicant could possibly achieve. Several respondents depicted the Orthodox approach to Confession and Communion favorably in comparison with the Roman Catholic approach. In the focus group discussions, respondents tended to view the Orthodox and Catholic traditions as opposing each other. The Orthodox promote Eucharistic mercy, whereas Catholics adopt a juridical approach.

The Eucharist as a source of divine mercy and justice is a fertile area of research for liturgical theologians, as the people see the Eucharist as a source of both. A sense that God imparts mercy through Communion certainly prevailed in the sessions, but not without mention of fear that the human effort is somehow insufficient or not enough. Most people are familiar with the prayer recited before Communion. In many American parishes, this prayer is recited together by everyone. Even in liturgically conservative parishes, the prayer is recited aloud for the people to hear—it is customary for the deacon or priest to recite the prayer aloud, immediately following the invitation to Communion intoned by the deacon in the form of a command, "With the fear of God, faith [and love], approach!"[11]

An opportunity for the Orthodox academy to devote itself to a common project on the mystery of Confession and clarify the relationships between Confession and spiritual direction, along with canonical impediments to receiving Communion. The parish communities of our four focus groups have received the spirit of the Eucharistic revival. People are encouraged to receive frequently, if not at every Liturgy. The movement towards the frequent reception of Communion is attributable to the theological clarification on the relationship of Confession and Communion, primarily by Schmemann, whose essay on Confession was influential among some Orthodox in the United States. Schmemann followed the teaching of Nicholas Afanasiev, who had argued that the rigorous process of repentance observed by many Orthodox (*govenie* in Russian) in preparation for Communion did not cohere with the spirit of Communion in early Christianity, as all of those who attended the Liturgy would be expected to participate in all of its rites, including Communion. Afanasiev and Schmemann viewed strict observance of *govenie* as an obstacle to encouraging frequent Communion, as faithful would be largely unwilling to receive the mystery of Confession on a regular basis. Schmemann's proposal on Confession resulted in the permission for parishes to institute the practice of general Confession on Saturdays, prior to the Sunday Liturgy. A service of General Confession involves the assembly confessing its sins together, with the clergy imparting absolution to each participant at the end of the rite. General Confession was never envisioned to function as a replacement for personal Confession; it functions as a meaningful communal rite of penance designed to prepare one for the Divine Liturgy. Its implementation meant that individual Confession was no longer a prerequisite for Communion. Each communicant at Liturgy was still expected to prepare through prayer and fasting, and repenting for their sins.

When the Holy Synod of the Orthodox Church in America received and approved Schmemann's proposal on Confession, the absolute requirement of Confession for Communion was removed from the process, and clergy had the freedom to encourage people to partake of Communion without fear of being denied. Communities that practiced regular reception of Communion passed that tradition on to the succeeding generations. Frequent Communion and advance preparation through prayer and fasting remained part of the process, but the rite of General Confession was not observed everywhere. Questions have also emerged on the rigor required for fasting before Communion. In general, the minimal requirement for fasting is to abstain from all food and drink from midnight until Communion at the time of the Liturgy. For some people, this means that they shouldn't brush their teeth in the event they accidentally swallow some water. The requirement of strict fasting is especially problematic for people on medication, who need food and water with their medicine. There is also the matter of people who suffer from low blood sugar and the onset of illness when they refrain from food for too long. Some Orthodox clergy assert that Eucharistic mercy supersedes the rule for fasting and that those who ate or drank for medicinal purposes should approach Communion without hesitation or doubt. Other clergy believe that the tradition of absolute fasting trumps all exceptions and depict breaking the fast as an example of a lax attitude on the Eucharist. Parishes that received and encouraged frequent Communion tend to approve exceptions to the rules of rigorous fasting. Critics claim that relaxation violates Orthodox tradition, but a closer examination suggests that the approach to fasting is pragmatic. In parishes where most people do not receive Communion, there is no need to address the question of fasting since it is not required for those who will not receive. Communities of the Eucharistic revival are addressing the reality of regular fasting that accompanies Communion: the people of those parishes might be fasting more often than those in parishes of infrequent Communion. Reception of frequent Communion and encouragement of a healthy approach to fasting is also indicative of an openness to change. Parishes that have embraced change have been influenced by leaders formed by theologians like Schmemann. The motivation for change was to restore an older stratum of liturgical tradition that coheres with the theological synthesis of the actual rites. One theological idea prevails in the spirit of Eucharistic revival: God's mercy overcomes all of the reasons one might enumerate to abstain from the Eucharist.

Not all Orthodox parishes resemble those of our study, and many have not embraced the Eucharistic revival. In some parishes, the mystery of Confession and absolution are required before each Communion, even if the communicant wants to receive every Sunday. Some clergy are hesitant to encourage people to receive frequently, for fear that they will begin to view the Eucharist as something to which they are entitled. Proponents of a rigorous approach to Communion do not deny that God imparts mercy, but caution that those who are not prepared yet receive anyway are taking the path to damnation, not salvation. A rigorist approach to Communion refuses to diminish the specter of damnation: judgment is at the door for those who dare to approach, knowing that they have not repented of their sins or prepared to receive God's gift. Advocates of a more cautious approach assert that this is a matter of pastoral care, to infuse a habit of repentance and gratitude for God's gift among those wish to approach God in Communion.

These two divergent approaches to Communion are illuminated by the older respondents of our focus groups who experienced the transition from infrequent to frequent Communion. They recalled the rigorous approach to Communion handed on to them by their parents. Some of them feel uneasy about receiving Communion frequently to this day. On the one hand, they appreciate the Church's official recognition that breaking the fast to take medicine is no longer prohibitive for Communion. On the other hand, they worry that those who do not partake appraise them with disapproval. Their tension demonstrates that the mutual exclusivity of the two approaches to Communion exists within their own generation. There is gratitude for mercy, but the fear of reproach suggests that the tension between mercy and justice has yet to be resolved.

The Orthodox Church is in the early stages of the Eucharistic revival, since its introduction and reception occurred in contexts where Orthodoxy is a minority among other Christian denominations. One might conclude that the Church is still adjusting to the changes introduced by the advocates for liturgical renewal. At the international level, the Russian Orthodox Church has embraced the spirit of Eucharistic renewal while urging faithful to remain faithful to the rigors of preparation and penance. As the Orthodox Churches of the West navigate this period of adjustment to the Eucharistic revival, liturgical theologians have an opportunity to address the seemingly unresolvable tension between mercy and justice faithful encounter in the Eucharist.

The matter of penance is fertile soil for theologians to address this topic. It is possible that Schmemann's proposal for penance may be revived, but it might be more advantageous to focus on the place of the mystery of individual Confession in the Church's liturgical life. The matter demanding attention is the notion that Confession prepares one for the reception of Communion. The mystery of Confession originated as a way to reconcile penitents who were separated from the Church because of the severity of their sins. After engaging the penitential process—the duration of the process depended on the degree to which the penitent had strayed from the Church—the penitent would be readmitted to the Eucharistic community, with receiving Communion as the final ritual act that washes away the penitent's sins. Eventually, the mystery of Confession evolved into a process that all faithful were to engage, even though they were not separated from the Church community. As Confession evolved, it retained a crucial component, the idea that Communion was granted as a way of readmitting those who had confessed and received absolution. The problem with this paradigm is that the process of Confession suggests that the faithful are temporarily separated from the Church, even though they are not, in reality. The faithful are not actually expelled from the community, a fact that reveals the flaw in this process.

A second aspect of contemporary Confession is relevant to this discussion. For most faithful, Confession is not a matter of returning to the Church—it is an opportunity to check-in with the confessor, to confess one's sins and receive counsel on how to amend one's way of life. This process is quite enriching when the confessor is capable and well-trained, but it has become more a rite of spiritual direction than Confession. Many faithful find these sessions to be quite valuable, so this is not a critique of Confession, but an opportunity to acknowledge the presence of desire among the people for personal spiritual direction from elders in the Church. Sometimes this spiritual direction occurs in the context of Confession, but the two should not be confused.

Theologians have an opportunity to provide clarity on the diverse rites of penance and processes of spiritual direction, and how they relate to participation in the Eucharistic community. I suggest three initial steps as a way of inaugurating a discussion among theologians on this topic. The first step is to devote energy to studying the art of spiritual direction in the Orthodox tradition and making it available to the people.[12] Traditionally, spiritual direction is the domain of monks and monasteries, and there has been much effort in attempting to plant monastic communities in North America. Encouraging people to visit monasteries and meet the monks and nuns of the Church is one way of facilitating spiritual direction. Theologians should also explore ways that spiritual direction might be expanded beyond monasteries and planted in parish life. The temptation is to add spiritual direction to the list of presbyteral duties, and it is one task presbyters attempt to perform within the context of Confession, to varying degrees of success. Given the current movement for revitalizing the diaconate in Orthodoxy, one might imagine deacons mastering the practice of spiritual direction, especially since this ministry does not require liturgical presidency.

The second step is to illuminate the existing rites of penance already practiced by the Church as legitimate ways of preparing for Holy Communion. There are several liturgical components that express and encourage penitence that are part of the process of preparing for Communion. The Divine Liturgy itself includes the kiss of peace that takes place immediately prior to the anaphora, an ancient and organic rite of mutual forgiveness that is often ignored or performed only by the clergy. The third and sixth hours contain many penitential psalms and hymns, especially Psalm 51 of the third hour. Perhaps the most undervalued penitential rite is the entire office of Vespers prayed in many parishes on Saturday evening. The prayers that occur towards the end of Vespers—especially the prayer at the bowing of the heads—is penitential and could be interpreted as preparing one for Communion. The Orthodox Church does not have a rite of penance within the Divine Liturgy as the revised Roman rite practices in Mass—the absence of a specific component that is defined and commonly understood as penitential and preparatory is one of the reasons the Church tends to turn to individual Confession as the preparatory rite, par excellence. Confession is a private office, and it seems that a readily identified communal rite of penance that prepares the assembly for Communion is missing. This rite needs to be positioned within the context of the Divine Liturgy, since attendance at Vespers or any office on the eve before Communion will not compare with the gathering for Divine Liturgy.

I have not mentioned the prayers of preparation for Holy Communion because these are recited privately. Some communities have introduced the practice of reciting the prayers together, along with the prayers after Communion. The issue with this practice is that the prayers contain numerous references to fear of judgment or condemnation if the communicant is unworthy, a pattern that exacerbates the unresolvable tension between divine mercy and justice.[13] Theologians should identify an existing liturgical component, or series of components, that encourage the faithful to repent and prepare for Communion. The most obvious existing component is the kiss of peace—adding more time to this component, encouraging all to participate, and accentuating the promise of divine forgiveness of sins for those who forgive others of their trespasses (Mt. 6) would allow the penitential quality of this rite to break through. Another possibility is to enhance a rite that occurs in some parishes in two liturgical soft spots: the very beginning of the Divine Liturgy and before the Great Entrance. Some parishes maintain the custom of the presider asking the people for forgiveness before beginning the Liturgy: this is a good opportunity to enhance this simple rite into one of communal penance and forgiveness. Orthodox Eucharistic theology has recovered a sense of the parts of the Divine Liturgy coming together as a cohesive whole. While some people are unable or unwilling to arrive for the beginning of the Liturgy, emphasis on a particular moment of consecration at the epiclesis of the Eucharistic Prayer is no longer universally observed among Orthodox clergy. The restoration of the Liturgy of the Word with emphasis on preaching illuminates an acknowledgment of divine activity throughout the course of the entire Liturgy. It is therefore essential to avoid positioning a communal act of penance before the Great Entrance because God is present from the beginning. In honor of the notion of the Divine Liturgy itself as an epiclesis (or a series of epicleses threaded throughout the Liturgy), I have composed a communal rite of penance (appendix B) to take place before the beginning of the Liturgy. This rite has the capacity to set the tone for the Divine Liturgy: instead of a collection of individuals saying their own private prayers exclusive of one another, all together stand in the same place (as the clergy descend from the sanctuary to the nave) and pray that God would bless the assembly to hear the word, offer God praise, receive the gift of Christ in Communion, and witness to God through service in the world. This rite is offered in the spirit of Jesus' teaching in the Gospel of Matthew (5:23–24), that Christians should forgive one another their trespasses before presenting their offering.

The last step is to liberate individual Confession from frequent Communion.[14] This is an appeal to frame Confession as a mystery to be approached with hope and courage, and not fear. Many priests handle Confession quite ably, as demonstrated by the respondents from St. Anthony parish who expressed gratitude for the mercy imparted to them in Confession. Their testimony confirms Confession as the rite through which God imparts divine mercy to the penitent. It is the affixation of Communion and one's unworthiness to receive it to Confession that instills fear of judgment. When Confession evolved, it became a mystery that acknowledges human weakness and invites people to receive divine grace anew, even when they have fallen from it repeatedly. Faithful should be invited to receive this grace without fearing that it will be withdrawn because they are not worthy of Communion. Theologians can reset the relationship of Confession to Communion by explaining both mysteries as rites that enable the participant to gain strength to become like Christ. On some days, the temptations and struggles of life render the participant weak after falling from grace, and God renews that strength in the Christian's quest to take up the cross and follow Christ. On other days, the reception of grace adds another layer of energy to the participant. The point is to acknowledge that the participant is always in a process of becoming and always in need of God's grace—approaching both mysteries is a penitential act in itself. Resetting the mysteries so that they are understood as mysteries that nourish Christians through the duration of their lifetimes shifts the paradigm from mysteries to be feared to mysteries to approach with confidence and hope.

The prayers of preparation for Communion demand our remarks as well. At minimum, these prayers need careful and gentle pastoral explanation, as many of the prayers were written in a milieu of Communion as a spiritual arena. Many of these prayers promote fear of condemnation and damnation for those who approach unworthily: adopting a new approach to these prayers, or composing new prayers that express hope and confidence instead of fear or condemnation.

LENT, HOLY WEEK, AND PASCHA AS THE
ONLY HOLY SEASON

It came as no surprise that respondents reflected at length on Lent, Holy Week, and Pascha as the feasts that were most meaningful to them. Like all Christian traditions, Pascha serves as the axis for the Orthodox Church. The intensity of the season may be even more pronounced in Orthodoxy than it is in other Churches, given the number of services and the grueling schedule of Holy Week. When respondents spoke fondly of the Good Friday processions and the rites involving the epitaphios, they fit right in with the larger Christian tradition that is always anticipating the good news that Jesus is risen. There are two implications from the focus group sessions that I will address as opportunities here: evidence that this season might be too intense, and the absence of references to other parts of the liturgical year.

Multiple respondents reflected on the grueling character of Holy Week and Pascha. This was particularly true for the choir directors, who had increased their workload of musical leadership significantly only to find themselves irritable and exhausted by Pascha. Two respondents confessed feelings of irritation when singers joined the choir for Pascha after being absent for all of Lent and Holy Week. One respondent marveled at the clergy's energy, and wondered how they could sustain such a pace. A few respondents mentioned feeling flat and disappointed when the joy of Pascha could not be sustained with the same intensity for the following weeks.

Holy Week and Pascha are solemn occasions that are largely untouchable. People revere Church traditions on the most solemn holidays, so it is unrealistic to propose that the Church would embrace major changes to this season. Liturgists could examine the offices of Holy Week to identify repetitions in the readings and commemorations. The readings for the offices of Good Friday are repeated from one office to another, a result of the current tradition absorbing the Holy Week liturgical components from both Jerusalem and Constantinople.[15] One respondent's suggestion that the Gospel readings could be adjusted to remove the repetitions is notable: his remark suggests that the repetitions add unnecessary length and weight to the services. A modest trimming of the readings could result in the improvement of the pace of the services and their transitions from one station to the next.[16] There is also a repetition in the celebration of Pascha itself. The current Vesperal

Liturgy of Holy Saturday is actually the original cathedral Paschal Vigil celebrated in both Constantinople and Jerusalem. The Vigil was designed to initiate new Christians into the Church so the first Gospel proclamation they heard would be the announcement, in Matthew, that Jesus is risen.[17] In contemporary practice, this office is usually celebrated on Saturday morning, and the people continue to fast until the main liturgy of Paschal Nocturne, Matins, and Eucharist begins at midnight (or at dawn among some Orthodox). In other words, there are two resurrection services, with the first interpreted as a commemoration of Jesus' sabbath in the tomb that leads to the second as a way to justify keeping both offices. In reality, the first is the retention of the cathedral Vigil—moved to Saturday morning—to be followed by the monastic Paschal offices featuring the canon of St. John of Damascus.

It would be sensible to maintain both services for parishes that have Baptisms on Pascha, or in communities that would embrace liturgies of several hours. For the latter, the Paschal Vigil could be moved to Saturday night, followed by a break, and continued with the next Paschal offices. Such a schedule would be enormously demanding for clergy even in large parishes, and it would prove difficult for people who are cooking and baking in preparation for the holiday, a crucial non-liturgical component of the holiday. The challenge is that most Orthodox parishes are small, and the liturgical leaders are expected to be on hand for all of these services.[18] One can see how an exhausted leader can become irritable given the additional rigors of these services. Musicians and leaders tend to tire quickly and are unable to sing well for Pascha because of the fatigue.

The Challenges of a Universal Ordo

The primary problem with the Holy Week schedule of services is the assumption that the ordo demands absolute observance by all parishes. The ordo represents a historical amalgamation of multiple traditions, which is why it is so lengthy, but it also provides a pattern for parishes. This means that parishes should be permitted to adapt the pattern to fit their reality. Many parishes omit the first part of Holy Week, but do so much from Thursday through Sunday that all leaders are exhausted. Clergy tend to dismiss the fatigue—even when it afflicts them—and this attitude ignores the human ability to perform for an extended period of time. In non-liturgical contexts like athletics or musical performance, athletes and performers experience similar challenges. Athletes participating in a series of games or a long game rely on adrenaline to sustain their energy, but even the best athletes tire, and in the worst circumstances, work themselves to such exhaustion that they become ill or injured. An even more crucial component is the thrill of competition and performance: artists revel in completing a series of concerts, but the ecstasy is simply not sustainable beyond a day or two. The proverbial image of "falling back to earth" applies to everyone, including clergy and musicians.

The challenge for our task of mitigating the drop-off from the height of Pascha is to make the celebration manageable and sustainable without excising beloved traditions. A reduced celebration of Pascha would still result in some kind of post-holiday drop-off. The objective is to revise the week so that Pascha does not amount to the end of the solemnity, but becomes the beginning of a fifty-day period of rejoicing, the season of Pentecost. Theologians can achieve this objective by exchanging liturgical rigidity for flexibility (a parish is not "Orthodox-light" if it has a less intense Holy Week ordo), and by featuring Pascha as the first announcement of the risen Lord, who is revealed to the Church in beautiful images throughout the fifty days of rejoicing, especially on each Sunday of Pascha. Earlier, I highlighted the power of the lectionary for the Sundays of Pascha: theologians could contribute to a rejuvenation of this liturgical season by reframing Pascha as the kickoff in a season of celebration, encounter, and renewal.

This objective of reframing Pascha leads to the second opportunity, for the people to receive the benefits of the rest of the liturgical year. The only other holiday mentioned by respondents was Theophany, and it is likely that this occasion comes to mind because it is particular to the Eastern Christian tradition. The absence of references to Christmas or Mary's Dormition was notable as well. The hegemony of Pascha in this discussion might have been influenced by the environment of the focus groups. When respondents began to talk about Holy Week and Pascha, others contributed to the discussion. However, I pointedly asked respondents to comment on other seasons and celebrations of the liturgical year, and the responses were generally quiet. My observation of parishes shows that people participate in other feasts and seasons, especially Mary's Dormition. But there is also a sense of disconnection between Pascha and the other holidays. The task posed to liturgical theologians is to demonstrate the liturgical year as a cohesive unit, with all of the feasts disclosing the Incarnate Christ and communion of saints to the people through a diverse array of narratives.

THE MYSTERY OF THE EXTRAORDINARY

One of the questions posed to the focus groups concerned "strong" liturgical and non-liturgical moments. My intent was to tease out particular moments people remembered as having a profound effect on their lives. I knew that the question might require clarification before people would respond, so I offered my own examples. In my case, I was struck by deeply personal events that involved Church and liturgy in some way, but did not occur during liturgical celebration. The first such event happened after my mother was diagnosed with breast cancer in 1989. After the initial news of the diagnosis, we attended Liturgy as always, and *after* the Liturgy, while people were still slowly making their way from the church to the hall, my mother knelt and prayed on her own while we stood beside her. It was an intimate family moment, and it was dramatic, since she cried and sobbed. I was seventeen years old at the time, and recall my father's anguish—he pulled my brother and me to the side and said sternly, "boys, this is serious." It was indeed serious, and I still have the image of my mother kneeling and praying, begging God to cure her and let her live. My memory includes more than an image of her and her crisis: it happened after Liturgy, so my picture is of her kneeling in church with the iconostasis in the background, illuminated only by the sunlight coming through the stained-glass windows in the historic building in St. Paul, the smell of incense and wax from candles lingering in the air.

My second memory is of an event that took place in my grandparents' backyard in 1996. We had received the tragic news of my uncle's sudden and untimely death of a heart attack and had to report it to my grandparents. We came with heavy hearts and deep anxiety, since they had lost their youngest daughter (my aunt) to sudden death in 1981. I feared they would both die on sight. After we told them, I expected hysteria, even from my grandfather, who had been a priest for 44 years at that time. His response shocked me—he crossed himself three times and said, "совершалось"—quoting Jesus on the cross, "it is finished." We pleaded with him to take the next day off from serving Divine Liturgy, as he was pastor of a small parish nearby. Not only did he serve, but he also presided over a memorial service for his departed son. I am struck by this memory to this day to see how people of faith responded to the fundamental sorrows of human daily life: with faith, yet not without sorrow. To this day, I believe that these moments of faith were formed by Liturgy, even if the relationship to actual liturgical celebration is implicit.

Respondents were generally quiet and hesitant to answer this question: maybe they needed more time to think it through. Besides the expected references to memories of Baptisms, Chrismations, funerals, and weddings, respondents tended to talk about extraordinary moments. A medical emergency in church during Holy Week, feeling struck by God in the body at Communion and during the Liturgy, and struggling to return to the world following the intimacy of a burial were some of the memories shared by respondents. In all of these cases, respondents were positive that their bodily experiences were spiritual, and even the medical emergency was not coincidental, but needed to happen in church.

The discussion on the extraordinary relates to this analysis of Liturgy because focus group respondents did not mention the typical phenomena one might expect in a conversation about the extraordinary. Contemporary Orthodox Liturgy is deeply saturated with commemorations of extraordinary events and celebrations of such manifestations in the present. The liturgical year contains several commemorations of wonderworking icons. These liturgies are not only sensational in the places the icons streamed myrrh, but the sensation is shared when the wonderworking icons travel to other places of the world. A regular review of the news in the Orthodox world yields multiple reports on clergy and faithful taking a wonderworking icon and bringing it to a parish in another city or country for a weekend of liturgical celebrations. The phenomenon of traveling icons is a continuation of the ancient tradition of translation of relics, as a local church shares its precious saints with the rest of the Church, so the saint can become a patron of many communities. When wonderworking icons arrive, the news is occasionally sensational. The local pastor invites people in the surrounding areas to join the celebration, and less frequently, the occasion can become quite public.

When the Vatopedi Monastery of Mount Athos brought the belt of Mary, the Mother of God, to Moscow in 2012, the Church invited the public to come and venerate her belt, and even hinted that those who approached with faith could be cured of diseases and infertility. The most renowned liturgical phenomenon occurs annually when Christians flock to Jerusalem to receive the "holy fire" in preparation for Pascha. The patriarch goes into the tomb at the Church of the Holy Sepulchre and receives a fire ignited by God—this fire is used in many churches to light the first candles in honor of Christ's resurrection.[19] In Orthodox culture, receiving the holy fire is a mark of prestige: bishops send delegations to Jerusalem to obtain the fire and bring it to their native communities in a gesture of solidarity. The phenomenon of the holy fire and the liturgies commemorating wonderworking icons are practices continuing the tradition of the translation of relics. These liturgies are also official Church events celebrating the extraordinary and inviting the faithful to share and witness to the manifestations of God in icons and relics.

It is telling that the respondents of our focus groups tended to drift towards the personal in their testimonies of the extraordinary. There was not one reference to the official Church events honoring the extraordinary, even though these liturgies are promoted broadly and familiar to the people. The absence of references to wonderworking icons does not necessarily mean that the people dismiss these events, especially since these commemorations in the liturgical year tend to originate from lay eyewitness accounts of theophanies in parish life. People sense that God is working in their lives by addressing the fundamental issues confronting humanity: life, death, crisis, health, and so on. The Liturgy produces theophanies, but they are not limited to tangible and material evidence that God is with us. Liturgical theophanies involve people and relationships, and illustrate that God is active in the ordinary business of daily life.

Of the accounts shared by the people, I found the testimony about their experience at a funeral from several respondents at HTC to be the most intriguing statement, especially since it was remembered by more than one person. They did not mention a tangible material theophany, but instead collectively acknowledged that everything had changed when they resumed everyday life after the funeral. The theophany was manifest not in icons or relics, but in the transformation of the people who had sung the departed to heaven at the burial. Their transformation was evident in the way they were seeing the world and encountering it following a death. They observed that nothing was the same, since God had taken someone from the world into the kingdom. Implicit in their description of their burial experience was their own need to confront the remainder of life following the death of a loved one. Their description of this adjustment resonated with my own experience of adjustment ignited by my mother's and grandfather's responses to illness and death. These testimonies suggest that God is quite active in the process of our transformation as we journey through the stages of this life. Most of the testimonies suggest that transformation is sparked by responses to events or experiences taking place with other people, or in dialogue with them.

The Legitimacy of Theophanies in Everyday Life

The opportunity for liturgical theologians here is to explore the phenomenon of theophany that occur among ordinary people encountering the struggles of daily life. Theologians would also be wise to explain the significance of theophanies in official Church events commemorating wonderworking icons, relics, and the holy fire. The primary issue with these events is the explosion of political interpretations that arise.[20] Church leaders have used such events to demonstrate God's favor among the people—this is not a new ploy, as leaders made such assertions in the fourth century, to assure the people that God is among them.[21] In the contemporary context, the triumphalism that accompanies miraculous relics and icons contradicts the core message of the Gospel calling for masters to become servants and all to adopt the way of the cross. The current generation of theologians has an opportunity to offer a theological critique of political theologies coalescing around liturgical com-memorations of miracles and relics.

LITURGY AND THEOLOGICAL ANTHROPOLOGY

The focus group discussion waded into the dangerous waters of the culture wars affecting the churches today. Exchanges on the possibility of ordaining women to the order of deaconess and expanding the liturgical roles for girls were animated and occasionally heated. In chapter 4, I indicated that advocates of both sides seemed to view the liturgy as a bearer of the Church's theological anthropology. Those who would like to sustain the status quo see the liturgy as honoring the differences between men and women and view gender complementarity as good. Proponents for ordaining deaconesses and assigning girls to roles reserved for boys (altar servers) suggest changes so that the Liturgy would express a theological anthropology that has become distorted. This second view depicts the status quo as promoting patriarchy, since men exercise almost all of the leadership roles in liturgy, with the exception of musical leadership.

The liturgical academy is busy at work on the matter of the order of deaconess, so in a sense, this particular topic of the deaconess could be described as a strength. Several liturgists, including me, have publicly indicated their support for the restoration of the order of deaconess. [22] The movement to restore the deaconess has existed in Russia, Greece, much of the West, and is most vibrant today in the Patriarchate of Alexandria. The primary question requiring clarification is assigning liturgical ministries to the deaconess. Will she simply be a female copy of the order of deacon, or will she resume the ministries previously performed in the medieval Church? Would the restoration of deaconess open the door to permit girls to be altar servers in all Orthodox churches? Liturgists rely exclusively on history to address these issues, and they will need to expand their horizons by addressing them theologically as well, because history is not formidable enough to offer a solution to a controversial question that could be received by the Church. I would add only that the discourse on this matter must include a discussion of renewing all of the orders, episcopate, presbyterate, and diaconate, because restoring one entails an adjustment in the ministry performed by the rest. This is particularly true for a larger discussion of the diaconate.

Respondents of our focus groups lamented the burdens borne by parish priests, who seem to be the only ministers who can do everything in and for the Church. A renewal of the diaconate could deeply enrich the Church's ministry, especially if deacons resume the ministries of healing the sick, consoling the bereaved, and representing the Church to the public. Furthermore, deacons could expand their liturgical ministries by presiding at the offices of the Liturgy of the Hours which do not require the invocations of presbyters or bishops to consecrate. This expansion would facilitate more communal assemblies for the people to pray, and provide more space for the presbyters to attend to their particular ministries.

The Storm of Liturgy and Gender: Meet It Directly

The second task required of theologians is to confront the storm of theological anthropology head-on. Orthodoxy's tepid engagement of the role of women in the Church ignores the current issue of gender and sexual identity in the Church. At the official level, theologians have rejected same-sex mar-

riage and the legitimacy of neutral gender identities. Appealing to the antiquity of tradition will not stop LGBT people from coming out in parishes.
Orthodox clergy are already confronting the dilemma of how to address
LGBT people when the official Church position condemns these identities,
excommunicates them from the Eucharist, and develops programs to cure
them from same-sex attraction.[23] While obeying these policies will please
Church leaders and many people in the Church, others will be alienated and
will lament the exclusion of LGBT people from the Church, as evidenced by
the sentiments of the focus group respondents. The best way for theologians
to serve the Church on this matter is to engage the LGBT issue in an honest
dialogue within the boundaries of the Church. This proposed dialogue can be
productive only if it occurs in an environment prohibiting polemical attacks
and guided by the Spirit of love for all of God's children. This means that
Church leaders must be willing to end policies that exclude LGBT people
from receiving Communion. I do not know if the Church will adopt a new
mindset on this matter, but Orthodoxy cannot move forward unless it engages the LGBT community in a real dialogue where leaders will be willing
to hear the presentations of all perspectives. Theologians cannot change the
fact that the people view the Liturgy as a symbol of the Church's theological
anthropology; they can contribute to the discussion that assesses the adequa-
cy of the status quo of theological anthropology in Orthodoxy.

LITURGICAL CATECHESIS

Our final opportunity brings us back to the beginning of this project. The
bulk of this chapter provides a blueprint for the agenda of liturgical theology
in response to the people's descriptions of liturgical participation. The liturgical renewal movement was one of granting access to the people: they
received new access to Communion, many of the prayers and hymns of the
Liturgy, and were invited to partake more fully of its rites. A generation of
clergy presented the Liturgy to the people by emphasizing its lifegiving
potential. Liturgical renewal also increased the number of rites people could
attend and engage. There was more Liturgy for the people to engage and
absorb. The pioneers of liturgical renewal did not create structured programs
of liturgical catechesis, as we saw in chapter 2, as pastors customize liturgical formation to meet the needs of their communities.

Remove Opaque Liturgical Symbols and Components

The opportunity for theologians is to continue to remove obstacles that pre-
vent people from engaging the Liturgy. It is tempting to present official
explanations of the meaning of the Liturgy to the people, especially when
these texts are persuasive and beautiful. The Mystagogical Catecheses of St.

Cyril of Jerusalem represent an older explanation of the rites of initiation, whereas Schmemann's book on the Eucharist presents a contemporary view of its meaning. Pastors are free to encourage people to learn as long as the primary teacher remains the Liturgy itself. There is no need for pastors to impose rigid explanation defining liturgical components or the configuration of worship space on a program of liturgical catechesis. It is better for pastors to honor liturgical participation as a lifelong process that slowly engenders comprehension on the part of the people. In other words, Liturgy is not primarily informational; it is relational, and the people learn best when Liturgy illuminates the way they relate to family, friends, colleagues, and enemies. Information is helpful and pastors should encourage people to learn liturgical history to understand how the Liturgy came to find its current shape. But pastors and theologians are not bound to be slaves of that history, because a rigid commitment to sustaining the past is a way of stunting the organic development of the liturgy. The theologians can enrich the fluid Orthodox approach to liturgical catechesis by reminding clergy and laity that Liturgy has never been uniform, it has always been subject to change, it is relational, it is not a mimesis of the past, but a participation in the future life of God, and it is not a text, but a ritual event that includes the singing and recitation of some texts. When theologians stop short of canonizing one or another liturgical practice, interpretation, or aesthetic, they honor Liturgy's fundamental nature as an encounter with God that occurs through rituals employing the cultural and artistic idioms of the local community.[24] Being open to the possibility of change can cause anxiety, but theologians must take solace in the fact that the shedding of Byzantinisms from the Liturgy won't make it any less Orthodox.

CONCLUSION

This chapter has elaborated the agenda for theologians on the basis of the information yielded by our four focus groups. My proposed agenda is supposed to be the beginning of an ongoing discussion taking place in the local church. The point of the agenda is to consider and receive the observations of the people as legitimate and bearing a theological weight of equal value to the official theology espoused by Church leaders and canonized in published texts. Two observations summarize how the people's understanding of the Liturgy could contribute to specific aspects of its celebration. First, the Liturgy is much more than a text defined by official explanations: the experiences of the people who worship provide us with precious insights into what Liturgy really is, and I have attempted to illuminate this reality here and bringing it into dialogue with the theologians. Second, the people testified to a great deal of change in the Liturgy, and as time progresses, the Church is confronting more change. This chapter attempts to provide some guidance to theologians on how they might address change in and through the Liturgy.

NOTES

1. See also Senn, 211–14.

2. Paul Bradshaw and Maxwell Johnson, *The Eucharistic Liturgies: Their Evolution and Interpretation* (Collegeville, MN: Liturgical Press, 2012), 311.

3. Ibid.

4. Juan Mateos, *La célébration de la parole dans le liturgie byzantine: étude historique* (Rome: Pontifical Oriental Institute, 1971), 130–31. Daniel Galadza's research on liturgical sources of Jerusalem shows that an Old Testament reading is appointed for some ordinary Sunday liturgies in the manuscript Sinaiticus Graecus N.E. МГ 8 (10th century), "Sources for the Study of Liturgy in Post-Byzantine Jerusalem (638–1137 CE)," *Dumbarton Oaks Papers* 81 (2013), 81.

5. See Alexander Lingas, "Tradition and Renewal in Contemporary Greek Orthodox Psalmody," in *Psalms in Community: Jewish and Christian Liturgical, Artistic, and Textual Traditions*, ed. Harold Attridge, Society of Biblical Literature Symposium Series 25 (Atlanta: Society of Biblical Literature, 2004): 348–49.

6. Metropolitan Antony (Khrapovitskii) and New Skete monastery might not have much in common, but they share a common concern for the quality of liturgical celebration by the clergy. See my presentation of Antony in *Liturgical Reform After Vatican II*, 149–53, and also my treatment of New Skete, 267–69.

7. New Skete Monastery has published their lectionary on their web site: https://newskete.org/worship (accessed February 26, 2018).

8. Gabriel Bertonière, *The Sundays of Lent in the Triodion; The Sundays Without a Commemoration*, Orientalia Christiana Analecta 253 (Rome: Pontifical Oriental Institute, 1997): 45–50. Bertonière notes that the Jerusalem tradition had several lessons for the Gospel of Luke appointed to the Sundays of Lent.

9. Bertonière shows that the Sundays of Lent did not have major commemorations before the ninth century in ibid., 42–45.

10. Notable here is the recent teaching adopted and promulgated by the Moscow Patriarchate, "Об участии верных в Евхаристии" [On the Participation of the Faithful in the Eucharist], February 3, 2015, http://www.patriarchia.ru/db/text/3981166.html (accessed February 15, 2018). The Patriarchate adopted a somewhat restrained position by recommending Confession and fasting before Communion. It is notable, though, that the Patriarchate recommended that faithful receive Communion frequently—the prevalence of this spirit in the document demonstrates the influence of the Eucharistic revival on the mother Church. Practice has yet to catch up to teaching; the people's participation in church life is still at a low ebb.

11. Note that this prayer is normally recited twice, since the clergy recite it quietly in the altar before they receive Communion.

12. On this matter, see the excellent study of John Chryssavgis, *Soul Mending: The Art of Spiritual Direction* (Brookline, MA: Holy Cross Orthodox Press, 2000).

13. On this matter, see Nicholas Denysenko, "Death and Dying in Orthodox Liturgy," in "Inward Being and Outward Identity: The Orthodox Churches in the 21st Century," ed. John Jillions, *Religions* 8 (2017): doi:10.3390/rel8020025.

14. For more on this matter, see my article, "Orthodox Confession: Receiving Forgiveness for the Life of the World," in *Liturgy* (April 2018).

15. See Pott, 153–96.

16. Pavlos Koumarianos, "Liturgical Problems of Holy Week," *St. Vladimir's Theological Quarterly* 46, no. 1 (2002): 10.

17. Nicholas Denysenko, "Psalm 81: Announcing the Resurrection on Holy Saturday," *Logos: A Journal of Eastern Christian Studies* 50 (2009): 55–88.

18. I sang the responses to the Holy Saturday services by myself in many parishes to relieve the choir—this permitted the musicians to prepare for the holiday and rest.

19. For a historical overview of the holy fire, see Valentina Izmirlieva, "Christian Hajjis: The Other Orthodox Pilgrims to Jerusalem," *Slavic Review* 73, no. 2 (2014): 332–35. Also see Bishop Auxentios, *The Paschal Fire in Jerusalem: A Study of the Rite of the Holy Fire in the Church of the Holy Sepulchre* (Berkeley: St. John Chrysostom Press, 1993).

20. For example, see the comparison between the Orthodox belonging to the canonical Church and the so-called schismatics in "Priest Awarded for Defending Miraculous Icon from Vandals in All-Ukraine Procession," http://orthochristian.com/103963.html (accessed February 26, 2018).

21. Peter Brown, *The Cult of the Saints: Its Rise and Function in Latin Christianity* (Chicago: University of Chicago Press, 1981), 92–93.

22. "Orthodox Liturgists issued a statement of support for the revival of the order of deaconess by the Patriarchate of Alexandria," https://panorthodoxcemes.blogspot.ca/2017/10/orthodox-liturgists-issued-statement-of.html?m=1 (accessed February 22, 2018). See the rebuttal of this statement signed by dozens of scholars, clergy, and laity in "A Public Statement on Orthodox Deaconesses by Concerned Clergy and Laity," http://www.aoiusa.org/a-public-statement-on-orthodox-deaconesses-by-concerned-clergy-and-laity/ (accessed February 22, 2018). The authoritative study on the order of deaconess is Petros Vassiliadis, Niki Papageorgiou, and Eleni Kasselouri-Hatzivassiliadi, eds., *Deaconesses, the Ordination of Women, and Orthodox Theology* (Cambridge: Cambridge University Press, 2017).

23. "Holy Scriptures and the teaching of the Church unequivocally deplore homosexual relations," no. 12.9, in the "Basis of the Social Concept of the Russian Orthodox Church," https://mospat.ru/en/documents/social-concepts/xii/ (accessed February 22, 2018). The Assembly of Canonical Orthodox Bishops of the United States of America holds a slightly more irenic position in its 2013 statement on marriage and sexuality, stating that "Persons with homosexual orientation are to be cared for with the same mercy and love that is bestowed on all of humanity by our Lord Jesus Christ. Moreover, the Church is a spiritual hospital, where we all are called to find the healing of our fallen humanity through Jesus Christ, who assumed human nature in order to restore it," no. 3, 2013 Statement on Marriage and Sexuality, http://assemblyofbishops.org/about/documents/2013-assembly-statement-on-marriage-and-sexuality (accessed February 22, 2018).

24. Don Saliers, "Liturgical Aesthetics: The Travail of Worship," in *Arts, Theology, and the Church: New Intersections*, ed. Kimberley J. Vrudny and Wilson Yates (Cleveland, OH: Pilgrim Press, 2005), 187–88.

Conclusion

This review and analysis of the people's reflections on Orthodox liturgy yields several lessons. The people contributed diverse views on the Liturgy, an expected outcome since the study draws from four parishes covering a wide regional span of the United States. The previous chapter identified the strengths and opportunities for theological reflection with most of the attention devoted to changing our perception of liturgical understanding, addressing the ecumenical dimension of Eucharistic ecclesiology, enhancing a sense of divine compassion in the Liturgy, clarifying the connection between Confession and Communion, addressing liturgy as the bearer of theological anthropology, and examining the tendency to privilege Lent, Holy Week, and Pascha as the only solemn season of the Church year.

The conclusion to this book reflects on observations gleaned from the four focus groups that have implications for the enterprise of liturgical theology and the study of Orthodoxy in America in general. American Orthodoxy's context, expectations for the laity's contribution to liturgical theology, the people's response to authoritative theological teaching, and the dynamics of the people's sense of tradition are the topics rounding out this study.

THE UNIQUE CONTEXT OF AMERICAN ORTHODOXY

The small population of American Orthodox Christians does not do justice to the complex coexistence of liturgical schools in Orthodox America. One can encounter a variety of liturgical languages, icons, architectural styles, music, and customs from one parish to another.[1] Orthodoxy in America has communities that have functioned as curators of the tradition they received from their native countries deeply resistant to change, and also laboratories for liturgical renewal. As with other émigré communities, Orthodox diaspora parishes occasionally retain liturgical practices that are untouched by progress instituted in the Churches of the original native countries. Some parishes have embraced American life and attempted to fit in to the community, announcing their proverbial arrival by building new churches, with the purchase of property a sign of both vitality and longevity. In recent years, sociologists have included Orthodoxy when compiling profiles of the Orthodox Church as part of the broader American landscape. Alexei Krindatch has published the most material on Orthodoxy in America, and the Assembly of Canonical Orthodox Bishops in America (ACOBA) features Krindatch's results, many of which I have featured here to support this study.

What is missing from the ongoing study of Orthodox in America is a taxonomy of church life. The limited corpus of studies on Orthodoxy in America tends to examine either the primary theological figures at established theological schools, or statistics within individual jurisdictions. Topical studies are also oriented towards jurisdiction—to date, there is no effort to construct a cross-jurisdictional study of parishes and parish life, so there is no existing taxonomy of practices. For the purposes of this reflection, I will draw from the modest taxonomy I constructed on the basis of the architectural models I examined from seven Orthodox communities in America.[2] These models offer an initial foundation for further examination of liturgical life in America. The immigrant Church, the American Church, and the liturgical renewal church are the three models.

The strongest witness to the immigrant Churches comes from the people of Greek descent from SG and SK. These immigrants offer an important witness to the migration of liturgical traditions from their native countries to America and the ensuing development of those traditions here. They witnessed to important changes, especially the gradual introduction of English to the Liturgy. The immigrant respondents recalled the liturgical rigor instilled in them as children: they were instructed to fast absolutely in preparation for Communion, but their education in Orthodoxy was uneven—one immigrant attended a school in Cyprus with instruction on the fundamentals of Orthodoxy, whereas another learned very little about the Bible. The sense that something was lost when the Church came to America was striking. The respondents stated that an English translation of the liturgy is just that—a translation—and simply cannot connote the meaning of the original Greek. It is likely that these respondents had the formidable task of transplanting the fullness of Church life in the new world as it was experienced in their mother countries.

Yet these same immigrants embraced opportunities to learn about their faith in America, with one participating in a Bible study with non-Orthodox colleagues at work, and another expressing her desire that pastors would share their knowledge with the people. The immigrant model is complex:

immigrants desire to sustain their memories of the past and pass them on to the next generation, but they are also willing to learn new things. For these respondents, the process of migration yields two insights: some change was inevitable when community life was established in America, especially in liturgical language, and some loss was going to accompany that change. But arriving in America offered a new opportunity to learn: the witness of SG5 is striking, since his encounter with biblically oriented Christians inspired his desire to learn about his own faith. The immigrants who embraced arrival and exploited it as an opportunity to learn were open to some American assimilation in Church practice.[3] Ironically, this assimilation is contradicted by converts who desire a restoration of traditional Orthodox practices, especially Byzantinization.

In my study on architecture, I was struck by parishes that wanted to blend into the American religious landscape. The features of American religiosity are inscribed on architecture, especially when structures do not have an overtly Orthodox style on the exterior, but blend with the buildings of the surrounding neighborhood. The aspects of Americanization are subtle in our study. Americanization appears in social dimensions: the gathering of a Bible study group in which participants learn more about liturgy, in the use of pews in church, the use of the organ or other instruments during the Liturgy, and the desire for an increase in the liturgical participation of the people in the liturgy. Liturgical participation is also a feature of liturgical renewal and it is not particularly American, but its connection to egalitarianism and democracy—especially for parishes based on conciliarity as their ecclesiology—makes it compatible with American values. It was not only normal, but pleasant for the focus groups to come together and have an open discussion about liturgy. The respondents seemed perfectly at home debating the pros and cons of female ministry: this is not to claim that the notion of female presidency is American strictly speaking, but the spirit of open discussion on these matters without censorship in the focus groups is compatible with American values. Therefore, when respondents express joy at assembling together for Liturgy and remorse for prohibiting others from joining in, they represent features of American Church life that values inclusivity and community. The fact that discussion on these issues did not always result in consensus but yielded difference is also a staple of the American affinity for plurality.

Churches of the liturgical renewal are also rooted in conciliar ecclesiology. Most of the respondents of this study experienced liturgical renewal in one way or another, especially in receiving encouragement to partake of Communion frequently. This study shows that liturgical renewal remains a process—it is not completely implemented by parishes that practice it, since people express some discomfort, that others view them with disapproval, or that they are unworthy. America has provided fertile soil for Orthodox liturgical renewal, and this study demonstrates that the people are relieved that they are encouraged to participate more, but that this invitation challenges their faith in new ways, as they are becoming more attuned to the human condition, to the way they interact with others in their company, and to their own unworthiness before God. In other words, liturgical renewal demands more from participants; it appears to be minimalist on the surface, but it is actually more rigorous than the liturgical status quo.

Furthermore, liturgical renewal is not limited to the Eucharistic revival. Some parishes are dismissing the absorption of non-Orthodox elements of worship and parish life, and have turned to Byzantinization as a way to restore a sense of authentic liturgy, especially in iconography and Church music, but also in Eucharistic discipline. This is a veritable liturgical change, and some tension between adherents of the Eucharistic revival and Byzantinization was evident in some of the respondent comments, especially those who did not understand why new traditions they had adopted needed purification. In sum, this study has illuminated the liturgical diversity in the small Orthodox churches of America and has especially shown how people adjust to their new environments in liturgical migration, and how they seek to sustain their identity through varying and often contradictory approaches to liturgical renewal.

TRADITION: LOCAL, PERSONAL, RECENT

In the Eastern Orthodox world, liturgical practices have not remained static. Before the ninth century, the primary Liturgy of Constantinople was St. Basil's, the Great Church of the imperial city set the pace for the rest of the churches, and churches were not painted wall-to-wall with icons. By the eleventh century, the liturgical status quo had changed, as icons filled the domes, apses, and chancel barriers of churches, and the liturgy of St. John Chrysostom became the primary Sunday liturgy of the Church. Events that changed society had an effect on liturgy: monks were the leaders of the triumph over iconoclasm, so the monastic liturgy became pre-eminent in Byzantine liturgical practice. Just as no single event was responsible for changing the composition and rhythm of daily life, liturgical change cannot be traced to a single act. The Latin sack of Constantinople in 1204 CE changed the shape of Church life enough that the monastic rite came to be the dominant partner with cathedral liturgy in the fusion that resulted in the wake of the capital's turbulence. The pattern of political and cultural events affecting liturgical life occurred at other times in the history of the Orthodox Church. One outstanding instance was the introduction of polyphonic music to Orthodox Liturgy. This was not a simple change to the practice of liturgical music effected by an episcopal decree, but the result of a shift based on cultural encounter within Central Europe. When Ukrainian and Belarusian youth studied at Central European centers such as Prague, Leipzig, and Krakow, they learned the forms of religious poetry and drama, and liturgical and paraliturgical music that were cultivated in those centers in the Protestant and Catholic Reformations. Religious pluralism caused cross-pollination: religious dramas with catechetical or even polemical purposes performed by Protestants were copied by Jesuits and adopted by Orthodox young people. The singing of hymns set to polyphony in these contexts eventually permeated Orthodox liturgical practice, migrated from central into Eastern Europe, and became permanent fixtures of liturgical music.

These examples provide the historical nuts and bolts for a simple fact concerning liturgical development: multiple factors contribute to changes in tradition, which means that traditions can and do change. This study has queried selected groups of Orthodox laity for their sense of tradition, and as a result, we have learned that focus group participants are witnesses to an important period of liturgical change. The participants in this study witness to the forms, styles, and language of liturgy established in America by immigrants from mother countries. They witnessed to change effected in those liturgies caused by a series of intellectual movements, including the opening of Church borders in ecumenism, the movement for the use of the vernacular in liturgy, a desire to restore tradition through the study and application of liturgical history, and a related movement of Byzantinization that sought to restore authenticity to Orthodox liturgy. Each movement resulted in tangible changes in ritual acts experienced by the people: these changes also unearthed fundamental questions of belonging, theological anthropology, and the assembly's relationship with God and their surrounding world.

Since the eighteenth century, Christian theologians have adopted new methods of critical research, examining texts and communities through new methods that provide new information on the sacred texts and practices. Manuscript studies provide much more information on how texts are written, revised, translated, and distributed in many places of the world. The same methods of critical textual and ritual examination have enhanced the development of liturgy. Christians have access to precious details on how liturgies develop, how they are received, and how they change in response to environmental factors. In other words, the traditions held by Christian communities are complex: rarely are they handed on from one generation to the next with no changes or revisions, even within a single community. The academic methods used to illuminate tradition are employed by experts within the Church who desire to understand tradition.

In Church communities, the narrative on tradition developed by academics occasionally comes into conflict with prevailing myths about tradition. The prevailing myth is common to religious communities: beloved and sacred rites, rituals, and customs are handed down directly from one generation to the next, without blemish or change. These traditions become untouchable when they are shaped by narratives defining them as universally held and honored by recognizable heroes of religious communities. Such views are held even by well-educated academics. The notion of a universal Christian tradition held by all is epitomized by the Commonitory of Vincent of Lerins in the fifth century, in which he claimed a universal orthodox consensus held everywhere, always, and by all (ubique, semper, ad omnibus).[4] Vincent's classical treatise exemplifies the power held by a critical mass of theologians to affirm the authority of tradition. If Vincent symbolizes the hegemony of a synthetic authority in the patristic era, Schmemann is an example of a modern theologian who sees the fathers as speaking univocally. In this sense, Schmemann used the supposed consensus of the fathers on the liturgy as the epiphany of the Church's faith to reposition the liturgy as the primary source for theological reflection.

Non-experts in Church communities might not know the names of the high-profile theologians who supposedly adhere to a theological synthesis, but they tend to lean towards the myth of traditions as being held by all the forebears of their own communities. Lay men and women might not claim that the fathers viewed the liturgy as the epiphany of the Church's faith, but they will claim that multiple generations honored the traditions observed by their communities of the present. The people's notion of tradition is shaped by what they have received from the previous generation. When I began discussing what I was learning in courses on liturgical history with my grandfather, who had been a priest for over fifty years, he gave me an abridged typikon for parish clergy published in the early twentieth century, and said, "here is the Church's tradition of worship for the last 2,000 years." He was educated in history, but when it came to the ritual practices and customs of his Church community, he trusted the authority of those who reared and formed him in those customs.

Parish people, then, tend to honor the authority of those who led and taught worship in their native communities, even if the information one can obtain from experts on the history or theological quality of a given practice suggests that revision might be in order. The people of our focus groups felt the weight of responsibility to honor the tradition they had received from their parents and elders, and to pass that tradition on without blemish to the next generation. In most of these cases, some kind of personal touch enhanced the weight of the sense of responsibility. Respondents from HTC and SG reflected on the admiration and respect they held for pastors of their communities. In the case of HTC, the pastor's style of liturgical celebration resonated personally with the respondents, who knew the contours of their local tradition. There is a direct connection between the pastor's relationship with the people and their ability to speak eloquently and even lovingly of the liturgy they celebrated. It is also clear that respondents honored the traditions received from the lay elders of the previous generation. The recollection of elderly people bowing as low as possible to walk under the epitaphios during the Matins of Holy Saturday is a good example. Respondents were sensitive to the elders' fidelity to observing the tradition, even when it was difficult for them to participate on account of their age.

Love for a community tradition is enhanced when beloved and respected elders of that community passed it on. It is impossible to disentangle the meaning of the tradition from the personal characteristics of the people who passed it on. The love people hold for the elders of their community—parents and grandparents, but also the other people—becomes affixed to the actual tradition itself. This type of veneration for tradition has domestic roots, and it is related to the traditions honored by all local cultures, especially family meals. Children often choose lives that depart from the conditions of their family cell, but they will come together to host a family meal even if it is difficult for them to find the time to prepare it because of their love for the family member who hosted the meal.[5] For some reason, the tradition of venerating the epitaphios on Holy Saturday became beloved in the global Orthodox community, and the elders of the community passed this tradition on to the succeeding generation. Liturgical scholarship demonstrates that the epitaphios tradition is one of the newest arrivals in the Byzantine world, and liturgical scholars might agree that the Scripture readings form the core of the Holy Week liturgical offices. In this instance, the people would honor the authority of the tradition they received from beloved elders over the weight of academic findings on the novelty and relative importance of the epitaphios rites.

The participation of converts in this study offers a helpful dimension in learning how the laity honors liturgical tradition in the Church. Converts learn about liturgy differently from people born in the Church because many converts are introduced to Orthodoxy through literature. For many converts, their first impression of tradition comes from literature and not participation in parish life. Amy Slagle mentions the occasional tensions between converts and established parishioners when converts critique liturgical traditions dear to the parish.[6] The picture of parish liturgy painted by literature is not always compatible with the realities of local parish liturgy. This reflection on converts and their sense of tradition simply illustrates how varying experiences result in different views of tradition. For the case of some converts, literature has more prestige in their sense of tradition than it does among people born and raised in the Church.

In our focus groups, tensions between converts and others on parish liturgical practices did not rise to the surface, but instead, some converts compared Orthodox worship with the rites of their previous Church affiliation. The remarks of two respondents from SA on the blessings of Orthodox Confession and their claim that it is superior to Catholic reconciliation are good examples. Since Vatican II, the Roman Church has intentionally strengthened the therapeutic components of Confession, partially as a result of the ecumenical mindset of the council. For the two convert respondents from SA, Catholic and Orthodox Confession are mutually exclusive: Catholic Confession promotes fear of judgment, whereas Orthodox Confession encourages hope and healing. Individual reflections on church experience cannot represent the entirety of a tradition: it's possible that the two respondents' experiences of Confession in the Catholic Church did indeed emphasize the juridical and fear of damnation over hope and healing. But it's also possible that one could have the opposite experience, and emerge from Orthodox Confession with a heavier heart, fearful of eternal punishment.

What's important here is the tendency to identify Orthodox liturgical and sacramental practices as the only bearers of authentic Christian tradition. In other words, because the Orthodox Church is the true Church, all of its practices are the only legitimate ones by definition. This tendency to depict Orthodoxy as a repository of truth manifest in its liturgy was particularly powerful in the somewhat heated debates on the question of women and the diaconate in our focus groups. In the focus groups, only self-identified converts to Orthodoxy voiced a belief that the disappearance of the order of deaconess in Orthodox was a result of witnessing to the true faith. In each instance, the same opponents offered ominous warnings of the perils coming to Orthodoxy if the Church restores the deaconess, given the catastrophes that had stricken the Churches to which they belonged previously, when they began to ordain women. Today, proponents for the restoration of the order of deaconess dismiss the argument that a series of evils will accompany the admission of women to ordination as a fatuous slippery slope argument. But I believe that the discussions that took place in our focus groups show that opposition to ordination is galvanized because that would require either change to liturgical practice or the introduction of something new. Note that the same people tend to love certain traditional Orthodox liturgical practices, such as the restoration of Byzantine or neo-Novgorodian iconography. These restorations are permissible and desirable because they come from within Orthodoxy. Deaconesses are not permissible because the opponents perceive that this is an importation of a flawed practice from Western Churches that would diminish the authenticity of Orthodox identity, even though deaconesses were once a part of Orthodox tradition. In this sense, the introduction of a tradition of women engaging ministry to communities remained fresh in the minds of those who rejected the tradition. For them, the anti-tradition of women's ordination supersedes any historical justification of its restoration because it was handed on to them by the previous generation.

In summary, the focus group sessions illustrate a complicated view of tradition held by participants. The liturgical traditions that resonate most powerfully with them are those that have been handed down by beloved elders of the previous generation. Their love for the people who taught them how to participate in liturgy generally supersedes the lessons presented by liturgical history. But tradition works in different ways, too—for some people, rejection of a tradition experienced in a non-Orthodox Church heightens the authority of the present Orthodox tradition, and this view can depict the Orthodox tradition as the absolute and only bearer of truth. The implications of this observation for the liturgical theologian are manifold. First, theologians cannot dismiss living practices, even if their research on a ritual practice informs them that it is relatively new and does not have deep roots in history. Second, the dynamic connection between the personal experience and fidelity to tradition exhibits the deeply communitarian nature of Liturgy. Liturgical participation is rooted in domestic rites of family meals, the narration of stories, and celebrations with singing. These are also dimensions that tend to characterize practices of popular religion. The key for theologians is to honor the power of lived ritual and to demonstrate respect for it by working with the people to understand how beloved rituals relate to the rest of the liturgical office. This does not mean that theologians are to abandon the hard work of liturgical history; rather, they are to gently teach people to recognize the connections between their favorite liturgical practices and the larger context of the liturgical office. For example, the practice of walking underneath the epitaphios can be connected to the proclamation of the word at that same Gospel so the two ritual components enrich one another.

Addressing the myth of tradition as observed everywhere, always, and by everyone is a more challenging task, especially since experts know that all liturgy is local. Some of the respondents exhibited openness to learning about tradition during these sessions, as people praised fathers Arida and Courey for explaining the history of liturgy and iconography to them. People become more defensive about traditions that are dear to their hearts. Some clergy perpetuate the myth of eternal liturgical traditions that are universally held. Theologians perform a great service to the Church when they teach people the details on the development of traditions; that service is undone when theologians use the history to propose revoking a tradition that has taken root in a local community. The controversy surrounding serving festal Divine Liturgies in the evening is a good example: even though there are historical precedents for evening Divine Liturgies on the feasts of Holy Thursday, Pascha, Christmas, Theophany, and Annunciation, some theologians view these as exceptions that were not intended to become modular for any feast, whereas others viewed the tradition as a pattern that could be applied. Regardless of one's view on the matter, some parishes began to celebrate evening Vesperal liturgies. Once such a tradition becomes a part of a parish's rhythm and order, there is no good reason to discontinue it if it is building up parish life. In this sense, theologians need to beware of depicting historical practices as bearing absolute authority: revoking beloved practices on the basis of historical research only leads to a decrease in the laity's trust in academic research and its capacity to enrich parish liturgy.

THE LITURGICAL THEOLOGY OF THE LAITY IN THE FUTURE: DANCING TO THEIR OWN TUNE

The people's sense of tradition shapes their attention to and interest in the authoritative theology of the Church. There are many levels of authoritative theology in Orthodoxy, and pastors instruct the people primarily from the pulpit, and secondarily through distribution of literature in bulletins. Authoritative theology is akin to magisterial theology, or theology promoted by the Church. Authoritative theology includes dogmatic definitions and conciliar declarations, especially those of the seven ecumenical councils, and theological works promoted by bishops and parish pastors. Such theological works can include patristic writings, such as homilies by St. John Chrysostom, and contemporary historical or theological monographs on the Liturgy.

Amy Slagle's study reminds us that the people tend to learn about Orthodoxy on their own, by consulting a customized selection of online sources. The survey of pastors and respondent feedback from the focus groups suggests that the process of instructing people through selected readings takes place in some parish settings, but is not universal in Orthodoxy. The Orthodox Church simply does not have an organizational apparatus devoted to varying levels of catechism akin to those of the Catholic and Protestant Churches. Therefore, one cannot draw any firm conclusions about the people's reception of authoritative theology. This study suggests that some clergy make an effort to instruct people in the basics of liturgical theology by reading the works of theologians like Schmemann, or sacramental theology by reading the likes of St. Cyril of Jerusalem. This kind of instruction is not directed towards the entire parish, but occurs in the context of small groups within parishes consisting of people who want to learn more about the Liturgy. The Bible study group at parishes like St. Katherine's in Redondo Beach exemplifies the kinds of small groups within parishes that seek catechetical instruction. It is a voluntary exercise, not optional. Furthermore, the Orthodox Church does not have an official catechism distributed to the people for instruction on authoritative theology. There are informal catechisms published in individual independent Orthodox Churches one can purchase in a parish kiosk or online, but Orthodoxy's position on authoritative theology is that it is located in the legacy of the seven ecumenical councils, in their canons and declarations. As Petros Vassiliadis has observed, Orthodoxy does not have a Vatican II or Augsburg Confession to which one can refer faithful.[7] While many scholars and pastors refer to a type of patristic synthesis (or "the teachings of the holy fathers" in colloquial terms), there is no single text or publication that delivers these teachings. There have been recent systematic attempts to create an apparatus of Orthodox teaching that can be distributed to the people, exemplified by the Basis of the Social Concept of the Russian Orthodox Church.[8] This document is useful for identifying an Orthodox perspective on fundamental contemporary issues, but its authority is limited, as it is the teaching of the local Church of Russia, and does not represent the voice of the entire Orthodox Church.

The ordinary layperson in the pew encounters authoritative theology in the Liturgy, primarily through the frequent recitation of the Nicene-Constantinopolitan Creed, the Monogenes of the Divine Liturgy, and the hymnography of the Church. This study shows that the laity attends to some of the theology communicated by the actual Liturgy, especially in the examples of the reading of the vita of St. Mary of Egypt, and the narratives of the scripture lessons and hymns of Palm Sunday and Holy Week. The focus group discussions confirmed the notion of Liturgy as *theologia prima* when respondents referred to liturgical examples to reflect on real-life situations, especially in the joy of receiving Communion together, and the sorrow of realizing that some are excluded from participation. Some of the participants in the pastor's survey and the focus groups suggested that the Liturgy itself is the most effective teacher of Liturgy: this study suggests that the people learn the most from the actual Liturgy itself.

What, then, is the purpose of secondary literature on the Liturgy, the historical and theological books written by the likes of Schmemann, Taft, and other experts? Only a small sampling of pastors even mentioned secondary works, and if one considers the pastors of the focus groups alongside the survey of pastors, clergy who read monographs on the Liturgy for catechetical purposes are the exception, and not the rule. In the catechetical paradigm of the pre-digital epoch, the people would be exposed to literature on Liturgy through their pastor, who functioned as the gatekeeper of theological works contributing to the people's formation. Even now, many parishes have kiosks with pamphlets containing synopses of official literature, and in some cases, parishes have bookstores or small libraries of theological books. The digital age has expanded the reading options for the people, and for those who choose to learn more about the liturgy, they are most likely to read books on the basis of recommendation. Those who read independently have a plethora of online options available to them, including a lay-friendly site such as Public Orthodoxy, or Sister Vassa's YouTube channel and podcast.

The implications of the flexible process people engage to learn about Orthodoxy suggests that their reception of authoritative theology is inconsistent. On the one hand, the focus group sessions suggest that people have received some versions of authoritative theology. Perhaps the best example of this is the frequent participation in the Eucharist attributed to Schmemann. The process of exposing people to Schmemann's Eucharistic theology is manifold: the revival was introduced to the Church through pastors who encouraged and taught people to participate, and through the consistent dissemination of Schmemann's teachings and publications. Schmemann's theology can be described as authoritative here because he taught at an Orthodox seminary and his teachings influenced parish practice. On the other hand, there are cases in which the people are simply not attuned to authoritative theology. There have been many attempts within Orthodoxy to revive Saturday evening worship, especially through the revision of the Vigil service into an office combining Vespers with select components from Matins that proclaim Christ's resurrection.[9] Schmemann was an early proponent of a "parish" vigil that focused on resurrection: Paul Meyendorff also endorsed this office, and it was published and practiced in the liturgical ordo of New Skete Monastery. One can identify this liturgical practice as authoritative because it is rooted in the finest methods of comparative liturgy, but it has been largely ignored within the Orthodox Church. The vast majority of people are not aware of similar authoritative works of the liturgical academy, including the baptismal Divine Liturgy on Sunday, the revision of the rite of Communion so that everyone received it from another (including the presider), and changes that would restore the inner meaning of the Holy Week offices. While the parish vigil has not been widely adopted outside of New Skete, in most cases, wise proposals for liturgical revision that would deeply enrich the meaning of liturgy in ways accessible to the people are ignored because they are not adopted and promoted by the clergy, who are the gatekeepers of liturgy. The people cannot entertain the possibility of receiving a liturgical teaching if they are unaware of it. The second reason for the people's alienation from authoritative theology is the absence of a real connection between teaching and their everyday lives. Many liturgical theologians and clergy continue to insist that increasing the number of hymns sung at the liturgical offices will expose the people to more of the theological legacy of the Orthodox Church. There is no evidence that the people can perceive the theology proclaimed by Byzantine hymnography. There are many potential reasons for this lack of communication: the hymns are often sung or chanted incomprehensibly, the texts tend to be long, and the number of hymns appointed to a given office makes the Liturgy saturated with texts. One has yet to see a liturgist publicly suggest that the people's capacity to retain multiple themes proclaimed at Liturgy is incompatible with the sheer amount of text that is sung. That said, many liturgists call upon clergy to simplify their sermons so that the people can identify and reflect upon one central theme. The appeal for more hymnography—which is understood to be a hymnographic echo of patristic preaching—contradicts the "less-is-more" commonsense approach to preaching.

The tendency for liturgists and pastors to pack teaching and their publications with theological jargon foreign to the people contributes to the people's perception of authoritative theology as esoteric, and encourages them to tune it out. The people, therefore, receive authoritative theology that is encouraged by pastors and resonates with their daily lives. They tend to ignore theological texts that are inaccessible.

This study shows that the people have developed their own liturgical theologies. In some cases, these theologies are compatible with and even traceable to the influence of theologians in the academy like Afanasiev, Schmemann, and Calivas. In other cases, the people's theology develops on its own. In the penultimate chapter, I identified areas that theologians might explore with greater vigor. It is tempting to read that chapter as a formula to develop new theological treatises through which the experts will dictate the meaning of liturgical celebration to the people. Such an interpretation is misinformed and would not capture the spirit of this book. Even if the theologians who have expertise in academic methods work in the areas defined as opportunities in this book, the laity's understanding of the liturgy will continue to evolve independently of experts. It is necessary for the people's theology to have a life of its own, but the point of that life is neither to counterbalance the hegemony of authoritative theology nor to demonstrate the equality of popular religion with official doctrine. The point is to restore the proper relational dynamics among the people who participate in offering the Liturgy to God and receiving God's gift. In this dynamic environment, theological experts stand together with the nonexperts, and they are "done unto" by God just as God acts upon the nonexperts. The point of the exercise is for the liturgical theologians to learn how to recognize the liturgical theology of the faithful, how to receive it, and how to respond in word (spoken and written), thought, and deed for the glory of God along with the people. The liturgical theologians are to perform their work in the midst of the assembly, with the people, and not from above.

WHAT IS TO BE DONE?

Since the people will continue to contribute to liturgical theology on their own, does the role of the theologians in the academy become moot? The enterprise of liturgical theology engaged by the experts can only be enriched when they are fully attuned to the actual responses of the people to the Liturgy. This review of focus group reflections on the Liturgy suggests that the people thirst for divine compassion, feel uneasy about their worthiness when they stand before God, and yearn to strengthen their bonds with others who are outside of the assembly. A liturgical theologian who translates another patristic mystagogy into English is offering valuable scholarship to the Church, but it's possible that the translation could be ignored by the people, even if it is theologically sound and offers a new insight on the Eucharist heretofore unknown. The theologian whose scholarship is inspired and informed by participation in the local assembly will be attuned to concerns that are both vertical and horizontal, coming from God and the people in their midst. In other words, if the people of the assembly yearn for divine compassion, there is no good reason for the theologian who worships alongside of them to be unaware that people hope for reassurance that God is suffering with them through the tumults of everyday life.

This study concludes, then, with a brief description of three concrete steps to be taken as a new initiative in the enterprise of liturgical theology of the Orthodox Church in America. These three steps are more of an elongated process than simple steps—the effective production of the enterprise depends on changing the mindset of the primary agents of liturgical theology.

The first step concerns these agents whose work in liturgical theology is so crucial. The status quo assumes that nothing needs to change because the system is intact, and that system depends on seminaries training pastors who lead liturgy in the parish. While pastors are still the most significant agents of liturgy and liturgical theology, the digital age and the people's thirst for knowledge about the liturgy and access to information provide an opportunity for theologians who are not in the seminary system but produce original academic research on the Liturgy to apply the fruits of that work to the pastoral life of the Church. This is possible only if pastors are open to the contributions of theologians who labor in the academy, but not necessarily in the seminary system. While Schmemann's and Calivas's legacies loom large on the American Church scene, there is no reason to limit Orthodox reflection and direction on the liturgy to these two figures. Opening up the forum to include a wider variety of experts requires pastors to trust theologians outside of the seminaries, and that seminaries themselves honor the work of academic theologians who do not belong to their faculties. There are many voices of the liturgical academy who have something to offer the Church: their contributions could do much good if the primary agents of the Church, seminary staff and pastors, change their mindset to trust the liturgical academy that exists outside of the seminary's orbit.

The second step is a continuation of the first step. This is the simplest of the three steps, but it is necessary for the enterprise to achieve its full potential. The liturgical formation of the clergy must be an ongoing process; likewise, the liturgical formation of the people should occur year-round. The status quo assumes that two or three seminary liturgy classes plus participation in chapel services can compress everything the pastor needs to know about liturgy for his ministry of presidency and teaching. The actual outcome of seminary formation is that pastors are introduced to the fundamentals of liturgy—an introduction is designed to develop into a body of learning. Many pastors receive formation informally through apprenticeship to senior clergy, but in the twenty-first-century era of pluralism, the liturgical formation of pastors should continue each year. This is yet another area in which the experts of the liturgical academy who are not trained in seminary can contribute. Liturgical theologians could work with clergy in an annual series of symposia that take place quarterly, to broaden pastoral competence not only in liturgical history, but also in preaching, knowledge of liturgical structures, music, and performance. Currently, the only post-seminary liturgical formation of clergy is for deacons who need to learn how to celebrate the hierarchical liturgy led by the bishop. Working with liturgical theologians could broaden clerical liturgical leadership and ultimately enrich the people's experience of the liturgy. Furthermore, an enhanced emphasis on the centrality of liturgy in parish life should translate into intentional liturgical formation of the people. Costs are no longer an obstacle in the digital age, as lectures, classes, and other materials can be administered through file transfer, audio, and video presentations.

The final step concerns respect for the people's contributions to liturgical theology. The ascendance of popular religion and its serious consideration by experts are significant hallmarks of the theological academy, but this is not a matter of acknowledging the existence of devotions or popular pieties in the assemblies. Nor is this an instance of equating popular religion with authoritative liturgical theology. The argument here is that the people's theology is just that: authentic liturgical theology. Their theology may lack the historical precision and the linguistic sophistication of authoritative liturgical theology, but it is just as legitimate as any treatise, statement, or declaration. If the achievement of twentieth-century liturgical theology was a type of conciliarity that returned the privilege of participation to the whole people of God, the legacy of the twenty-first century will be accomplished when the appointed representatives of the Church and the academy give the people time and space to reflect on the liturgy.

The Church has heard the Amens and Alleluias of the people, and in a few projects mentioned in this study, scholars have taken the time to hear what the people have to say about the liturgy. This study marks a modest achievement in approaching selections of parishioners from four distinct parishes in America to hear how they experience and understand the Liturgy. The boldest claims made here are that the people's words have reoriented our understanding of the Eucharist to account for those who are prohibited from partaking, that the people continue to feel uneasy about obeying Christ's command to "do this in remembrance of me" because they sense they are unworthy, and that the people want the Liturgy to reassure them that God is with them always, each and every day. This study is a beginning, as it only scratches the surface: imagine how much more the academy could learn about how people relate to God and with one another in Liturgy if new and more expansive studies followed this one. One can only hope that this study might inspire theologians to practice some silence so that they might hear the voice of the people, and to join the people in both offering God and praise and receiving God's gift in return. Then, and only then, can one claim that liturgical theology is indeed *theologia prima*, since theological reflection on the liturgy will find its source in the midst of those complex bodies who praise and worship God side-by-side, the laity, clergy, and theologians forming one people of God together.

NOTES

1. In northwest Indiana, where I now reside, the medium-sized community of Merrilville has no fewer than four Orthodox parishes with large edifices: Romanian, Serbian, Greek, and OCA.

2. Nicholas Denysenko, *Theology and Form: Contemporary Orthodox Architecture in America* (South Bend, IN: University of Notre Dame Press, 2017).

3. I am not arguing that all immigrants embrace change; many parishes seek to sustain their inheritance to a stronger degree than others. See my study of three immigrant parishes in *Theology and Form: Contemporary Orthodox Architecture in America* (South Bend, IN: University of Notre Dame Press, 2017).

4. See Jaroslav Pelikan, *The Christian Tradition: A History of the Development of Doctrine, vol. 1: The Emergence of the Catholic Tradition (100–600)* (Chicago: University of Chicago Press, 1971), 333.

5. For a beautiful example of this fidelity to tradition, see the personal essay by Carolyn Beans, "On Christmas Eve, Pass the Pierogi and the Memories," NPR, December 20, 2017, https://www.npr.org/sections/thesalt/2017/12/20/571156134/on-christmas-eve-pass-the-pierogi-and-the-memories (accessed March 2, 2018).

6. Amy Slagle, *The Eastern Church in the Spiritual Marketplace: American Conversions to Orthodox Christianity* (DeKalb: Northern Illinois University Press, 2011), 48–53.

7. Petros Vassiliadis, "Orthodox Theology Facing the Twenty-First Century," *Greek Orthodox Theological Review* 35, no. 2 (1990): 153.

8. "The Basis of the Social Concept of the Russian Orthodox Church," https://mospat.ru/en/documents/social-concepts/ (accessed March 14, 2018).

9. Nicholas Denysenko, "The Revision of the Vigil Service," *St. Vladimir's Theological Quarterly* 51 (2007): 236–41.

Appendix A

A Eucharistic Prayer

A Eucharistic Prayer for Churches of the Byzantine Rite[1]

Deacon: [Let us stand aright! . . .]

People: [Mercy, peace, a sacrifice of praise!]

Presider: "The grace of our Lord Jesus Christ, the love of God the Father, and the Communion of the Holy Spirit, be with all of you."

People: [And with your spirit.]

Presider: Let us lift up our hearts.

People: [We lift them up to the Lord.]

Presider: Let us give thanks to the Lord.

People: [It is meet and right.]

Presider (aloud): It is meet and right to stand before You, O Almighty One, who stretched the heavens like a tent; You appeared to the Prophet Moses, who stood on holy ground, in your presence, hiding his face; the disciples could not behold the divine light of your son, as they stood on holy ground; today, you have granted us, flesh and blood, worthy to stand before your throne, with your holy ones, the angels and archangels, together singing the triumphant hymn, shouting, proclaiming, and saying:

People: [Holy, Holy, Holy, Lord of Sabaoth! Heaven and earth are full of your glory! Hosanna in the highest! Blessed is he who comes in the name of the Lord. Hosanna in the highest!]

Presider (aloud): O giver of life, you are holy, and the life you have given us is holy. As the giver of life, you created order out of chaos, and filled the earth with vegetation and animals, calling them good. You created humankind, endowing us with your image and likeness. In your steadfast love for us, you sent us your eternal word. He poured himself out for us, the life of all hanging from a tree, for the life of the world. We bow down in worship before you, and your only-begotten Son and your all-Holy Spirit. We thank you for gathering us for this holy supper; in obedience to his command, we remember the supper with his disciples, when he took bread, blessed and broke it, saying "take, eat, this is my body which is broken for you, for the remission of sins."

People: [Amen]

Presider (aloud): When supper was ended, He took the Cup, saying: drink of this, all of you, this is my blood of the new covenant, which is poured out for you and for many, for the remission of sins.

People: [Amen]

Presider (aloud): Father, you so loved the world that you sent us your-only begotten Son. The eternal word took on flesh and dwelt among us, without knowing sin. He endured the passion, the cross, and the tomb; death could not contain the life of all, and he rose from the dead, ascending to you and sitting at your right hand. We await his second coming, and his kingdom shall have no end. Giving thanks for the gift of your Son, and offering you your own of your own, on behalf of all and for all:

People: [We praise you, we bless you, we give thanks to you, Lord, and we pray to you, O God.]

Presider (aloud): God, you sent your spirit on the waters and your holy springs nourished the fertile soil, feeding us and quenching our thirst. You sent your Spirit to your Son in the tomb; he rose from the dead and appeared to us, as the prophets foretold. O holy God, Lover of humankind, send your Spirit upon us and these gifts we offer, [+] revealing them as the body and blood of your risen Christ. Grant to those who partake of them remission of sins, communion of the Holy Spirit, and strength to praise your holy name together with the bodiless powers, all the days of our lives. May this same Spirit raise us up to become lovers of humankind who care for the orphan and the widow and delight in fulfilling your divine law. [2]

People: [Amen. Amen. Amen.]

Presider (aloud): Remember, Lord, the holy patriarchs, prophets, apostles, martyrs, confessors, and hierarchs who repose in You, and the righteous made perfect in faith. Especially for our most holy, pure, blessed and glorious Lady, the Theotokos and ever-virgin Mary.

The Choir sings the Theotokion "It is truly meet."

Presider: In honor of St. John, the Baptizer of our Lord, [saint N.], patron of this holy temple, saints [N] whose memory we commemorate today. Remember, Lord, your Church, all patriarchs, bishops, presbyters, deacons, monastics, and laity; remember our Metropolitan [N.] and our Bishop [N.], our civil authorities and armed forces; our parish community, the choir, servers, our visitors, and all our men, women, and children; remember, Lord, this city and all who live, work, and visit here; remember, Lord, all of those who are sick and suffering; addicts, alcoholics, depressed, injured, bereaved, and mentally ill; remember, Lord, widows and orphans, divorced and single people, the lonely, forgotten, and homeless among us; grant them peace, comfort, and healing, and bless the physicians and therapists who tend to them; remember, Lord, children and students, and bless the teachers who instruct them; remember, Lord, Christians of other Churches, and grant that we would be one, as you and your Son are one; remember, Lord, Jews, Muslims, Buddhists, Hindus, Sikhs, and people of all religions: grant us to live together in peace and reconciliation; remember, Lord, atheists and all those who do not know or seek you, and abide with them; remember, Lord, our enemies, those who love and hate us; grant us to love them as you have commanded. Remember, Lord, those who are in prisons, captives, and slaves; remember, Lord, the poor among us and outside our borders, the vulnerable; remember, Lord, all victims of war, violence, rage, and exploitation; grant them justice and bring their offenders to repentance. Remember, Lord, those who travel by land, sea, air, and space; send your angels with them. Remember, Lord, your creatures and plants that you have called good; make us into your stewards who care for and befriend them. Remember, Lord, all of your people, for you, Lord remember the age and name of each. Grant us peace and prosperity, and may your kingdom come.

And grant to us with one mouth and one heart to glorify and praise Your all-honorable and magnificent Name, of the Father and of the Son and of the Holy Spirit, now and forever and to the ages of ages.

People: Amen.

NOTES

1. The presider recites the entire prayer aloud for all to hear; he may recite or chant the prayer, according to parish custom. This prayer assumes that the people sing the responses as is customary, guided by chanters or a choir.

2. The entire anaphora is an epiclesis; therefore, this prayer *does not contain the diaconal commands* that the presider bless the bread and the cup; the prayer emphasizes the fullness of Christ's presence in the gifts accepted by God and sanctified through the descent of the Spirit. The Triple Amen occurs at the end of the entire section, marking the community's affirmation that partaking of Communion results in our transformation.

Appendix B

A Communal Rite of Penance

Before performing the kairos ("It is time . . ."), the priest, deacon, and servers descend from the sanctuary to the middle of the nave, standing before the tetrapod.

Deacon: Let us pray to the Lord!

People: Lord, have mercy!

Priest: Lord our God, we stand before you to offer you this liturgy in remembrance of your Son, as you have commanded. We know that we are not worthy of the gift of your Son because we have sinned; yet we dare to approach, hoping in your mercy. O Lover of humankind, who forgives sins up to seventy times seven, wash us, make us clean, forgive our sins, and ever teach us to forgive those who trespass against us. Grant us to hear your Word, to offer you praise, and to receive the body and blood of your Christ so that we may be one as you and your Son are one. Send your Spirit upon us so that we would serve you with joy, gladness, and thanksgiving all the days of our lives. For to you we send up glory, together with your only-begotten Son and your All-holy and lifegiving Spirit, now and forever and to the ages of ages.

People: Amen.

The clergy and servers turn to face the people.

Priest: Brothers and sisters, forgive us, sinners! *(The clergy and servers bow their heads low before the people.)*

People: May God forgive you! We forgive you! Forgive us, fathers! *(The people bow before the clergy.)*

Clergy: May God forgive all of us! *(All turn and bow to the high place.)*

The clergy perform the kairos in the middle of the nave: the deacon takes his place before the icon of the Theotokos and priest ascends to the holy table for the beginning of the Divine Liturgy.

Select Bibliography

Afanasiev, Nicholas. *The Church of the Holy Spirit*. Translated by Vitaly Permiakov, edited by Michael Plekon, foreword by Rowan Williams. South Bend, IN: University of Notre Dame Press, 2007.

———. "Una Sancta." In *Tradition Alive: On the Church and the Christian Life in Our Time*, edited by Michael Plekon, foreword by John Erickson, 3–53. Lanham, MD: Rowman & Littlefield, 2003.

Alexopoulos, Stefanos. "The Influence of Iconoclasm on Liturgy: A Case Study." In *Worship Traditions in Armenia and the Neighboring Christian East: An International Symposium in Honor of the 40th Anniversary of St. Nersess Seminary*, edited by Roberta Ervine, 127–40. Crestwood, NY: St. Vladimir's Seminary, St. Nersess Armenian Seminary, 2006.

Ammerman, Nancy. *Pillars of Faith: American Congregations and Their Partners*. Berkeley: University of California Press, 2005.

———. *Studying Congregations: A New Handbook*. Nashville: Abingdon Press, 2006.

———. *Work, Family, and Religion in Contemporary Society: Remaking Our Lives*. Hoboken, NJ: Taylor and Francis, 2014.

Auxentios, Bishop. *The Paschal Fire in Jerusalem: A Study of the Rite of the Holy Fire in the Church of the Holy Sepulchre*. Berkeley: St. John Chrysostom Press, 1993.

Barnard, Marcel, Johan Cilliers, and Cas Wepener. *Worship in the Network Culture: Liturgical Ritual Studies; Fields and Methods, Concepts and Metaphors*. Liturgia condenda, 28. Leuven, Paris, Walpole, MA: Peeters, 2014.

Beans, Carolyn. "On Christmas Eve, Pass the Pierogi and the Memories," NPR, December 20, 2017. Accessed March 2, 2018. https://www.npr.org/sections/thesalt/2017/12/20/571156134/on-christmas-eve-pass-the-pierogi-and-the-memories.

Belcher, Kimberly Hope. *Efficacious Engagement: Sacramental Participation in the Trinitarian Mystery*. Collegeville, MN: Liturgical Press, 2011.

Bell, Catherine. *Ritual: Perspectives and Dimension*. Oxford: Oxford University Press, 2009.

Berger, Teresa, ed. *Liturgy in Migration: From the Upper Room to Cyberspace*. Collegeville, MN: Liturgical Press, 2012.

Bertonière, Gabriel. *The Sundays of Lent in the Triodion: The Sundays without a Commemoration*. Orientalia Christiana Analecta 253. Rome: Pontifical Oriental Institute, 1997.

Betts, Richard. "From America to Russia: The Myrrh-Streaming Icon of Tsar Nicholas II." *Road to Emmaus: A Journal of Orthodox Faith and Culture* (2000). Accessed November 15, 2013. http://www.roadtoemmaus.net/back_issue_articles/RTE_01/From_America_to_Russia.pdf.

Bradshaw, Paul, ed. *Foundations in Ritual Studies: A Reader for Students of Christian Worship*. Collegeville, MN: Liturgical Press, 2007.

Bradshaw, Paul, and Maxwell Johnson. *The Eucharistic Liturgies: Their Evolution and Interpretation.* Collegeville, MN: Liturgical Press, 2012.

Brown, Peter. *The Cult of the Saints: Its Rise and Function in Latin Christianity.* Chicago: University of Chicago Press, 1981.

Calivas, Alkiviadis. *Essays in Theology and Liturgy*, vol. 3: *Aspects of Orthodox Worship.* Brookline, MA: Holy Cross Orthodox Press, 2003.

Chaves, Mark. *American Religion: Contemporary Trends.* Princeton, NJ: Princeton University Press, 2011.

Chryssavgis, John. *Soul Mending: The Art of Spiritual Direction.* Brookline, MA: Holy Cross Orthodox Press, 2000.

Chupungco, Anscar. *Liturgical Inculturation: Sacramentals, Religiosity, and Catechesis.* Collegeville, MN: Liturgical Press, 1992.

Congar, Yves. *At the Heart of Christian Worship: Liturgical Essays of Yves Congar.* Edited and translated by Paul Philibert. Collegeville, MN: Liturgical Press, 2010.

Cyril of Jerusalem, Saint. *Lectures on the Christian Sacraments: The Procatechesis and the Five Mystagogical Catecheses Ascribed to Cyril of Jerusalem.* Translated by Maxwell Johnson. Crestwood, NY: St. Vladimir's Seminary Press, 2017.

Demacopoulos, George, and Aristotle Papanikolaou, eds. *Orthodox Constructions of the West.* New York: Fordham University Press, 2013.

Denysenko, Nicholas. *Chrismation: A Primer for Catholics.* Collegeville, MN: Liturgical Press, 2014.

———. "Death and Dying in Orthodox Liturgy." *Religions* 8, 25 (2017), doi:10.3390/rel8020025.

———. *Liturgical Reform After Vatican II: The Impact on Eastern Orthodoxy.* Minneapolis: Fortress, 2015.

———. "Psalm 81: Announcing the Resurrection on Holy Saturday." *Logos: A Journal of Eastern Christian Studies* 50 (2009): 55–88.

———. "Retrieving a Theology of Belonging: Eucharist and Church in Postmodernity, Part 2." *Worship* 89, no. 1 (2015): 21–43.

———. "The Revision of the Vigil Service." *St. Vladimir's Theological Quarterly* 51 (2007): 221–51.

———. "Rituals and Prayers of Forgiveness in Byzantine Lent." *Worship* 86 (2012): 140–60.

———. *Theology and Form: Contemporary Orthodox Architecture in America.* South Bend, IN: University of Notre Dame Press, 2017.

Dinges, William D. "Ritual Conflict as Social Conflict: Liturgical Reform in the Roman Catholic Church." *Sociological Analysis* 48 (Summer 1987): 138–57.

Elchaninov, Alexander. *The Diary of a Russian Priest.* Translated by Helen Iswolsky, edited by Kallistos Ware, introduction by Tamara Elchaninov, and foreword by Dimitri Obolensky. London: Faber and Faber, 1967.

Espin, Orlando. *The Faith of the People: Theological Reflections on Popular Catholicism.* Maryknoll, NY: Orbis, 1997.

Fagerberg, David. *Theologia Prima: What Is Liturgical Theology?* Chicago: Hillenbrand Books, 2004.

Fisch, Thomas, ed. *Liturgy and Tradition: Theological Reflections of Alexander Schmemann.* Crestwood, NY: St. Vladimir's Seminary Press, 1990.

FitzGerald, Thomas E. "How to Understand Christian Unity (Ecumenism) in Relation to Orthodox Identity: A First Theological Approach." In *Orthodox Handbook on Ecumenism: Resources for Theological Education*, edited by Pantelis Kalaitzidis et al, 9–12. Volos: Volos Academy Publications, 2014.

———. *The Orthodox Church.* Denominations in America 7, edited by Henry Warner Bowden. Westport, CT: Greenwood Press, 1995.

Frost, Carrie Frederick. "The Churching of Mothers in the Orthodox Church." Accessed January 19, 2018. http://orthodoxdeaconess.org/women-church-praxis/.

Galadza, Daniel. "Sources for the Study of Liturgy in Post-Byzantine Jerusalem (638–1137 CE)." *Dumbarton Oaks Papers* 81 (2013): 75–94.

Gallagher, Sally. *Getting to Church: Narratives of Gender and Joining.* Oxford: Oxford University Press, 2017.

Gallaher, Brandon. "Ecumenism as Civilizational Dialogue: Eastern Orthodox Anti-Ecumenism and Eastern Orthodox Ecumenism: A Creative or Sterile Antinomy." Keynote lecture for "Questioning Ecumenism in the 20th Century: Who, When, Why," "The Desire for Christian Unity Research Program—2017 Research Conference," Fondazione per le Scienze Religiose Giovanni XXIII, Bologna, 13–15 November 2017. Convener: Prof Alberto Melloni.

———. "Great and Full of Grace." In *Church and World: Essays in Honor of Michael Plekon,* edited by William Mills, 69–122. Rollinsford, NH: Orthodox Research Institute, 2013.

Germanos, Patriarch. *On the Divine Liturgy.* Translated by Paul Meyendorff. Crestwood, NY: St. Vladimir's Seminary Press, 1984.

Gonosovà, Anna. "Epitaphios." In *The Oxford Dictionary of Byzantium,* vol. 1, edited by Alexander Kazhdan, 720–21. Oxford: Oxford University Press, 1991.

Graef, Hilda. *Mary: A History of Doctrine and Devotion, vol. 1: From the Beginnings to the Eve of the Reformation.* New York: Sheed and Ward, 1963.

Gray, Mark M., and Paul M. Perl. *Sacraments Today: Belief and Practice among U.S. Catholics.* Washington, DC: Center for Applied Research in the Apostolate, 2008.

Hall, David D. *Lived Religion in America: Toward a History of Practice.* Princeton, NJ: Princeton University Press, 1997.

Hart, David Bentley. "The Myth of Schism." In *Ecumenism Today: The Universal Church in the Twenty-first Century,* edited by Francesca Aran Murphy and Christopher Asprey, 95–106. New York: Routledge, 2016.

Haughton, Rosemary. *The Transformation of Man: A Study of Conversion and Community.* Springfield, IL: Templegate, 1967, 1980.

Heers, Peter. "The 'Council' in Crete and the New Emerging Ecclesiology: An Orthodox Examination." Orthodox Ethos, March 21, 2017. Accessed March 7, 2018. https:// orthodoxethos.com/post/the-council-of-crete-and-the-new-emerging-ecclesiology-an-ortho dox-examination.

Herbel, Dellas Oliver. *Turning to Tradition: Converts and the Making of an American Orthodox Church.* Oxford: Oxford University Press, 2014.

Hoffman, Lawrence. "Reconstructing Ritual as Identity and Culture." In *The Making of Jewish and Christian Worship,* edited by Paul F. Bradshaw and Lawrence A. Hoffman, 22–41. Notre Dame: University of Notre Dame Press, 1991.

Holy and Great Council of Crete. "The Orthodox Diaspora." Holy and Great Council. Accessed March 7, 2018. https://www.holycouncil.org/-/diaspora.

International Theological Consultation. *Sensus Fidei in the Life of the Church.* Accessed February 14, 2018. http://www.vatican.va/roman_curia/congregations/cfaith/cti_documents/rc_cti_20140610_sensus-fidei_en.html.

Irwin, Kevin W. *Context and Text: Method in Liturgical Theology.* Collegeville, MN: Liturgical Press, 1994.

Isasi-Díaz, Ada Maria. *En la lucha = In the struggle: Elaborating a mujerista Theology.* Minneapolis: Fortress Press, 2004.

Izmirlieva, Valentina. "Christian Hajjis: The Other Orthodox Pilgrims to Jerusalem." *Slavic Review* 73, no. 2 (2014): 332–35.

Jacobse, Johannes. "A Public Statement on Orthodox Deaconesses by Concerned Clergy and Laity." Accessed February 22, 2018. http://www.aoiusa.org/a-public-statement-on-orthodox-deaconesses-by-concerned-clergy-and-laity/.

John Chrysostom, Saint. "The Paschal Sermon. Accessed March 8, 2018. https://oca.org/fs/sermons/the-paschal-sermon.

Johnson, Clare, ed. *Ars liturgiae: Worship, Aesthetics, and Praxis: Essays in Honor of Nathan D. Mitchell.* Chicago: Liturgy Training Publications, 2003.

———. "Researching Ritual Practice." *Studia Liturgica* 35, no. 2 (2005): 204–20.

Kavanagh, Aidan. *On Liturgical Theology.* New York: Pueblo Publishing, 1984.

———. "Primary Theology and Liturgical Act: Response." *Worship* 57 (1983): 321–24.

Kelleher, Margaret Mary. "Liturgical Theology: A Task and a Method." *Worship* 62, no. 1 (1988): 2–25.

———. "Liturgy: An Ecclesial Act of Meaning." *Worship* 59, no. 6 (1985): 482–97.

Kodell, Jerome. *The Eucharist in the New Testament.* Collegeville, MN: Liturgical Press, 1991.

Kouli, Maria, trans. "Life of St. Mary of Egypt." In *Holy Women of Byzantium*, edited by Alice-Mary Talbot, 65–95. Washington, DC: Dumbarton Oaks, 1996.

Koumarianos, Pavlos, "Liturgical Problems of Holy Week." *St. Vladimir's Theological Quarterly* 46, no. 1 (2002): 3–21.

Krindatch, Alexei, ed. *Atlas of American Orthodox Christian Churches.* Brookline, MA: Holy Cross Orthodox Press, 2011.

———. "Orthodox Christian Churches in the 21st Century: A Parish Life Study." ACOBA. Accessed March 7, 2018. http://www.assemblyofbishops.org/assets/files/studies/2018-01-OrthodoxChurchesIn21CenturyAmericaFinal.pdf.

———. *The Orthodox Church Today: A National Study of Parishioners and the Realities of Orthodox Parish Life in the USA.* Berkeley, CA: Patriarch Athenagoras Orthodox Institute, 2004.

———. "Satisfaction and Morale among Parish Clergy: What American Catholic and Orthodox Priests Can Learn from Each Other." *Journal for the Scientific Study of Religion* 49, no.1 (2010): 179–87.

Lingas, Alexander. "Tradition and Renewal in Contemporary Greek Orthodox Psalmody." In *Psalms in Community: Jewish and Christian Liturgical, Artistic, and Textual Traditions*, edited by Harold Attridge, 341–56. Society of Biblical Literature Symposium Series 25. Atlanta: Society of Biblical Literature, 2004.

Makrides, Vasilios. "'The Barbarian West': A Form of Orthodox Christian Anti-Western Critique." In *Eastern Orthodox Encounters of Identity and Otherness: Values, Self-reflection, Dialogue,* edited by Andrii Krawchuk and Thomas Bremer, 141–58. New York: Palgrave Macmillan, 2014.

Manalo, Ricky. *The Liturgy of Life: The Interrelationship of Sunday Eucharist and Everyday Worship Practices.* Collegeville, MN: Liturgical Press, 2014.

Mary, Mother, and Kallistos Ware, trans. *The Festal Menaion.* Introduction by Georges Florovsky. South Canaan, PA: St. Tikhon's Seminary Press, 1990.

———. *The Lenten Triodion.* South Canaan, PA: St. Tikhon's Seminary Press, 2002.

Mateos, Juan. *La célébration de la parole dans le liturgie byzantine: étude historique.* Rome: Pontifical Oriental Institute, 1971.

Mazur, Eric Michael, and Kate McCarthy. *God in the Details: American Religion in Popular Culture.* New York: Routledge, 2001.

McGann, Mary E. *A Precious Fountain: Music in the Worship of an African American Catholic Community.* Virgil Michel Series, edited by Don Saliers. Collegeville, MN: Liturgical Press, 2004.

McGowan, Anne. *Eucharistic Epicleses, Ancient and Modern: Speaking of the Spirit in Eucharistic Prayers.* Alcuin Club Collections, no. 89. London: SPCK, 2014.

McInerny, David. "Identity, Divine Filiation, and the Eucharist." *Assembly: A Journal of Liturgical Theology* (March 2009): 29–32.

McPartlan, Paul. *Sacrament of Salvation: An Introduction to Eucharistic Ecclesiology.* Edinburgh: T & T Clark, 1995.

Meyendorff, Paul. "The Liturgical Path of Orthodoxy in America." *St. Vladimir's Theological Quarterly* 40, nos. 1–2 (1996): 44–49.

Mitchell, Nathan. *Liturgy and the Social Sciences.* Collegeville, MN: Liturgical Press, 1999.

Nelson, Gertrude Mueller. "Christian Formation of Children: the Role of Ritual and Celebration." In *Liturgy and Spirituality in Context*, edited by Elanor Bernstein, 114–35. Collegeville, MN: Liturgical Press, 1990.

"Orthodox Liturgists issued a statement of support for the revival of the order of deaconess by the Patriarchate of Alexandria." Accessed February 22, 2018. https://panorthodoxcemes.blogspot.ca/2017/10/orthodox-liturgists-issued-statement-of.html?m=1.

Pelikan, Jaroslav. *The Christian Tradition: A History of the Development of Doctrine, vol. 1: The Emergence of the Catholic Tradition (100–600).* Chicago: University of Chicago Press, 1971.

Permiakov, Vitaly. "Чин освящения храма в восточных традициах" ("Rite of the dedication of a temple in the Eastern Traditions"). In *православное учение о церковных таинствах* (Orthodox teaching on Church Mysteries), edited by Michael Zheltov, vol. 3, 346–67. Moscow: Synodal Biblical-Theological Committee, 2009.

Pew Research Center. "Orthodox Christianity in the 21st Century." Pew Research Center Study, November 8, 2017. Accessed March 7, 2018. http://www.pewforum.org/2017/11/08/orthodox-christianity-in-the-21st-century/.

Phan, Peter. *Being Religious Interreligiously: Asian Perspectives on Interfaith Dialogue in Postmodernity.* Maryknoll, NY: Orbis Books, 2004.

———. "Liturgy of Life as the 'Summit and Source' of the Eucharistic Liturgy: Church Worship as Symbolization of the Liturgy of Life?" In *Incongruities: Who We Are and How We Pray,* edited by Timothy Fitzgerald and David A. Lysik, 5–33. Chicago: Liturgy Training Publications, 2000.

———. "Religious Identity and Belonging Amidst Diversity and Pluralism: Challenges and Opportunities for Church and Theology." In *Passing on the Faith: Transforming Traditions for the Next Generation of Jews, Christians, and Muslims,* edited by James Heft, 162–84. New York: Fordham University Press, 2006.

———. "To Be Catholic or Not to Be: Is It Still the Question? Catholic Identity and Religious Education Today." *Horizons; Journal of the College Theology Society* 25, no. 2 (1998): 159–80.

Pitt, David, Stefanos Alexopoulos, and Christian McConnell, eds. *A Living Tradition: On the Intersection of Liturgical History and Pastoral Practice.* Essays in Honor of Maxwell E. Johnson. Collegeville, MN: Liturgical Press, 2012.

Pius XII, Pope. "Munificentissimus Deus." *Acta Apostolicae Sedis* 42 (1950): 753–71.

Pivarnik, Gabriel. *Toward a Trinitarian Theology of Liturgical Participation.* Foreword by Kevin Irwin. Collegeville, MN: Liturgical Press, 2013.

Plekon, Michael. "Belonging to the Church in the Twenty-First Century, When 'The Church Has Left the Building'." In *The Church Has Left the Building: Faith, Parish, and Ministry in the Twenty-First Century,* edited by Michael Plekon, Maria Gwyn McDowell, and Elizabeth Schroeder, 1–16. Eugene, OR; Cascade Books, 2016.

———. *Living Icons: Persons of Faith in the Eastern Church.* Foreword by Lawrence Cunningham. South Bend, IN: University of Notre Dame Press, 2002.

———. *Uncommon Prayer: Prayer in Everyday Experience.* South Bend, IN: University of Notre Dame Press, 2017.

———. *The World as Sacrament: An Ecumenical Path toward a Worldly Spirituality.* Collegeville, MN: Liturgical Press, 2017.

Poole, Stafford. *Our Lady of Guadalupe: The Origins and Sources of a Mexican National Symbol, 1591–1797.* Tucson: University of Arizona Press, 1995.

Pott, Thomas. *Byzantine Liturgical Reform: A Study of Liturgical Change in the Byzantine Tradition.* Translated by Paul Meyendorff and preface by Robert F. Taft. Orthodox Liturgy Series 2. Crestwood, NY: St. Vladimir's Seminary Press, 2010.

Raiche, Diana Dudoit. "Liturgical Catechesis as an Essential Dimension of Initiatory Catechesis in the *Rite of Christian Initiation of Adults* Adapted for Children." PhD dissertation, The Catholic University of America, 2011.

Rapp, Claudia. "Spiritual Guarantors at Penance, Baptism, and Ordination in the Late Antique East." In *A New History of Penance,* edited by Abigail Firey. Boston, MA: Brill 2008.

Russian Orthodox Church. "The Basis of the Social Concept of the Russian Orthodox Church." Accessed March 14, 2018. https://mospat.ru/en/documents/social-concepts/.

Saliers, Don. "Liturgical Aesthetics: The Travail of Worship." In *Arts, Theology, and the Church: New Intersections,* edited by Kimberley J. Vrudny and Wilson Yates. Cleveland, OH: Pilgrim Press, 2005.

Schmemann, Alexander. *The Eucharist: Sacrament of the Kingdom.* Translated by Paul Kachur. Crestwood, NY: St. Vladimir's Seminary Press, 1987.

———. *The Journals of Father Alexander Schmemann, 1973–1984.* Crestwood, NY: St. Vladimir's Seminary Press, 2000.

———. "Problems of Orthodoxy in America: The Liturgical Problem." *St. Vladimir's Seminary Quarterly* 8, no. 4 (1964): 164–85.

Searle, Mark. *Called to Participate: Theological, Ritual, and Social Perspectives.* Edited by Barbara Searle and Anne Y. Koester. Collegeville, MN: Liturgical Press, 2006.

Senn, Frank. "The Constitution on Sacred Liturgy and Lutheran Book of Worship: What Was Renewed?" In *Liturgy in a New Millennium*, edited by R. Schuler. Valparaiso, IN: Institute of Liturgical Studies, 2006.

———. *The People's Work: A Social History of the Liturgy.* Minneapolis: Fortress Press, 2006.

Skobtsova, Maria. *Mother Maria Skobtsova: Essential Writings.* Translated by Richard Pevear and Larissa Volokhonsky, introduction by Jim Forest, Modern Spiritual Master Series. Maryknoll, NY: Orbis, 2003.

Slagle, Amy. *The Eastern Church in the Spiritual Marketplace: American Conversions to Orthodox Christianity.* DeKalb: Northern Illinois University Press, 2011.

Slater, Wendy. "Relics, Remains, and Revisionism: Narratives of Nicholas II in Contemporary Russia." *Rethinking History: The Journal of Theory and Practice* 9, no. 1 (2005): 53–70.

Stokoe, Mark, and Leonid Kishkovsky. *Orthodox Christians in North America: 1794–1994.* Syosset, NY: Orthodox Christian Publications Center, 1995.

Stout, Daniel A., and Judith Mitchell Buddenbaum. *Religion and Popular Culture: Studies on the Interaction of Worldviews.* Ames: Iowa State University Press, 2001.

Taft, Robert. *Beyond East and West: Problems in Liturgical Understanding*, 2d ed. Edizioni Orientalia Christiana. Rome: Pontifical Oriental Institute, 2001.

———. "Byzantine Communion Spoons: A Review of the Evidence." *Dumbarton Oaks Papers* 50 (1996): 209–38.

———. *A History of the Liturgy of St. John Chrysostom, vol. 2: The Great Entrance, A History of the Transfer of Gifts and Other Pre-anaphral Rites*, 4th ed. Rome: Pontifical Oriental Institute, 2004.

———. *A History of the Liturgy of St. John Chrysostom*, vol. 5: *The Precommunion Rites.* Orientalia Christiana Analecta 261. Rome: Pontifical Oriental Institute, 2000.

———. "In Faith and Worship Can Orthodox and Catholics Ever Be One? Communion, Not Reunion, in a Future Church of Sister Churches." *Worship* 89, no. 1 (2015): 2–20.

———. "In the Bridegroom's Absence: The Paschal Triduum in the Byzantine Church." In La celebrazione del Triduo pasquale: anamnesis e mimesis. Atti del III Congresso Internazionale di Liturgia, Roma, Pontificio Istituto Liturgico, 9–13 maggio 1988. Studia Anselmiana 102 (1990): 71–97.

———. "The Liturgical Enterprise Twenty-five Years after Alexander Schmemann." *St. Vladimir's Theological Quarterly* 53, nos. 2–3 (2009): 139–77.

———. "The Liturgy of the Great Church: An Initial Synthesis of Structure and Interpretation on the Eve of Iconoclasm." *Dumbarton Oaks Papers* 34 (1980–81): 47–75.

———. *The Liturgy of the Hours in East and West: The Origins of the Divine Office and Its Meaning for Today*, 2d ed. Collegeville, MN: Liturgical Press, 1993.

———. "Monogenes." In *The Oxford Dictionary of Byzantium*, vol. 2, edited by Alexander Kazhdan, 1397. New York: Oxford University Press, 1991.

———. "Mrs Murphy Goes to Moscow: Kavanagh, Schmemann, and 'the Byzantine Synthesis." *Worship* 85, no. 5 (2011): 386–407.

———. "A Tale of Two Cities: The Byzantine Holy Week Triduum as a Paradigm of Liturgical History." In *Time and Community, in Honor of Thomas Julian Talley*, edited by J. Alexander, NPM Studies in Church Music and Liturgy, 21–41. Washington, DC: National Pastoral Musicians, 1990.

———. *Through Their Own Eyes: Liturgy as the Byzantines Saw It.* Berkeley, CA: InterOrthodox Press, 2006.

Torrance, Alexis. *Repentance in Late Antiquity: Eastern Asceticism and the Framing of the Christian Life c. 400–650 CE.* Oxford: Oxford University Press, 2012.

Vassialidis, Petros, Niki Papageorgiou, and Eleni Kasselouri-Hatzivassiliadi, eds. *Deaconesses, the Ordination of Women, and Orthodox Theology.* Cambridge: Cambridge University Press, 2017.

———. "Orthodox Theology Facing the Twenty-First Century." *Greek Orthodox Theological Review* 35, no. 2 (1990): 139–53.

Vrame, Antone, ed. *The Orthodox Parish in America.* Brookline, MA: Holy Cross Orthodox Press, 2003.

Ware, Kallistos. *The Inner Kingdom.* Crestwood, NY: St. Vladimir' Seminary Press, 2000.

Wilbricht, Stephen. *Rehearsing God's Just Kingdom: The Eucharistic Vision of Mark Searle.* Foreword by Kevin Irwin. Collegeville, MN: Liturgical Press, 2013.

Winchester, Daniel. "Converting to Continuity: Temporality and Self in Eastern Orthodox Conversion Narratives." *Journal of the Scientific Study of Religion* 54 (2015): 439–60.

Winner, Brother Stavros. "The Monastery and Applied Liturgical Renewal." In *Worship Traditions and Armenia and the Neighboring Christian East: An International Symposium in Honor of the 40th Anniversary of St. Nersess Armenian Seminary*, edited by Roberta R. Ervine, 307–23. Crestwood, NY: St. Vladimir's Seminary Press, St. Nersess Armenian Seminary, 2006.

Index

About the Author

Nicholas E. Denysenko is Emil and Elfriede Jochum Professor and Chair at Valparaiso University. A graduate of St. Vladimir's Orthodox Theological Seminary (M.Div., 2000) and The Catholic University of America (Ph.D., 2008), Denysenko specializes in liturgical theology and Orthodox Christianity. His books include *The Blessing of Waters and Epiphany* (Ashgate, 2012), *Chrismation: A Primer for Catholics* (Liturgical Press, 2014), *Liturgical Reform After Vatican II: The Impact on Eastern Orthodoxy* (Fortress, 2015), *Theology and Form: Contemporary Orthodox Architecture in America and Theology* (University of Notre Dame Press, 2017), and *The Orthodox Church in Ukraine: A Century of Separation* (Northern Illinois University Press, 2018). In his research, Denysenko explores the intersections of liturgical history, ritual studies, and pastoral theology, and writes for an ecumenical audience. The grandson of immigrants from Ukraine, Denysenko also writes about the contemporary Ukrainian Orthodox Church. He has been a deacon of the Orthodox Church in America since 2003.

CPSIA information can be obtained
at www.ICGtesting.com
Printed in the USA
LVHW101542161022
730828LV00001B/3